I0827275

The Christian Counselor's Commentary

Proverbs

Jay E. Adams

Institute for Nouthetic Studies, a ministry of Mid-America Baptist Theological Seminary, 5640 Airline Road, Arlington, TN 38002
mabts.edu / nouthetic.org / INSBookstore.com

Proverbs: The Christian Counselor's Commentary
by Jay E. Adams

ISBN: 978-1-949737-21-9 (Paper Cover)
ISBN: 978-1-949737-22-6 (eBook)
ISBN: 978-1-949737-31-8 (Hard Cover)
Old ISBN: 0-889032-03-4
Editor: Donn R. Arms

Library of Congress Cataloging-in-Publication Data
Names: Adams, Jay E., 1929-2020
Title: *Proverbs: The Christian Counselor's Commentary* / Jay E. Adams
Description: Memphis: Institute for Nouthetic Studies, 2020
Identifiers: ISBN 978-1-949737-21-9 (paper)
Classification: LCC BS1465.3 .A18 | DDC 223.7

Published in the United States of America

Introduction

Proverbs is a teaching manual. It might be called *Truth for Youth* since it speaks as if a father is addressing a son. However, the words **father** and **son** were used frequently to designate the relationship that existed between a teacher and his pupil. This indicated the closeness of that relationship and the large responsibility that a teacher assumed: he was to become all that a parent is to his pupils. That is quite a different view than that which is recognized by many parents and teachers even in Christian schools today. It has ramifications for parents as well as for teachers. Most of this I have discussed in some depth in my book *Back to the Blackboard*, which is a book about biblical methods of teaching.

Be that as it may, the important thing to understand about Proverbs is that, as a piece of wisdom literature, it inculcates *truth for life*. Indeed, the book must not be thought to be merely a book for youth, since there is so much that every Christian and (in particular) every Christian counselee may learn from its pages. All Christians are ever students of God's Word. Many subjects apply best to more mature readers. For an understanding of how the New Testament writers used the book, applying it to the whole church, see Hebrews 12:5 (a quotation from Proverbs 3:11 in which, interestingly enough, the words "my son" are used in a non-familial context). Indeed, in the book, at times father and mother seem remote (cf. 23:22-25).

Moreover, Proverbs is a book that every counselor should consider his good friend. It is a book with which, if he is wise and wishes to impart wise counsel, he will want to become as familiar as possible. And as he becomes increasingly familiar with its teachings, he will discover himself using it more and more in the process of counseling. Indeed, soon he will want to learn the whole of it as quickly as possible so that he may have all its wisdom at his disposal at all times. There are few books as valuable for direct use in counseling. I commend the study of the book to you.

One of the principal reasons why Proverbs is so valuable is its emphasis on folly. It exposes the ways of folly, covering many—if not most—of those that you will meet in the counseling room. The consequences of folly and the ways of avoiding foolish thinking and behavior alike are considered. Indeed, a sub-theme, running opposite the major theme of acquiring the ways of wisdom, is how to confront the failures of folly. This two-sidedness of the book makes it doubly valuable as the ways of wisdom and the failures of folly are frequently compared and contrasted, the proverbial form of the contrasting couplet being the principal method of structuring the comparison.

The Book of Proverbs is not merely good advice, though surely you won't find better anywhere. More fundamentally, it is a book of revealed morality. It contains divine wisdom from God for His covenant people. It is a book in which the saint may learn from God how he ought to conduct his life before other men. As the Psalms focus on *man* in relationship to *God*, the Proverbs focus on *man* in relationship to *man*. But the relationships one bears to other men are always against the backdrop of one's relationship to God, which affects these lesser ones at all points. God revealed this truth, and what one does with it is clearly an issue between him and God. Moreover, as sanctification occurs through following biblical, proverbial wisdom, one honors his heavenly Father thereby. And it is the power of the Holy Spirit, enabling him to do what he is instructed by the writers of the book to do, that is working in and through their writings. Though God is directly mentioned occasionally throughout the book, there can be no doubt all that is written has ramifications that relate to Him. Jesus Christ is the Wisdom of God. He it is, therefore, into Whose likeness one grows as he appropriates and incorporates Proverbs' teaching into daily living. As a result, it is a thoroughly Christian, Christ-honoring book.

Often the proverbs given are the result of a process of compacting truth tightly into one unit. To interpret and apply the truths thus compacted one must understand this process and be able to utilize it. The process looks something like this:

The **writer** structured the proverb
out of *particulars* from which he formed a *generalization* that he applied to *one particular* in which he encapsulated the *generalization* in the form of a pithy proverb
from which, in turn, the **interpreter**
must again abstract the *generalization* behind it and then apply it to that or any number of other *particular* situations to which it also validly applies.

In I Corinthians 9:9, you see the apostle Paul at work interpreting an Old Testament verse in exactly this way. Referring to Deuteronomy 25:4, Paul quotes an instruction about not muzzling the ox that is treading out the grain. That is a *particular* situation to which the *generalization,* that the worker should benefit (live) from his work, is applied. Paul sees the *generalization* behind the *particular* and applies that to a *different* particular:

the preacher should be paid out of his work. Indeed, in the discussion he goes so far as to suggest that God was not talking about oxen. What he means, of course, is that He was not talking exclusively (or, perhaps, primarily) about oxen.

Why is the proverbial form with its compactness valuable? And, especially, why is it of such great value in counseling? One major reason is that a proverb is portable truth. Compacted into that easily-memorized, often vivid or picturesque particular situation that the proverb addresses is a generalization that may be readily learned, carried about in one's mind and then applied to any number of life situations as they occur. Both the general principle and the method of application are transportable. For counselees who are in the process of learning how to address a variety of circumstances day by day in a truly biblical way, the potential capability for such practical use that this provides is just short of phenomenal. We may say that proverbs of this sort are, in effect, portable, practical principles.

Well, why not simply learn principles? You couldn't retain abstract principles in your thinking so easily. Which is easier to remember: the principle that "doing a good deed in the wrong way or at the wrong time ruins the good deed," or Proverbs 27:14, "He who blesses his neighbor with a loud voice, rising early in the morning, will have it reckoned to him as a curse?" The former, along with scores of other such principles, is difficult to retain; the latter, because of the picture presented (and the touch of humor in it) is readily recalled. Many of the proverbs, you will notice, are not only short and picturesque, but at times also sharply-worded and salty. And because they are filled with so much tightly-compacted truth, some have more than one application. Notice, for instance, how Proverbs 10:12 is applied in the New Testament: in I Peter 4:8, it is used to stress brotherly love; in James 5:20, it is applied to the restoration of the erring. There is more than one principle embedded in it, each of which has a life of its own.

Moreover, Proverbs are thought starters. They get you started thinking along certain lines. They don't always tell you all that you would care to know, but they get you going in the right direction and expect you to fill in the rest (cf., for instance, 21:2). They are especially useful at all sorts of times and places. The important point to be learned is that they are not static, one-dimensional thoughts having to do with only one incident. Truth, applied to the specific case mentioned, is beneath the case and broader than the case to which it adheres in the proverb. That is why a proverb is, as someone has said, like hard candy. You have to suck on it, turning it over and over with your tongue, until you have sucked all there is out of it. The application to a specific case makes it portable and memorable, but remember, it also shows you *how* a given principle is to be applied.

The Hebrew noun translated **proverb** is *mashal.* Solomon spoke 3,000 of them (I Kings 4:32). To what, exactly, does this Hebrew word refer? Well, it was a large word that encompassed any sort of saying or writing that was out of the ordinary. Anything that was said in an enigmatic, unusual or roundabout way could be styled a proverb. A gnomic or aphoristic saying, a simile, a metaphor or even a parable could be referred to as a *mashal*. While a variety of *mashals* are employed in the Book of Proverbs, the most usual form is the simple comparison. That is why the word *mashal*, which means "likeness" or "comparison," is so appropriate as a title to the book.

The English term *proverb*, from *pro* (meaning "for, instead of") and *verba* ("words"), also readily describes the contents of the book. Proverbs is, indeed, a brief saying that takes the place of many words. This English term aptly refers to the compacting process.

By these comparisons (and likenesses) the proverbs warn, instruct, expose folly, point the way to wisdom, tell you what to expect in life (describing what it is like), show you how to live life in ways that please God and give you an idea about how things *tend* to work out without always being absolute about it. Proverbs is a thoroughly enjoyable book. Don't fail to make the most of it in your counseling. In this exposition, I have tried not only to explain what the author is saying at each point, but often to observe the underlying truth or principle and show something of how it may be applied in the counseling context. If you have never before studied the Book of Proverbs from the perspective of counseling, get ready for a treat—and I guarantee that as soon as you begin to use its contents freely in your counseling work, your counselees will know the difference! *Bon voyage.*

NOTE: The text of Proverbs cited in this commentary is from a new translation which I prepared. Throughout, the Lord's name, Yahweh, is used. This is according to the Hebrew. In the New Testament, verses employing this covenant name are applied to Jesus Christ. That means throughout Proverbs where "Yahweh" occurs you might as readily use the name Jesus Christ.

CHAPTER 1

Part One: Chapters 1-9

1 The proverbs of Solomon, David's son, king of Israel—
2 To know wisdom and disciplined training;
to understand words of discernment;

For basic information concerning the purpose, forms and methods used in writing and interpreting the Book of Proverbs, kindly see the Introduction. But more to the point of this chapter is the fact that the author gives us his own introduction to the book. He opens with a title (v. 1): **The proverbs of Solomon, David's son, king of Israel**. Plainly, this designation of the author means that Solomon composed and/or selected the proverbs of the first section. Later we shall see that the contributions of other inspired writers also are included. And indeed, other proverbs of Solomon himself are appended. The next six verses (vv. 2-7) provide a fitting general introduction to all that follows, describing the purpose for which the book was written. Verses 8 and 9 urge youth to heed to the counsels of their parents, verses 10 through 19 warn against those who would tempt them to get involved in bloodthirsty robbery, verses 20 through 23 echo with the call of Wisdom, and the chapter concludes with a description of the terrifying results of a failure to heed her call (vv. 24-33). It is a powerful introduction to the words of the first nine chapters in particular and to the Book of Proverbs as a whole.

Let us look now at verses 2 through 6. The main purpose is clearly set out: **to know wisdom and disciplined training; to understand words of discernment** (v. 2). Note what is up front. If you want wisdom and knowledge, there is wisdom and knowledge to be had. That means that the counselor and his counselees may find instruction about the will of God in this book. It is a book of revealed truth. To communicate knowledge of God's will for His covenant people, then, is one aim of the author. Secondly, that will of God is called **wisdom**, a key term in this book. Proverbs belongs to a genre of biblical writing referred to as wisdom literature. By reading this material, learning from its insights and following its instructions, one will become wise. The word **wisdom** means more than the attaining of knowledge; it carries the idea of skillful use of knowledge in the service of God. The wise man is one who competently lives for Him. This wisdom, however, does not come easily; it is attained only by

3 To receive disciplined training in prudence,
right living, judgment and uprightness.
4 To give clear perception to the naive,
knowledge and discretion to the young man.

---

disciplined training in righteousness (see II Timothy 3:16). As one reads again and again the wisdom that is inculcated in Proverbs, and prayerfully, and consistently applies it in life, he trains himself in righteous living. This is a training manual. The word for **discipline** here *(musar)* is also used in 22:15. But there is also a concern for the reader to **understand words of discernment** (lit., "to discern the words of discernment"). The word *bin*, from which these terms are derived, means instruction or understanding that comes with the ability to separate or distinguish between things that differ. One of the principal ways in which counselees run into trouble is from their lack of discernment. For more on this matter in general, and the use of the word in particular, see my book, *A Call to Discernment.*

In verse 3, a string of related words appears: **to receive disciplined training in prudence, right living, judgment and uprightness.** Not only will one learn the best ways of doing something from Proverbs, so that he may act **prudently** when doing so, but in addition, he will discover what **right living** means, how to make good **judgments** and what it is to be **upright** in all things. He will be able to settle questions of right and wrong, will know what is morally right in God's sight and will be able to move through life with the care and patience born of prudent action. Wow! Isn't that precisely what your counselees—just about all of them—need? Think of those who stumble and bumble into trouble because they lack **prudence**. The acquisition of that characteristic alone would reduce the number of counselees that you see by at least a third—wouldn't it? Consider the thoughtless manner in which they go about living their lives, the ways in which they drift, stumble and hurt others unintentionally. Think too of the counselees who cannot tell right from wrong, who are unable to understand how to acquire and apply truth from the Bible. They are at sea most of the time; they never seem to reach harbor. And if and when they do make landfall they come crashing into rocks and barriers instead of gliding safely into port. They lack the very qualities in which this book purports to be able to train them. How useful Proverbs is for counselees!

5 The wise person hears and increases his learning,
and those who exercise discernment will acquire wise counsel to guide them,

---

Now the sort of person who needs the teaching of this training manual is mentioned: **to give clear perception to the naive, knowledge and discretion to the young man** (v. 4). The "simple" or **naive** is the one who is highly impressionable, who is open to all sorts of influences—both good and bad. He lacks the know-how and the **discretion** to distinguish the one from the other. He is in a dangerous place; he lives in a fallen world that continually beckons him in addition to the call of **wisdom**. He has trouble knowing which voice is which; he does not know how to distinguish the two. That is what this wisdom book will provide if he reads and heeds.

Counselees abound who have been scammed into all sorts of things thinking that they were doing right only to wake up too late to the fact that they were "had." They, like the **young man** who lacks experience, are **naive**, gullible. That is understandable in one who is only beginning life, but if they have for years possessed the Book of Proverbs and remain so, there is no excuse for the sort of **naivete´** that leads to trouble and sin. It is time for them to grow up; time to learn what the world is all about. As a counselor, you are fortunate to have a book that will enable you to help them do so.

Verse 5 reads: **The wise person hears and increases his learning, and those who exercise discernment will acquire wise counsel to guide them.** The fool drifts along with what **knowledge** and **discernment** he has (which generally is little to begin with, and even that is slipping away). No wonder many persons need counsel about even the simplest matters. But the **wise** man is ever **increasing** his store of information and sharpening his intellectual and social skills in ways that please God. He wants to know about the teachings he will discover in Proverbs, and will find waiting to put them into practice difficult. He will devour new truth from God and improve his life as a result. Counselees like him soon find that their problems will melt away. Others, however, who lack such enthusiasm for learning God's Word, will not progress in counseling. Therefore, you must encourage this trait for learning. You must show them how the very acquisition of a new truth from God can change everything. Just recently, a counselee said to me, "Now that's a new thought," as I used a passage from Proverbs to illuminate his situation by showing him what

6 to understand a proverb and its interpretation,
the words of the wise and their dark sentences.

God wanted him to do about it. You could see how this one fact newly awakened hope in him concerning a matter about which he had all but given up. In fact, that new insight was a turning point in the counseling session.

Those who exercise discernment are always glad for **wise counsel,** no matter who may give it. Here, it is Proverbs that is the source of such **counsel**. But, note well, the Bible firmly stands on the side of using counsel that one obtains from the Scriptures. Here is a source of counsel, then, that the counselor neglects only at peril to his counseling and to his counselees. Counselees, on the other hand, who are not interested in such **counsel** may be shown from this passage (and many others in this book) how unwise their disinterest is.

It is not always easy to interpret the Bible on one's own (though it is the obligation of every believer to growingly become able to do so), so it is necessary for many to consult with those who can make sense of those things that are difficult for them. They seek **wise counsel** in order **to understand a proverb and its interpretation, the words of the wise and their dark sentences**. Now, there is your commission counselor. You are to become one who not only understands and can interpret **proverbs,** but who also is able to penetrate into the meanings of those verses that many find too **dark** (i.e., unintelligible). A big order? Why, certainly. But what could be of greater benefit to you and to your counselees than for them to be able to come to you uncertain about the meaning of God's Word, and to find you able to enlighten them? Much of counseling at one point or another involves enlightenment about various aspects of Scripture. To counsel well, you must interpret well. Every counselor must consider it his duty to become a good interpreter of the Bible.

Why isn't all Scripture equally perspicuous? Some of its **sentences** are **dark**. God may have many reasons for this. Certainly all those things that have to do with the way of salvation and with basic Christian living are patent on their surface. But there are other passages into which one must delve, diving very deeply for understanding. These He may have given in the form of parables and enigmatic sayings *in order to fix their richness in one's mind once he understands them.* It is possible too that He reveals truth in such a manner in order to induce us to engage in more serious study of His Word. Whatever God's purposes in this matter may

7 The fear of Yahweh is the beginning of knowledge;
but stupid fools despise wisdom and disciplined training.

---

be—and we do not need to inquire into them more fully—we know that the **dark** sayings of the Bible do serve to nudge us into deeper study of it.

Now, the climax of the purpose statement with which the Book begins: **The fear of Yahweh is the beginning of knowledge; but stupid fools despise wisdom and disciplined training** (v. 7). There, in one sentence, is the nub of all that is being said. The wise man will come to **know** God and His **wisdom** through the proper state of mind and the proper relationship to God. To attain to **wisdom** (which comprises all that series of words whose meanings we have been exploring) one must **fear** God. He must understand that God is His **Yahweh—**the covenant making and the covenant keeping God Whose slogan is, "You are My people and I am your God." To be in the relationship of fellowship with **Yahweh** through salvation and openness to His will as it is revealed in the Bible, is the condition for learning. The **fear of Yahweh** is not some servile fear, but a holy awe that flows from a healthy acknowledgment of His might and power. In certain places the phrase has become a semi-technical term meaning *to be in a right relationship to God through saving faith.*

Counselor, don't miss the point here: counseling for change that pleases God is not an academic matter. Nor is it merely a matter of behavior change. Good counseling begins by bringing counselees into a proper relationship with God. It is a moral-relational matter.

But, sadly, there are **stupid fools**[1] who **despise wisdom**. They **despise wisdom** because they are **fools**, and they are **fools** because they **despise wisdom**. Cyclically, the two feed one another. In counseling, however, you may need to determine which is dominant. Is one a fool, and therefore, one who stupidly despises wisdom? That is to say, does he have no interest whatsoever in wisdom because he is a fool? Or is it the other way round—is he a fool *because* he has turned his back on wisdom? There may be more hope for the latter than for the former, if you can help him to repent and turn around.

At any rate, it is important to recognize that here Solomon is making a plea for the reader to enter into the study of that which will bring him

---

1. There are three words for **fool** in Proverbs. I have distinguished them by adding an adjective to each: The *ewil* (used here) I translate "stupid fool;" The *k^e^sil*, "stubborn fool" and the *nabal*, "shameful fool."

8 My son, listen to your father's disciplined training,
and do not neglect your mother's law.
9 They will be an attractive ornament adorning your head,
and like chains for your neck.

---

the **wisdom** he needs for life. He urges a pious attitude that submits to and delights in the truths that God has revealed in his Word (in this case, in Proverbs in particular). To learn **wisdom** means first of all to love **Yahweh**, the Fountain from Whom all true wisdom flows (James 1:5ff.).

But what is it to ***despise*** **wisdom and disciplined training**? The word in the original is a strong one indicating that the **fool** in question has stupidly slighted and even acted contemptuously toward wisdom and the training by which it is acquired. To **despise** it is more than the sour grapes attitude of one who has failed to learn as he ought; rather, it is to take a positive delight in showing contempt (probably by outward words and actions) for something. He has abandoned (or never begun) the search for wisdom, not so much out of lethargy (though that is where his antipathy toward wisdom and training may have begun) as out of a definite dislike for it. He is, according to the word for **fool** used here, one who will have nothing of the counsel of others; he is self-confident to the point of **despising** wisdom out of self-importance and pride. To submit to a teacher or counselor is the height of stupidity in his mind, whereas exactly the opposite is true. He is stupid for failing to do so. So, Solomon's admonition is to heed Wisdom's call to come and drink to the fill. If you do not, you will end up in the company of fools, and become like them.

Verses 8 and 9 are directed to an application of the commandment to honor father and mother. Indeed, the very first word is the *shema* of the Book of Proverbs: **hear.** It is a plea to accept the wisest counsel that any youth can ever receive; it is a plea to listen to the words of one's **father** and **mother**. He urges the reader, **My son, listen to your father's discipline** (*musar*) **and do not neglect your mother's law**. The beginning of wisdom is to fear Yahweh. One who does will respect his father and mother and heed their commands because in His Word Yahweh tells him to do so. Thus, the next step in wisdom occurs: next to fearing God, the wise son obeys his parents.

Why should one obey? Because God commands it, of course. But what will it do for him? Obedience to the disciplined training and the law of his parents will cause others to note that the results are like **an attractive ornament adorning your head** (or headdress) **and like chains for**

10 My son, if sinners entice you, do not willingly consent.
11 If they say, "Come walk with us; let's lie in wait for blood.
Let's ambush some who have no reason to suspect it.
12 Let's swallow them alive like Sheol does,
whole, like those going down into the pit.
13 We'll find all sorts of valuable stuff;
we'll fill our houses with loot!
14 Throw your lot in with us;
we'll all share one bag."
15 My son, don't walk in the way with them;
keep your foot off their path.
16 Their feet are rushing toward evil;
they are hurrying to shed blood.
17 It's useless to spread out the net in the sight of any bird,
18 but these men lie in wait for their own blood;
they are ambushing themselves!
19 So are the ways of every one who is out to get gain;
it takes away its owner's life.

---

your neck (v. 9). The **chains** are not to be thought of as binding, but rather as adorning one's neck. In other words, the one who accepts his parents' instruction and obeys their will is going to live a beautiful life. His ways and his words will be attractive to others. Not only is he likely to attract the right sort of marriage partner, but also friends and working associates who are pleased to know someone like him. He will be a delightful person who exhibits a lifestyle that is like fair jewels in his headdress and beautiful **chains** around his **neck**. What a magnificent goal for a young person—or anyone! How worthwhile is the study of the Word. How important for the youth (or older person) whose lifestyle is anything but attractive to others. On the other hand, you may find it necessary to explain to the one who wonders why no one wants to associate with him, that it is because of the absence of these adornments. If he is older, and has grown up in rebellion against his parents, he may still have to learn all those lessons they might have taught him, at this late date. A rebellious person, one who wants only his own way and will not listen to others, is not a person who attracts others. They will turn from him as soon as they discover what he is like. Part of your work as a counselor is to size up the situation and learn which **chains** and **ornaments** are missing. In effect, then, you must become his surrogate parent, helping him fit these into the costume of his life.

Coming to verses 10 through 19, we are introduced to a longer section having to do with robbery and violence. It is virtually a picture of what we see on TV every night. If ever a passage of Scripture were appropriate to our day this is it. Let me set forth the picture as a whole, in uninterrupted sequence as the author sketches it. He begins with a plea that is also a warning: **My son, if sinners entice you, do not willingly consent.** He then goes on to the description of the temptation, even using dialog to add to the drama:

They say: **Come, walk with us; let's lie in wait for blood. Let's ambush some who have no reason to suspect it. Let's swallow them alive like Sheol does—whole, like those going down into the pit. We'll find all sorts of valuable stuff; we'll fill our houses with loot! Throw your lot in with us; we'll all share one bag.**

Father: **My son, don't walk in the way with them; keep your foot off their path. Their feet are rushing toward evil; they are hurrying to shed blood. It's useless to spread out the net in the sight of any bird, but these men lie in wait for their own blood; they are ambushing themselves! So are the ways of every one who is out to get gain; it takes away its owner's life.**

This dramatic exchange, as I suggested above, is more than appropriate to our time. With the advent of street gangs in many large cities and the increase of crime—murder and robbery have become commonplace—no sounder advice could be given by a father/teacher to a young man. The public schools, in many places, have become a breeding ground for such activities, and the age of those participating in them has been falling every year. The method for warning here is powerful. The counselor takes the counselee behind the closed doors of those thugs who would like to recruit his pupils. He lets them listen in to their enticing spiel. He makes it sound every bit as exciting as it might be; his words are realistic. If and when his students are ever faced with such a proposition, they cannot fail to remember his warning. At the outset, he even makes it sound easy, challenging, inviting, sure to produce gain. But then he turns the tables. These people actually are lying in wait for their *own* blood; they can't wait to rush to their own death. They are hurrying toward trouble. If you spread a net in the eyes of a bird to trap him in it, your efforts will be in vain. A bird is smart enough to recognize the danger. But these people are so ignorant that they fail to see—what ought to be in full view of their eyes—that they are setting a trap for *themselves*. They will end up *dying* for their gain! Those who take the sword will die by the sword.

When counseling, drawing a vivid, accurate picture of the trouble toward which one's counselee is heading, as a warning to call him off, is a powerful method. For instance, you may find yourself describing life in a mental institution toward which a counselee may be heading if he fails to assume responsibility for his life. And, when you do something like that, why not embellish it the way Solomon does—with *dialog*? Dialog is an important means of making principles come to life; it is almost as good as recreating the actual scene itself. And it is impressive; it leaves a deeper dye in the mind of the hearer than the mere repetition of a principle. By example, the Book of Proverbs shows a counselor much about how to best reach his counselees (for more, see the Introduction).

Notice the contrast between the two perspectives from which the speakers view the proposed criminal way of life. On the one hand, the gang leader sees only money, easy living and the horrid thrill of theft and murder. He is short sighted; blinded by the glare of sin. The teacher, in contrast, sees beyond the temporary gain to the ultimate, dismal outcome of it all: utter ruin and death. The one sees the enterprise as a rushing toward quick wealth; the other as a path down which one recklessly runs toward death and destruction.

Any counselor worth his salt will be able to see more in an evil scheme than the gains that may tempt his counselee. He will, therefore, be able to sketch a bigger picture. No counselee, contemplating an unsavory course of action (adultery, theft, etc.) willing or unwilling to listen, should ever leave your office without having been shown such contrasting scenes as you dramatically paint them for him. It is part of good teaching to do so. And remember, every counselor (to the extent that he is a faithful and successful counselor) by virtue of the nature of the task of counseling, *is* a teacher (for more on this, see my book, *Teaching to Observe: The Counselor as Teacher*).

Following hard on the heels of the call of the wicked to obtain gain (actually to obtain death) comes the call of **Wisdom** (personified) to the naive who is satisfied with his naiveté and the fool who has been rejecting knowledge. Presumably, the call issued in verses 20 through 23 to such persons means that there is hope for them, even though they are in such an advanced state of sin, lethargy and scorn. Let's listen to Wisdom who (again in dramatic dialog) seeks to win the heart of the reader. Verses 20 through 21 is what is said about her by way of introduction.

20 Wisdom shouts loudly in the street;
in the public squares she raises her voice.
21 At the most prominent spot of the noisy gathering places she calls;
at the openings of the city gates she speaks her message:
22 "How long, you naive ones will you love naiveté—
scorners delight in their scorning,
and obstinate fools hate knowledge?
23 Turn in repentance at my rebuke!
Look, I will pour out my Spirit toward you;
I will make my words known to you."

What a powerful speech that is! **Wisdom** is not for the few; it is not found only in esoteric places. No! Indeed, wisdom **cries out loudly** in all sorts of **prominent** public places where everyone can hear and respond. No one may complain that wisdom is inaccessible to him. He fails to listen to its call. The simple, inexperienced, naive person who doesn't want to progress, as well as the scorner who mocks at knowledge which he hates (because it would condemn him), alike are called to repentance. **Turn**, the graphic Hebrew word for **repentance**, pictures one who is following a wrong course of action and is called by Wisdom to turn back and get on the right one. According to this invitation, even the worst sinner (see Psalm 1:1, where the **scorner** is at the top of the heap) may repent and be saved to a productive life of honoring God. How is he to turn back? He is to recognize that the call of God comes to him, that his sinful way of life is futile and that God can change him dramatically. All of this is achieved by the Word (**message**) of **Wisdom** and the **Spirit.** God promises to those who want to change not only His good counsel but also the power of His Spirit of holiness to enable them to make the needed changes. That is a promise that any counselor may hold out to counselees, no matter how sordid, how hardened their previous attitudes and behavior may have been.

But if they refuse to heed the call of wisdom their doom is sure. There comes a time when God will cease calling. And a time when He will hear them no more. Counselors need to warn stubborn counselees that light rejected is a serious matter, that what they are hearing from the Bible (presupposing, of course, they are) ought to be given full consideration because it *may* be the last opportunity they will ever have to respond. Listen as Wisdom continues in verses 24 through 28.

24 "Because I called and you refused,
stretched out my hand but nobody responded,
25 you ignored all my counsel
and didn't want my rebuke,
26 I too will laugh—at your calamity.
I'll mock you when your terrifying fear comes—
27 when your terrifying fear comes like a storm—
and your calamity arrives like a tornado;
when distress and despair come upon you."
28 Then they will call to me and I won't answer;
they will search for me early, but won't find me.

These riveting words are intended to extend a powerful warning to all who continue to reject truth and reproof. In the face of rejected light and offered help, those who persist in their foolish ways will discover that the time will come when it is too late to turn; repentance will give way to mere regret. Though they **call on** God He will not **answer**. Though they get up **early** (i.e., make it a priority—a matter of first importance) to search for God, it will be too late; they will not find Him. He will **laugh** at their **fear** and **distress** which will come like a **tornado**, like a hurricane—with devastating force. All they will receive from God is the same sort of **mocking** and jeers that they, themselves, directed at Him and His Word for so long! These are terrifying words. And because they are, it is best for you in using them merely to read them, and not try to paraphrase them. People need to hear directly from God's Word itself about the jeopardy into which they are plunging themselves. Therefore, when dealing with a scorner in counseling (usually, it will be at the last session—unless this warning has a salutary effect), you might close the discussion in a powerful way by reading this section. I urge you not to avoid such portions of the Scriptures; they are given precisely for such purposes and ought to be so used. There are few other places in which you will find a more pointed warning about the danger of rejecting God as He implores them with outstretched hand to repent. As a consequence, those who fail to do so will be rejected by Him.

Wisdom concludes her speech in verses 29 through 33:

29 Because they hated knowledge
and did not choose the fear of Yahweh,
30 Because they didn't want my counsel,
despised my every reproof,
31 They will eat of the fruit of their ways
and be filled with their own schemes.
32 Now, the turning away of the naive will kill them,
and the ease of the stubborn fools will destroy them.
33 But the one who listens to me will dwell securely
and will be at ease from the terrifying fear of evil happenings.

Again, I can only commend the use of these concluding remarks by Wisdom in circumstances such as I have described above when looking at her earlier warning. Do, however, note the final word of hope in verse 33. To **listen** (i.e., heed)—which is the burden of the entire section—is to reap the fruit of **security** and true prosperity—and **ease**. The **ease** of the wicked is unsteady, perilous, ready at any moment to rip apart. That of the one who hears Wisdom when she calls is lasting and certain. That does not mean that all will be a bed of roses, you might want to observe. Rather, it may mean **ease** of soul in the midst of persecution or trial. Yet, there will be nothing to **frighten** or **terrify** the heart of those who have placed their trust in Yahweh. That is true ease and security (cf. III John 2, "even as your soul is prospering").

What a forceful beginning to the Book of Proverbs. If you use the book at all in counseling, surely you will want to use this chapter. Is there any other book of the Bible that so aptly describes the lure and the danger of violence, criminal activity, and gang membership? Here you have a remarkable, almost unique, source of help in this area; don't fail to recognize and deploy it!

Chapter 2

1 My son, if you will receive my words and store my commands within you,
2 so as to bow your ear to wisdom, you will stretch your heart toward discernment.

In chapter two, we are treated to a very positive exposition of the benefits, results and other advantages of following the way of wisdom. Chapter two, presumably, is for those who, having heard of the two ways set forth in chapter one and being inclined to follow the way of wisdom, want to learn more about it. Solomon doesn't hesitate to expatiate. This chapter is designed, then, to consolidate early gains in those who have responded well so far.

It is wise for counselors not to take too much for granted. People sometimes opt for proper courses of action on the basis of too little information. So unless you take the time to fill them in on additional aspects of what you have said, this insufficiency may have the effect of leading them to question their decision later on. Learn to buttress early gains with solid, biblical facts on which they may rely when trial or temptation faces them in the future. That seems to be what the writer does here. If one has been inclined to read on to this point after those severe warnings of chapter one (which, in part, were designed to separate those who are serious from those who aren't), it is time to lay some more solid groundwork beneath his feet.

The father/teacher once again addresses his son/student: **My son, if you will receive my words and store my commands within you, so as to bow your ear to wisdom, you will stretch your heart toward discernment** (vv. 1, 2). To **store** up God's truth in one's **heart** is to learn it not only in the sense of being able to repeat verses parrot-like, but to be able to recall the substance of that teaching in times when it is needed for analyzing situations, making decisions, answering questions, etc. To be **discerning**, one needs the words and commands of the Scriptures at ready at all times. This, then, is a notice that what is about to be said is not merely to be read; rather it is to be pondered, understood and thought through, assimilating it into the very thought life and lifestyle of the reader. Solomon is calling for a serious study of what he is about to offer.

There may be counselees who can recite verses perhaps better than you can. Yet, they have no idea what those verses mean. In assigning the

3 So, if you call out for discernment and lift up your voice for discernment,
4 if you will seek her as silver and search for her as hidden treasure,
5 then you will know the fear of Yahweh and find the knowledge of God.

---

memorization of verses in counseling, I advise you to assign few (so that they may be truly learned), together with a clear explanation of the meaning of each. In addition, I suggest that you learn to give instances of how each verse (or unit of verses) may be applied and implemented. For more on a method of Scripture study, see my book *What to Do on Thursday*, which also might be used as a handout to help counselees become more adept in assimilating the Bible into their lives. The idea behind the title of that book is that we have not taught people how to move from the problems that occur on Thursday (or any other weekday) to the Bible to find a solution. Rather, we have taught people only to memorize for next Sunday's Bible quiz! The book is designed to remedy the situation.

The passage continues, citing the reason why storing up God's truth will lead to this end: **So, if you call out for discernment and lift up your voice for discernment, if you will seek her as silver and search for her as hidden treasure, then you will know the fear of Yahweh and find the knowledge of God** (vv. 3-5). So the fear of Yahweh involves **discernment**—the ability to distinguish right from wrong, truth from error—which, in turn, comes from an understanding of the **words** and **commands** of God. Unlike others, our faith is based solidly on data. It involves an acceptance of the truth. The basic data, you know, are those facts about the death and resurrection of Jesus Christ Who, in bearing the sins of His people, effected the atonement with God. Likewise, all progress in the Christian life is based on data. One may not acquiesce in a life of drifting about in some "spiritual dreamland" that consists of mouthing pious-sounding platitudes and smiling a lot, but that does not require one to do the hard work of coming to understand and learning to apply the Scriptures. One wonders, from the way that many Christian counselees lead their lives in avoiding all serious study of God's Word, how they expect to grow and go in the ways of righteousness. Presumably, because of how he speaks in this chapter, God assuredly thinks His Word is necessary! Tell them so. The passage is "fragrant with hope" for all those who do not turn their nose up at the thought of Bible study.

And as you note the emphasis on searching for wisdom as one would search for treasures, you understand something of the urgency, dedication,

6 This is because Yahweh gives wisdom; from His mouth come knowledge and discernment.
7 He stores up sound wisdom for the upright; He is a Shield for those walking in integrity

---

time, energy and thought that God expects us to devote to the project. Treasure hunters are persistent! Counselees, who fail to exert much effort and who show little enthusiasm for the endeavor, give evidence of what is behind the problems that they bring to the counseling room. In addition to helping them resolve specific problems, therefore, if you want to avoid the necessity for counselees to return over and over again for help, instill a love and concern for biblical study in counselees. Do you? If not, is there not something drastically lacking in your counseling that you need to remedy?

Verse 6 says it all; these things are true **because Yahweh gives wisdom; from His mouth come knowledge and discernment** (v. 6). There is only one source of wisdom—God. And He dispenses it one way alone: **from His mouth**. And it comes from Him in the form of **knowledge and discernment**. "Man cannot live by bread alone!" Drive that home to every counselee who is starved for truth, discernment and knowledge from trying (unsuccessfully) to do so apart from that heavenly bread. Strongly emphasize the great affirmation that he also must live "by every word that comes from God's mouth" (Matthew 4:4). The sole way of accessing those soul-nourishing words today is from a study of the Bible in which they are recorded. In the story of the acquisition of wisdom by Solomon (I Kings 4:29ff.), it is clear that, as we read here, Yahweh is the One Who ***gives* wisdom**. Wisdom is a *gift,* graciously imparted to those who seek it for the right reasons, from the right Source, in the right way.

But that is not all. The prospects of wisdom are manifold: **He stores up sound wisdom for the upright; He is a shield for those walking in integrity** (v. 7). God has all the **wisdom** any of His children could ever need; and He has **stored** it **up** for their use. Where? As we have already seen, in the Bible. It is for those whose lives are **upright** (i.e., "straight"; note our expression, "He's a straight shooter"). To say that God is a **shield** is to speak of His protection of those who walk in **integrity** (i.e., "who have it all together;" who are growing in every area of their lives. See comments in the *Christian Counselor's Commentary on James* having to do with the *teleios* man). It is possible from an examination of the Hebrew and the agreement of the Septuagint, that the words translated **sound wis-**

8 to guard the ways of judgment and protect the path of His saints.
9 Then you will understand righteousness and judgment and uprightness—indeed, every good path.

---

dom should be translated **help**, thus paralleling the second clause. All sorts of **help**—the various ways in which God provides it—then would be the idea. There is no end of the ways in which God is able to bring **help** to those who walk in a straight way, turning neither to the right nor to the left. Counselees may take heart in this fact. Be that as it may, which ever way it is better to translate, both are true.

God acts as a Shield and Helper **to guard the ways of judgment and protect the path of His saints** (v. 8). The **ways of judgment** are the **ways** on which the just travel. They are the **paths** that are taken by those who piously serve Him. Many counselees fear; they are running from this or that. But they fail to understand that the **paths** of righteousness are the **paths** of safety. They are those that God Himself patrols both to help those who stumble and to protect them from thieves and cutthroats. The answer to their problems, therefore, is not so much a matter of doing this or that (though any action commanded in Scripture must be followed) as it is making sure that one is traveling the right **path** in the right way.

Then you will understand righteousness and judgment and uprightness—indeed, every good path (v. 9). Following the way of wisdom leads to discernment; one is enabled by it to **distinguish** between **paths** of **righteousness, justice and honesty** and those that are not. Indeed, embracing biblical **wisdom** makes it possible to find **all the paths of goodness**. That is to say, counselees receive guidance in doing those things that please God from the wisdom of the Word. The Bible, not some mystical way or other involving promptings or hunches, is the source of guidance. That, of course, is in strict accord with everything taught in the New Testament as well. Counselees who fall into the various traps associated with false means of guidance need to be instructed in the import of these words. They constitute *an infallible guide to guidance*!

There is much in this next section (vv. 10-15), some of which, however, we have dealt with already. The new element is the appearance of an unexpected threat to those walking on the paths of righteousness. It is the influence of those who **leave the paths of righteousness to walk in the ways of darkness**. Obviously, their profession of faith was false; they were wolves in sheep's clothing. They go out from us to make it known that they were not of us (I John 2:19). These apostates, leaving the path, can be a serious enough jolt to believers; their defection itself can cause

10 When wisdom enters your heart and knowledge is pleasing to you,
11 discretion will protect you; discernment will watch over you
12 to deliver you from the evil way, from the men who speak perverted things,
13 who leave paths of uprightness to walk in ways of darkness,
14 who rejoice to do evil and delight in the perversities of evil persons,
15 whose ways are crooked and who are devious in their ways;

---

problems enough. But they do not leave quietly; they want to take others with them: they **rejoice in evil and delight in perversity, and *speak perverted things***. Their influence, their cutting words about the truth, spoken to justify their declension from it, can all have a strong influence on the young and weak if they are not careful to avoid such people, and if they listen to the **perverse things** they **speak**. Obviously, the writer warns the reader about this prospect so that when it happens he will be prepared and not surprised by it. And he will know what to do. He also wants him to avoid their influence. Warning ahead of time, again, is an important matter for counselors to be aware of.

This warning is apropos to many of the circumstances faced by your counselees. They are in trouble precisely because they have listened to those who have abandoned the ways of righteousness. Once more we are being warned about adverse influence exercised by others outside the faith; but, especially, from those who once professed to believe. Perhaps, more often than not, it is those people, rather than avowed skeptics, who are the most vitriolic and spew forth the vilest abuse. And because they have walked with the faithful, they are most aware of their shortcomings and are able to make out an apparently strong case against them. They are adept at pointing out inconsistencies, forgetting, of course, to mention their own! Counselors often fail to probe to discover whether anyone is exercising an adverse influence on their counselees. It is important to do so. And of chief importance is to try to find out if there are any apostates doing so.

Much can be said about the next verses (vv.16-19), as I have said already in my book *Marriage, Divorce and Remarriage in the Bible*. For here, therefore, I shall but summarize. Marriage is a Covenant of Companionship (see Genesis 2:18). The **companion** (or **guide**) whom the adulteress abandons later in life is her husband. She is called an **alien** and **foreigner** because harlotry was forbidden in Israel. Yet, it is possible for one of the covenant people to do the same as these heathen. Typically, she becomes a temptress who **flatters** men with her **words**. Believers are

16 to deliver you from the alien woman, from the foreigner who flatters by her words,
17 who abandons the companion of her youth and forgets the covenant of her God.
18 Her house settles down to death, and her roads to the departed.
19 None of those who go in to her return, nor do they reach the paths of life.
20 Thus you must walk in the ways of good people and keep to the paths of the righteous,
21 because the upright will dwell in the land and persons of integrity will remain in it.
22 But evil persons will be cut off from the land and hypocrites will be uprooted from it.

---

warned against getting involved with her. There is but one end to those who do—**death** (the writer will expand on this at a later point).

Since there will be more about the consequences of adultery later on, I shall wait until then to speak further of it. Nevertheless, again, it is important to observe that Proverbs is a prime source of instruction and warning about this prevalent evil in our society with which so much counseling is concerned.

Finally, God keeps you so that you may **walk in the ways of good men and keep to the paths of the righteous, because the upright will dwell in the land and persons of integrity will remain in it. But evil persons will be cut off from the land and hypocrites will be uprooted from it.** It is a good thing that by wisdom God **keeps** His own in the **ways** that **good** people **walk**; else we would all perish. This He does because He desires the **upright** to **dwell** in His **land**. After all, it *is* His land, and He has a right to say who will and who will not live in it. Those who have it all together (the *tam* or *teleios* people mentioned earlier) are the ones who will be allowed to **remain**. Those whose lives are **evil** and **hypocrites** will be **cut off from the land** and from the covenant people; they will be **uprooted** from God's holy soil.

All this had to do with the land of Israel, in the first place, but as Hebrews 11 repeatedly says, it had more far-reaching impact: it pertains as well to that land where God's own will dwell eternally. Again there is, at the conclusion of this chapter, both promise and warning. That is the way that God consistently deals with people—holding out both side by side. Counselors, speaking under conditions that warrant it, to be faithful to Him, must do the same.

CHAPTER 3

1 My son, don't forget my law;
but let your heart guard my commands;

The chapter is varied in its instruction, but has one unifying theme: wisdom is what you need to make it in this life. A general idea of what wisdom is, its great value and what it can do is presented.

In verses 1 and 2 the teacher urges the reader to remember his **law**. That is to say, his teaching. But, of course, it is not *his* teaching alone; he has in mind the *divine* teaching about **wisdom**; the law of God. Though one hears and hears, in the heat of the situation in which the law is so direfully needed, the pressure is to **forget**. That is why this reminder—one that counselors also must repeat over and over—is so necessary. Counselees *do forget.* Any and everything you can do, therefore, to help them remember is of value. And giving them reminders is the strategy we encounter here. The negative side is **do not forget**; the positive is **let your heart guard my commands** (here, **commands** is the parallel equivalent of **law**). It is easy for a **command** to be **forgotten** if one fails to make active efforts to **guard** it.

How does one guard God's commands? If he recognizes the value of God's commands, he will guard them so that no one may steal them from him. Frequently in the Proverbs wisdom is said to be worth far more than silver or gold—or even precious jewels. Until one recognizes their worth as Solomon does he will not take the trouble to **guard** the law. But, as one finds ways of guarding what is most valuable to him among his earthly possessions, the person who realizes the value of the teaching and instruction of God, also will find ways of remembering to guard the biblical treasures that he has learned. So, fundamentally, not forgetting and guarding is a matter of considering God's truth to be every bit as precious as it truly is. That is what the counselor must get across to his counselee: what he has learned here from the Scriptures about his problems and their solutions must be greatly valued! If he can get the counselee to recognize the worth of the teaching he has received, he will have achieved a great deal toward the end that is set forth in verse 1.

Every sort of influence in this wicked world is at work trying to wean a counselee away from God's way. Never forget these wise insights of Proverbs. That is why the admonition of verse 1 is so important. If he lets

2 they will add length of days, and years of life
and peace to you.

---

truth once learned slip from him, he will not have anywhere else to turn. He must retain it clear, unmixed, dominant in his **heart**. The issue is this: who will have his heart? To have the law of God in one's heart is to have it dominate the motivational center of his life. That is the point. When it guides and permeates the heart, continually before one in his thoughts, decisions and planning day by day, he will retain and not forget it. And as I said, when God's way is the way that is of the greatest significance to one, he will find the ways and means of remembering wisdom. "How can you be sure of this?" you ask. I am sure because Jesus said, "Where your treasure is, there will your heart be also." If God's revealed law and commands are your treasure, then your heart will be focused on them. Your **heart** *will* **guard** them.

But verse 2 tells you one fact that should encourage counselees to make the commandments of God their treasure: **they will add length of days, and years of life and peace to you**. That fact is a powerful incentive. And obviously it is true. Healthy living in terms of following biblical commands does, on the whole, lead toward longevity (something that the Proverbs continually emphasize). As this first part of the Book of Proverbs (chapters 1-9) teaches, robbery and murder as well as adultery lead to an untimely death. People who have disobeyed God's commands about homosexuality in our time have discovered the devastating effects of their behavior as the AIDS virus has swept through their communities. One could go on, but there is no need to do so. The facts are patent. Naturally, this statement must be qualified by the fact that persecution, physical defects, injury and other providential acts in God's plan do cut short the lives of some of His choice saints; the verse is not speaking of this fact. Jesus Himself was a victim of early death, as we all know. But, all other things being equal, the believer who observes the commands of God will tend to live longer. And the last element—**peace**—which in the Old Testament is a large concept including not merely tranquillity, but also a life of success in serving God, is the portion of those who guard the commandments of God by doing them and making them a part of their habitual lifestyle. That is what every person, down underneath, unknowingly seeks, but only the believer attains.

Verses 3 and 4 continue: **Mercy and truth must not forsake you; tie them about your neck, write them on the tablet of your heart.** To

3 Mercy and truth must not forsake you;
tie them about your neck, write them on the tablet of your heart,

---

be merciful is one of the beatitudes. Blessing comes to those who show mercy, kindness and thoughtful consideration to others. That is the meaning behind the term. **Truth** in an individual is truthfulness, the dependability of one's word. He is trustworthy. But, though you may have acquired these habits, the verse indicates that you may lose them. Solomon warns: don't let them **forsake you**. It is almost as if they had a will of their own and were all the time attempting to get away. That is, of course, what it is like in this life. When we think we have attained to something, we tend to take it for granted and, if not careful, will gradually abandon it. It is almost as if you had a dog on a leash and when you let go of the leash, it took off. The verse is saying don't let go; hold on tightly.

How? The second half of the verse gives the answer: **tie them about your neck, write them on the tablets of your heart**. When you buy a beautiful necklace that you prize, you are careful not to lose it. Rather, you will wear it on all appropriate occasions. So too should it be with mercy and truth. Whenever a situation calls for either, you must make it a practice to exhibit it. You must not lay your necklace aside, but wear it whenever it is proper to do so. You may lay it aside only to find that you have lost it. Compassion is easy to lose; the practice of shading truth may be readily adopted without realizing what is taking place. There is danger of losing either or both, or you can be sure that this word of warning would not have been issued. Has your counselee lost his necklace? Did he ever own it? These are questions to probe and matters with which he may need your help. Many counselees need to learn to think of others before themselves, showing mercy and kindness to them. There are all too many who fail in this regard. Check the matter out; it may be a large part of the problem your counselee is having with another. In addition (or separately) he may have difficulty with maintaining an altogether truthful lifestyle; the failure to do so can cause every sort of trouble.

But there is a second exhortation in line two of verse 3: **write them on the tablets of your heart**. I have discussed the **heart** already when considering verse 1. The **heart** is the inner you that determines your words, attitudes and actions. It is that which motivates you: out of it come the rivers (issues) of life. When **mercy** and **truth** pour forth from your life it is because these things were first found in your **heart**. If they are not embodied in the fabric of your life, they are not in your heart! That is why

4 and you will find favor and approval
in the eyes of God and man.

---

they should be written on your heart's **tablet**. The idea is to indelibly inscribe them in your thinking so that they will be always present in your living. To do so, you must be often thinking about your relationship to others and to the truth. You must continue to check up on yourself. Counselors can, in a sense, help a counselee to do just that by reminding them of these things and checking up from session to session. But they cannot do it for the counselee forever; he must be encouraged to take time each week (if not each day) to take stock of himself. We live such a hurried life, one that is so often filled with distractions, that a counselee may not ever take the time to go aside by himself to take thought for his life. Teach him the need to do so. Help him schedule such times. Check up on whether he did or not, etc. Help him to develop the habit of reading his heart to see what is inscribed there, and erasing what ought not to be, while replacing that with mercy and truth.

Suppose he does this; what will it do for him? What outcome may he expect? Verse 4 tells us: **you will find favor and approval in the eyes of God and man**. Certainly it is of the greatest importance to receive God's **approval**; *that* every counselee ought to be able to understand. And he ought to be driven primarily by nothing else. It ought to be uppermost in his concerns. But what of this word about **approval in the eyes of man**? Should we be motivated by what people think? Yes and no. We should never be concerned to receive human approval at the expense of God's. That is clear. But that is not the idea in the verse. The thought here is to attempt to find approval from others *in order to maintain a good witness for God.* When men praise your honesty and truthfulness, when they applaud you for showing mercy, you win the opportunity to tell them why you do as you do: that you serve the God from Whom you are ultimately seeking **approval**. In that way you may give the cup of cold water *in His Name*. You live as you do because you wish to please God. Counselees must be taught to put divine approval before human approval; all too often they tend to reverse the two. When they do, they will receive true approval from neither. Surely, the approval of men is good, but not at the expense of approval by God.

Verses 5 and 6 are well-known. I do not need to spend time, therefore, explaining their meaning. And they are probably well-known, often quoted and memorized, because they are easily understood and because

5 Trust in Yahweh with all your heart
and don't rely on your own discernment;
6 in all your ways acknowledge Him
and He will direct your paths.
7 Don't be wise in your own eyes;
fear Yahweh and avoid evil.

---

they contain a great promise. The promise is that when we stop **relying** on our own judgment and our **own** ways, and instead, rely on God (**acknowledging** Him by bringing Him into our decisions) He will **direct** us. Now, before you quote these verses to a counselee, be sure that you are careful to make it clear that God will not give direct revelation about the decision, or the way the counselee must go, beyond that which he reads in the Bible. Rather, this means that through all of the legitimate means (prayer, study and the application of biblical truth to the circumstance) God will so work out matters that the decision he makes will be the right one. That doesn't mean God will make the decision for him; the ways he takes are **His ways**. That is clear. But they are ways that in His providence He will bring about *by—not apart from—* his decision making. And there will be no promptings, sensings, feelings or the like. He will use the wisdom that is given in Proverbs as well as in the rest of the Bible. That is how God guides and directs—through His Word; not apart from it. That is important to emphasize. If that is not what He meant, then the entire thrust of this section and the rest of the proverbs concerning the written commandments of God would be foolish and unnecessary. One could simply pray and ask for some special revelatory sign from God. But there is nothing of that sort to be found in Proverbs. The counselee who thinks otherwise, believing he has a special pipeline to God, in the end will find that he is trusting in his own ways, relying on his **own discernment**, rather than God's. Make it clear that God dictates the terms by which He directs and guides; we have no right to do so.

Verse 8 raises an interesting question: why does the writer speak about the **navel**? When he continues the discussion of self-centered thought, he says that in contrast, the **fear of Yahweh** and the avoidance of **evil** that it will lead to, will also **bring health to your navel and moisture to your bones**. The word **navel** also may be translated "muscles, sinews." But **navel** is a good translation. Whatever the best translation, it is but a familiar biblical usage to speak of a part to represent the whole (as the second half of the couplet indicates when it refers to moisturized

8 That will bring health to your navel
and moisture to your bones.

---

bones). The idea is that the *body* will be healthy. Biblical living, in which (for instance) the body is cared for as the temple of the Spirit, tends to be **healthy** living. Rarely do Christians die of cirrhosis of the liver, lung cancer, etc. If one has a **healthy navel** and **bones**, he is healthy generally. The importance of the passage has nothing to do with the particular bodily part (or parts) mentioned, but rather with the health that the **fear of Yahweh** brings.

The phrase **fear of Yahweh** needs some explanation. This is an excellent place in which to give that explanation. Many reduce the word **fear** to mere awe or reverence. That is a mistake. Doubtless the effect of the **fear** in question is awe and reverence, but the word translated **fear** does speak of fright and dread. One must recognize that the **fear of Yahweh** is the result of man's sinful condition. A sinner—even a saved one—fears God. Whenever angels appear, the first thing they usually say is "Fear not." Why? Because the appearance of the supernatural reminds man of his relationship to the absolutely holy, the absolutely omnipotent and omniscient God Who created him and sustains his every breath. Man fears God for Whom He is in the light of what he is.

Now that fear is not a servile, groveling, cringing fear, but is a genuine recognition of Who God is in relation to the one fearing. It is a recognition of one's creaturely, utterly dependent relationship to the God Who made him. It is the recognition of the mighty power of God in relationship to one's utter frailty. It is a feeling of absolute dependence on Another—the fading of any self-trust or self-sufficiency that one may have possessed. To fear Yahweh, then, is precisely *not* to be wise in one's own eyes (v. 7), but to turn to Him for every explanation of the world and life itself. In short, it is to recognize God for Whom He is and one's self for whom he is. The phrase is used throughout the Bible, and especially in the Book of Proverbs, in a semi-technical sense to mean true religion, the faith that centers in Yahweh.

The word Yahweh (or Yahveh; we're not altogether sure of the correct pronunciation) means the ever-existing One. He is the One Who is the same yesterday, today and forever. When Jesus said, "Before Abraham was I am" those to whom He spoke fell backwards. Why? Because He had spoken the forbidden Name of God, Yahweh, when he pronounced those last two words, "I am." The Jews held the Name so sacred they

9 If you honor Yahweh with your money
and with the firstfruits of all your produce
10 your barns will be filled with plenty
and your vats will burst with new wine.

---

refused to pronounce it. If they were reading a verse, such as verse 7 here in Proverbs, they would use the vowels of another name of God along with the consonants of the word Yahweh, so that it would be pronounced *Jehovah.* So, to be as accurate as possible, I have translated the four consonants Yhwh, "Yahweh."

One will **avoid evil** when, indeed, he has the fear of Yahweh in his soul. He will not want to do anything that would displease the God of the universe. A respectful, reverent fear of God will cause one to refrain from evil. Self-exaltation is the opposite of this fear. It is an attempt to become autonomous, which was Adam's sin—the attempt to go one's own way, being **wise in his own eyes**, rather than God's. All other sin stems from the idea (expressed or otherwise) that one can know better than God what is best for himself. That is the thing that every counselor must watch for in his counseling of Christians. Every unbeliever depends on his own wisdom or on the wisdom of some other man (or men). Christians know that they should rather depend on God. But there is still much of the old ways in the believer. It is these that become the hindrance to growth and success in pleasing Christ. Whenever a counselee puts his—or another's—ideas before God's it is time to bring the session to a screeching halt. Point out what is happening. Make it clear that among others, this is a serious problem that he has that must be dealt with. Then do so. In one sense, all problems involve a measure of self-wisdom and self-will. We are all born thinking that we are more than we are and that God is less than He is. It takes the grace of God and the resultant **fear of Yahweh** to change that.

There are two more verses in this section of the chapter (vv. 9, 10). They have to do with giving. The one who gives **money** and the **firstfruits** of his field, in return, will receive even more from Yahweh. His **barns** will be **filled** with more **grain** and his **vats** with even larger amounts of oil and wine. In other words, one cannot outgive God. Many counselees need to be taught this lesson. They are stingy, self-serving and fail to give as they should. But God wants grateful, joyful givers; not those who give grudgingly. Your task, then, in cases where little is received because little is given, is to do all you can to induce gratitude in the counselee, so that he gives gladly. The Lord loves a cheerful giver. Begging is

11 My son, don't despise Yahweh's discipline,
and don't resent His correction.
12 Those Yahweh loves He reproves—
just as a father reproves a son in whom he delights.

---

not the right approach. While the fact that more will be given in return is a legitimate motive (as we see here), it must never be the *prime* one. Greed must not replace gratitude. Gratitude is always a by-product; it cannot be ginned up *de novo*. Gratitude stems from something else *for which* one is grateful. It is, therefore, that "something else" upon which you must concentrate. Instead of stressing giving, focus on the cross whenever you are attempting to encourage gratitude. In the long run, that is what everything else must come down to.

Verses 11 and 12 are quoted in Hebrews 12:5 and 6 and applied to the church in general, even though they are addressed to one called "My son" (see Introduction for implications of this fact). It is possible to take a wrong attitude toward discipline that comes from Yahweh. Like a good father, who out of love disciplines his sons, the heavenly Father disciplines all of us. Hebrews makes it clear that this is an indication that we are true sons of God. Moreover, though it is painful, discipline is also profitable: it leads to the peaceable fruit that comes from righteousness. All of the verbs used in these two verses for the **discipline** God exerts refer to unpleasant experiences. Because of that, it is possible for those who undergo it to become resentful and despise it. Children sometimes do this when their parents **discipline** them—though they too can be taught both to appreciate the fruits of **discipline** and the fact that it is exercised in their behalf out of love. **Discipline** is not a sign of God's displeasure with His own; it is a sign that He **delights** in them. It is evidence of His love.

That is the note that counselors must strike with complaining counselees. They must not allow or encourage them to continue with their complaints until they become resentful and learn to despise His **loving correction**. In conjunction with the Hebrews passage that explains more fully what is said here, the purpose and results of **discipline** can be set forth in some detail. For more information see *The Christian Counselor's Commentary on Hebrews*. It is dangerous for a counselee to develop resentment over the loving discipline of God; that is why this exhortation is of such great moment. If you detect it, deal with it before it grows and affects all you are trying to do to help. Remember, all change involves a proper relationship with God; those who **despise** His **discipline**, in

13 Happy is the person who finds wisdom
and the person who gets discernment.
14 The profit that comes from it will be greater than the profit from silver,
and the return that you get on it will be greater than from fine gold.
15 She is more precious than jewels,
and nothing you desire can be compared to her.
16 Length of days is in her right hand
and in her left hand are riches and honor;
17 her ways are pleasant ways
and all her paths are peace.

---

essence, **despise** and **resent** Him! It might be well also, to remember the words found in another piece of wisdom literature concerning God's discipline: **He makes sore and then binds up** (Job 5:17, 18). God is like the doctor who hurts in order to heal (see also Revelation 3:19).

Verses 13 through 17 speak of the benefits of **wisdom**: it is more valuable than, and yields greater **profit** than, **silver, fine gold and precious jewels**. **Wisdom**, as we have already seen, provides longevity **and riches, pleasant living and peace**. In fact, as Solomon—who ought to know since he had everything else as well—says, **Nothing you desire can be compared to her**. Did you feel the impact of that statement as you read it? ***Nothing*** can compare with **wisdom**. It is in a class by itself. Do you believe it? Then, as a counselor you must come to realize that the acquisition of divine **wisdom** should be foremost in your training and improvement as a counselor. Do you allocate the acquisition of this **wisdom** to that foremost place? Can counselees turn to you as a guide to *their* acquisition of God's **wisdom**? Are you a source for that **wisdom**? Does your counseling reflect it? In other words, do you put it before everything else in counseling? If not, you have some very basic changes to make in your study habits and your work as a counselor. Is there anything that you can think of that would make you a better counselor than an abundance of biblical wisdom? Think about it.

And remembering the words of verse 17, wisdom is of profit to you not only in your work of counseling, but also in personal living. When you experience the fruits of wisdom so operating for you, you will be able to model this for your counselees. What many of them lack is pleasant living and peace; that, you must make clear, is because they lack wisdom, or (having been taught it) fail to live by it. Fundamentally, if they have been taught wisdom, they don't really believe that it will bring these fine results; otherwise they would be living accordingly. Thus, they need to be convinced anew.

18 To those who seize her she is a tree of life,
and happy are those who hold on to her.
19 By wisdom Yahweh laid the earth's foundation;
He established the heavens by discernment.
20 By His knowledge the oceans broke forth
and the clouds dripped rain.

Turning now to the remaining verses in this section of the chapter (vv. 18-20) we read first that **To those who seize her she is a tree of life, and happy are those who hold on to her** (v. 18). The **tree of life** bears sweet fruit that is good to produce the joys of eternal life; and its leaves are for healing. There is hope for all in this image. Those who suffer from the effects of sin on their thinking can be healed by the pleasant, life-giving products that come from **the tree of life** that **wisdom** is. As the tree in the garden held forth the hope of eternal life with all its attendant benefits, so too, now does **the tree of life** hold forth the same for sin-weary creatures.

But like the **tree**, the needy sinner must move toward it; it is immovable: he must **seize** it. And once having done so, he must **hold on to** it. In other words, wisdom is as available as was the tree of life in the garden of Eden. But one must partake of it. And having done so—i.e., having learned wisdom concerning his problems—the counselee must **hold on to** it. He may not allow the wisdom that he learns from you in counseling to slip away from him. He must cling to and cherish it. The tendency is that, once having been relieved of the pain and pressures that sin brings, one may slide back again into previous ways, letting go of his/her **hold on** the **wisdom** that pleased God and that brought the peace and tranquillity. Warn counselees of this possibility and fortify them against it.

Verses 19 and 20 indicate that it was by wisdom that God created and molded the universe and the earth. If that **wisdom** had power do such things for God, think what it can do for you! By stressing such superb qualities of **wisdom** you may be able to help your counselees take care not to loosen their grip on it. What else in the world is available that will provide so much for so little expenditure of time and effort? After all, we are talking about God's own wisdom. Confront counselees, as the writer confronts the reader in this place, with the stupendous nature of the wisdom that is offered, and, therefore, with the foolishness of failing to grasp and cling to it.

Much in the next two verses is also repetitive. The reader is exhorted for the third time to **guard good judgment and discretion** (or discern-

21 My son, guard good judgment and discretion;
don't let them out of your sight
22 and they will refresh you
and grace your neck.
23 Then you will walk safely in your way
and your foot won't trip;
24 you won't be afraid when you lie down;
you will lie down and your sleep will be sweet.
25 Don't worry about sudden terror
or the coming overthrow of the wicked.
26 Yahweh will be at your side
and will keep your foot from getting caught.

---

ment) and not **let them out of his sight**. It is important to see how this danger is emphasized. There is no question that what one once attains by way of wisdom, he may also lose if he is not careful to maintain it. If this is true of preachers who will admit that they have forgotten much of what they learned in the past about the truth of Scripture when they fail to refurbish it, how much more of those who don't have as much time to do so?

These things—**judgment and discretion**—will **refresh** and, like an ornament, will **grace the neck**. They do good to the one who obtains and retains them in two ways: they continue to bring **refreshment** to the one who grows weary in the toils and trials of life. One who possesses **wisdom** may always turn to it anew and find **refreshment** for his soul. Moreover, his wisdom is as conspicuous to others as a valuable piece of jewelry worn about the neck. The other day in a restaurant it was interesting to notice how two women at a table admired the necklace of a third. They pointed to and commented on it and, at length, asked her to remove it so they could try it on (which they then did). The necklace of wisdom (good judgment and discretion) cannot be worn without comment. People will seek you out, will ask help, etc., when they discover your ability. It will help your counselee to gain new respect from others as well as provide him opportunities to minister to them. That is precisely what many counselees need.

But having these qualities as his own also relieves the counselee of many of his fears (a very frequent problem from which many counselees suffer). Verses 23 through 26 provide that assurance. He will be able to walk safely along life's highway without fear that his foot will slip and cause him to fall. How can he be sure? Verse 26 says, **Yahweh will be at**

27 Don't withhold good from those to whom it belongs
when it is in the power of your hand to do it.
28 Don't tell your neighbor "Go away; come back later. I'll give it to you
tomorrow," when you already have it.

---

your side and will keep your foot from getting caught. What better assurance could there be than to know that when the temptations and trials of life must be faced, one need not face them alone. Rather, he may know that Yahweh, the mighty Creator of all, is at his side sustaining him throughout. How does Yahweh accomplish this? By working through the wisdom that He has provided and that the counselee is willing to accept and put into practice. God, by His Spirit, works through His wisdom-imparting Word!

But it is not only when one is out on the byways of life that he may confidently move ahead under this assurance, but also when he **lies down to sleep**. He need not worry about some **sudden terror** (as unbelievers and impenitent believers do), nor does he need to concern himself about being caught up in the certain **overturning of the wicked when it comes**. Wisdom will keep him far from the environs of those who are caught up in that devastation which, notice, is sure. Indeed, he may rest at night in **sweet** sleep. That is, the restful, refreshing sort of sleep that we all wish to enjoy; he need not toss and turn at night worrying as those who know nothing of God's wisdom do. His sleep can be truly restful and refreshing. How delightful a picture this is. When encountering counselees who have problems with these things, why not read this description of trust, confidence and peace. Hold out the prospects that God offers here. That ought to cause such counselees to yearn for wisdom, which is the **summary** word for the qualities of **good judgment, discretion** and the like.

Verses 27 and 28 address a common problem. If someone has rendered a service for which he ought to receive remuneration, the one who is obligated to pay should not make him wait for that pay. If he is able to pay, he should do so promptly: **when it is in the power of his hand to do it**. He sins if he holds on to it. Church treasurers are notorious for committing this sin. They should take the two verses to heart and make sure that payment is given at the earliest opportunity—not at their convenience. There are many other applications of the principle by which individual Christians might raise their credibility level with the world if they took these four verses seriously. Verse 28 warns against the all-too-common practice of saying *mañana*.

29 Don't plan evil against your neighbor
who lives alongside of you, trusting you.
30 Don't pick a quarrel with someone for no reason,
when he has done nothing evil to you.
31 Don't envy a violent person
or choose any of his ways.

Verses 29 and 30 have to do with unnecessary conflict. The Christian counselee must avoid being the one who provokes it (cf. Romans 12:18). Indeed, some don't only wrong a neighbor through their thoughtlessness, but deliberately **plan** to do so. Such malice of forethought is forbidden; it is especially heinous in the sight of God. Nor is one allowed to **plan evil** against a neighbor as vengeance. (Read all of Romans 12!) It is a sad thing when one wrongs another who was **putting his trust in** him (v. 29[b]); the statement, as it occurs in this verse is pathetic. He is vulnerable; you take advantage of it. That is to be strongly frowned upon and, if ever indulged in, to be followed up by genuine repentance and restitution. It will take some time before he will be able to rebuild the **trust** that was lost. Yet, he must work at it. Those who "love a good fight," as they sometimes put it, are wrong when they **pick a quarrel with someone for no reason**. This foolish sin cannot be countenanced. Yet, there are counselees who indulge themselves in it. They start a quarrel themselves, or between others, and then back off and "watch the fun." Both ways in which this command is violated are sin.

Another problem many have is **envy**. Because they see another getting his way by means of violence, they **envy** what he gets and adopt **his ways**. The violent person will end up in violence directed toward himself. Moreover, all of **his ways** are wrong; the counselee may not pick and choose among them. Instead, he must not **choose *any* of his ways**. In addition, notice that to do so is a matter of **choice**. Care must be taken not to allow anyone to blame his violent ways on the one he has chosen to emulate. He knew what they were like; they were violent enough to call attention to themselves. But, though he knew—and knew that they were sinful ways—he chose to adopt some (or all) of them *for what he could get* by doing so. **Envy** is a warped, evil attitude that can lead one into the grossest sorts of sin. You will encounter it in many counselees. Where you discover **violent ways** in a counselee, look for **envy**. Where you discover **envy** in a counselee, look for, or warn about, the possibility of future **violence**.

32 Yahweh hates perverted people,
but He takes the upright into His confidence.
33 Yahweh's curse is on the wicked person's house,
but He blesses the home of the righteous.
34 Surely, He mocks mockers,
but He shows favor to the humble.
35 The wise inherit honor,
but stubborn fools will carry away disgrace.

The next four verses are difficult for some Christians (even counselors) to accept. They teach that God **hates perverted people**, He **curses** the wicked's **house**, He **mocks mockers** and that He **disgraces fools**. They try to soften these facts by saying that God hates the sin but loves the sinner. That distinction is not only unbiblical, but also impossible to defend: God doesn't send sin to hell; He sends sinn*ers* there! To curse the wicked's house doesn't mean the building, but those who live in it. To contemplate God **mocking mockers** (or, this might be translated scorning scorners) they say brings God down to their level. That is not true. Nothing can do that. But what it means is that He gives them a taste of their own medicine; He turns the tables on them (cf. II Thessalonians 1: 6, 7 for another instance of the same principle). Most do not have much trouble with the other side of the contrasting couplets in this section. They are happy to hear that Yahweh **takes the upright into His confidence, blesses the home of the righteous, shows favor to the humble, provides an inheritance of honor for the wise**. But matters work both ways. You can't take only those portions you want and leave the rest; you must have it all or have none at all. The one is as sure and as true as the other. God does run His world government according to the principles of equity. There is mercy and forgiveness and cleansing with Him, it is true, but these may be obtained only on *His* terms through Jesus Christ. They will not be given in any other way.

To **take the upright into His confidence** is another way to say that they become His friends (cf. Jesus interpretive words in John 15:15. Note the operative thing about friendship is taking another into one's confidence).

If a counselee doesn't know God's will, he is probably not on friendly terms with God. He has not made His will known to him. But He sends His Spirit to help His friends understand His written Word in which that will is found.

If everything is going wrong in a person's family, one reason may be that God's **curse** is on it because of the wickedness of a family member. That is a fact to pursue when encountering circumstances like that. There is a family with which I am acquainted that is exactly in that condition. And, after several years of difficulty, it became clear that there was something radically wrong with one of the members of the household. Finally, the difficulties and calamities that had been descending on them were traced to the sin of that member who, at length, confessed and dealt with it. The proverb still holds true.

God mocks mockers by turning the tables on them. Voltaire declared that it took twelve men to establish Christianity, but that it would take only one to destroy it—he meant himself. After his death, the Geneva Bible society purchased his house and printed Bibles on his press! If that isn't mocking mockers, how about this one: Ingersoll claimed that twenty five years after his death there wouldn't be a church left in America. Well, Ingersoll is long gone but the churches aren't.

Do **stubborn fools** (the *kesilim*) **carry away disgrace**? Of course. Not always right away; some do while yet alive, but others only after their death when the truth about them is finally discovered. Paul alluded to this in I Timothy 5:24 and 25. When one is riding the crest of the wave, he will not hear you, but when the wave breaks and his snoot comes down in the gravel, he will know what **disgrace** is all about. There is no honor in **stubbornness,** yet fools exhibit it all the time.

This is a powerful chapter which, in many ways, is a prelude to the sort of thing encountered in chapters 10 and following. It is introductory, setting forth many of the themes that the writers of Proverbs will belabor until they have firmly fixed them in the minds of the reader. Repetition, sometimes in the very same words, is not beyond Solomon and those who write in this Book. Repetition, in similar words or in various figures and applications, is also found throughout Proverbs. That should teach every counselor the utter importance of repetition—of all sorts.

The Book of Proverbs is not the sort of textbook that you encounter today; thank God for ignoring that and doing things His way! It is full of divine wisdom, warning and good judgment; it enables one to learn much about the world and how men in it operate. It gives God's views of men's actions, and tells us what He does about them. It is preeminently practical. There is nothing like it anywhere in the world (including the Egyptian texts in which a few things that Solomon said have been copied, some of which were misunderstood—for more on this, see Gleason Archer, *A Survey of Old Testament Introduction,* 1994 edition, pp. 522, 523).

CHAPTER 4

1 Sons, heed a father's discipline
and pay attention in order to get understanding.
2 I give you good arguments;
don't forsake my law.
3 I was my father's son,
a tender, only child in my mother's eyes.
4 And he taught me saying,
"May my words cling to your heart;
keep my commandments and live.
5 Get wisdom; get understanding.
Don't forget or deviate from the words of my mouth.
6 Don't forsake her and she will protect you;
love her and she will guard you.

There is little in this chapter that is new. The same themes, having to do with the acquisition and retention of wisdom are echoed. It is the emphasis placed, the new ways of saying these things and the perspective (that of a true parent-child relationship) that gives it freshness.

In verse 1, **heeding and paying attention** to a **father's discipline** is the note first struck. That is the way to understanding. Few young people today think so; therefore, these words provide a new departure for youth—*if only you can get them to listen*! How does Solomon propose to get them to do so? By means of **good arguments** (some of which we have encountered and some that are yet to be set forth). The thrust is this: listen, pay attention and hold to **my law**.

Solomon says, "I was once where you are; **I was my father's son, a tender, only child in my mother's eyes** (v. 3). That is, I was considered very special by them and treated accordingly. So, out of his deep affection and evident concern, what did my father do? He **taught me**, as I now teach you. And what he taught is what I have said already; but for your sake I will repeat it (vv. 4, 5). In addition, let me urge upon you the fact that wisdom is the way to life—here, and hereafter (v. 4[c]). Wisdom protects and guards (v. 6). So **love** wisdom and **don't forsake her**. Instead, recognize in life that **wisdom is the principal thing**; put its acquisition before all else. And if you get anything at all, **get understanding**."

Counselor, if you can only impress upon your counselees the supreme importance of wisdom, and the part it ought to play in their lives,

7 The principal thing is wisdom;
get wisdom; and with all your getting,
get understanding.
8 Exalt her and she will lift you up;
hug her and she will honor you.
9 She will place a graceful wreath on your head;
she will provide a glorious crown for you."
10 My son, hear and accept my sayings
and you will have many years of life.
11 I have taught you in the way of wisdom;
I have guided you along straight tracks.
12 When you walk, your steps won't be impeded,
and if you run, you won't stumble.
13 Lay hold of discipline; don't let go.
Guard her: she is your life!
14 Don't enter the path of the wicked;
don't even make your way toward it.
15 Avoid it! Don't move onto it;

---

you will have done them a great favor. Try to help them to see that she is the real pearl of great price for which all else must be sacrificed, when necessary. To **exalt her** means that, in turn, she will exalt you (v. 8). She will bring you victories and power, which are suggested by mentioning the **wreath** and the **crown**. Those are but some of Solomon's **arguments** by which he summarizes what he has said thus far.

But he continues (vv. 10-19). **My sayings, heard and accepted**, he goes on to say, will bring longevity (v. 10); by walking in wise ways, he observes that he himself has modeled the way they should walk (v. 11). Modeling can be an important aid to counseling. And because counseling is to be carried on under the aegis of the church, it is possible for a pastor or elder in a congregation to show (by his own example or that of other well-known members) what a particular command of the Bible means in daily living. Modeling brings teaching outside of the building and onto the highways of life. Wisdom enables counselees to walk well, unimpeded, to run without tripping and falling (v. 12). Exhortations in verse 13 are not new. Those in verse 14, however, strike a new note: it is not merely a matter of walking on the right path; to assure this, it is better never to get near the wrong one in the first place. Many counselees never intended to choose the sinful lifestyles they eventually adopted, but because they played around the edges of sin, they soon became fascinated with it, and like Lot, who only intended to pitch his tent *toward* Sodom, ended up in

keep your foot off of it and pass by.
16 They don't sleep unless they have done evil;
they lose sleep if they don't cause someone to stumble.
17 They eat the bread of wickedness
and they drink the wine of violence.
18 But the path of the righteous is like the morning light
that gets brighter and brighter
until it is noonday.
19 The way of the wicked is like thick darkness;
they don't know what they stumble over.
20 My son, pay attention to my words;
bow your ear to what I say.
21 Don't let them out of your sight;
protect them in the center of your heart.
22 They are life to those who find them
and health to all one's flesh.

---

the midst of it. Verses 14 and 15, therefore, are an excellent addition to the advice already given: stay away!

In verse 16, we are given an insight into the way some people act. They are so bent on dragging others into sin, they **can't sleep** if they haven't caused the ruin of another. According to verse 17, their very staple of life (their **bread** and **wine**) is **wickedness and violence**. Now, contrast the two ways: verse 18 describes **the way of the righteous**, which, like the morning light, increases until the noonday when he is glorified. The **way of the wicked**, on the other hand, **is like dense darkness** where people stumble over objects because they can't see them. It is so thick that they can't even tell what it is they are tripping over (v. 19). That is to say, their ignorance is so great they don't have the faintest idea why their lives are so miserable, and why every seeming success turns out to be another failure. Impressive arguments, Solomon! These are arguments that every counselor should have tucked away for use whenever necessary.

One of the main contributions to the counselee who finds himself in utter darkness and is wondering why, is to throw biblical light on the question. Not only may this be an opportune time to present the gospel to those who come who are unsaved, but also to professed Christians who are so messed up that they are living in ignorance as well. Shine proverbial light on their situation; show them the objects over which they are falling, and that there is no reason to remain on the way of darkness, but every reason to abandon it for the path of light.

23 Above all that you guard, guard your heart
because it is the source of your life.
24 Put away a deceitful mouth
and put devious lips far from you.
25 Look straight ahead with your eyes;
with your eyes gaze directly in front of you.
26 Consider the tracks of your feet
and your ways will be established.
27 Don't turn right or left;
turn your feet away from evil.

The final section of this chapter runs from verse 20 through verse 27. The first three verses (20-22) are repetitious of teaching in chapter three. Verse 23, however, is a great summary of what is said elsewhere about the importance of the **heart** (the inner you). What does it mean? Just this: that all one thinks, decides, plans, does and says flows like streams from one common source—the **heart**. That is why one must keep his heart true to God's Word, pure and unpolluted by the world's poisonous springs. Jesus often referred to the heart as the basic source of one's life. In one notable passage He spoke of the heart as a storehouse from which everything comes; in another, it is pictured as the source of everything that defiles.

Because of its central place, what your heart is like is what *you* are like. Therefore, Solomon insists that the believer must **guard** it from every evil influence; guard it so that nothing good that the Spirit has done in the heart may be warped or lost. **Guard it above all that you guard**, is the way that he puts it!

The mouth and the lips are the outward expression of the heart (v. 24). Therefore, he urges your counselee to **put away a deceitful mouth and devious lips**, something that is accomplished by purging the heart of every intention to lie and deceive. Instead, he must determine to be honest and dependable in all he says. The latter must replace the former.

And as for his behavior, he must set his **heart** to walk a **straight course, looking directly ahead**, so that he will **turn** neither to the evil on the **right** nor to the wickedness that is on the **left** (v. 27). But unless he gives adequate consideration to the **tracks** his feet make, he is sure to go astray. It takes concentration on the goal to walk uprightly. This concentration, once more, is a matter of the heart. One's **ways** are **established** in rectitude, honesty and truth only by the proper heart activity. Heart care is a matter of regulating one's thinking, deciding and willing by the Scriptures. There is no other way to set the heart on a straight course and to keep it there. The Scriptures are the map and compass for the journey. Christ is the destination. Help counselees to get that sort of picture in their minds, to think of themselves on a journey that involves choosing the right path, and sticking to it ("staying the course"). Counselors who encourage heart care will urge counselees to study and assimilate such passages as Deuteronomy 6:4-6; 8:11-14, 17; 15:7-11 (to mention only a few from one book) that provide important information and direction pertaining to the heart. In short, it is necessary to help counselees develop a heart for God.

CHAPTER 5

1 My son, pay attention to my wisdom;
bow your ear to the understanding I have to give you,
2 that you may protect discretion
and your lips may guard knowledge.
3 The lips of an alien woman drip honey
and her mouth is smoother than oil.
4 But ultimately she is as bitter as wormwood—
sharp as a two-edged sword.
5 Her feet go down to death;
her steps take a straight course for the unseen world.

This chapter enlarges on the exhortations about fornication and adultery that were given so far. Few sins so dominate contemporary life as these do. Evidently, the age in which Solomon lived was a lot like ours. Indeed, the matter is of such great importance to him that he will return to it again and again, addressing it in various ways from differing perspectives. But for now, we shall consider the 23 verses in this chapter that are devoted to directions and warnings about illicit sex.

The first two verses plainly indicate that proper behavior in this area, as in others, depends on **wisdom, understanding, discretion and knowledge**—all matters of the **heart**. Why is a proper heart condition essential for avoiding sexual sin? Because, as he indicates, **the lips of an alien woman drip honey**. That is, they are filled with what we today refer to as "sweet talk." He continues: **her mouth is smoother than oil.** That is, by means of flattery and seductive words she can present a very convincing case (as we shall see acted out in chapter seven). Since this is how it is, counselees must be warned about the language and the ideas she speaks to induce unsuspecting persons to comply to her wishes. Before the act itself, there is much in the prelude to sin that a wise man may discern and turn from before he becomes ensnared. That is why wisdom in the heart is so important; sexual sin is not merely physical. One who is not wise will be unable to see through her facade.

It is significant also to know how flattery and **smooth** talk, that seemed so inviting, all too soon lose their appeal once the sin has been committed: **ultimately, she is as bitter as wormwood—sharp** (i.e., cuttingly harmful, indeed, deadly) **as a two-edged sword** (v. 3). Too late, many discover that her feet lead not to the pleasures she promised, but to

6 She doesn't consider the path of life;
her tracks wander, but she doesn't know it.
7 Now, my sons, listen to me;
don't turn from the words of my mouth.
8 Keep yourself far from her;
don't come near the door of her house
9 unless you want to give your vigor to others
and your years to the cruel one,
10 unless you want strangers to be filled with your wealth
and the results of your toil to end up in a foreigner's house.

---

death (v. 5). She, herself, may not realize the implications of her actions: **her tracks wander** from truth and righteousness because she has so rationalized everything that she **doesn't know it**. Sin blinds; it causes ignorance and foolishness to dominate one's thinking. A heart becomes hardened by it.

Because of these facts, Solomon urges, **listen to me; don't turn from the words of my mouth** (v. 7). Once more he urges his student to stay away from such women (v. 8). The point he makes is not that the student should fight temptation but, so far as possible, to remove himself from it so that fighting it is unnecessary. Good advice for many weak counselees, for counselors to advise and for all others to heed. None of us is so strong as to be able to successfully avoid falling when he gets as close to temptation as possible—intending, of course, to do nothing more than indulge himself in the cheap thrills involved in doing so. But in doing that, he has sinned already in the heart. It is to avoid this that our Lord directed us to pray "Lead us not into temptation."

If a counselee fails to heed this advice he will soon find his **vigor** (stamina and strength) dissipated and his life falling apart (vv. 9, 10). In time he will find the alien woman (called such because, since harlotry was forbidden in Israel, most prostitutes were foreigners) a **cruel** master, whose slave he has become. Falling into her power, she will bleed his wealth to the very last drop before casting him aside, and she (and possibly her husband or foreign friends acting as pimps) will end up with all that he previously owned (v. 10). Warn counselees by showing the outcome of prostitution as Solomon, who should have known about the wiles of loose women, does.

What will the end of it be like? Nothing but regrets and remorse. Often, that is the point at which the counselor first encounters his counselee (a pastor, counseling a member, however, should get to him much

11 And ultimately you will groan
when your flesh and muscle are consumed,
12 and you say, "How I hated discipline!
How my heart despised reproof!
13 I wouldn't listen to the voice of my teachers
or bow my ear to my instructors.
14 I was almost in total ruin
among the assembly and congregation."
15 Drink waters from your own cistern
and running waters from your own well.
16 Should your springs be dispersed outside
like channels of water running in the streets?
17 Let them belong to you alone,
and not to strangers.
18 Let your fountain be blessed
and take pleasure in the wife of your youth.

---

sooner). He is **groaning** under the ruin he has made of himself, his body and his life (v. 11). The consequences awaken him all too late to the fact that this has occurred because he **hated discipline, despised reproof** in his heart, when well-meaning parents and friends attempted to save him from ruin and misery, but he would **not listen** to his **teachers** and **instructors** (vv. 12, 13). And he confesses that his sin and ruin at length became apparent to everyone else, together with the **shame** that this brought in the presence of the **assembly** of God's people (v. 14). This section is a powerful piece when read to counselees who can identify with it.

Turning now to the positive side of things, the writer says, **Drink waters from your own cistern and running waters from your own well** (v. 15). Get your joy, satisfaction and thrills of sexual pleasure from relations with your own wife. This is the pure water from which you should drink, not the muddy, foul, polluted waters of prostitution or adultery. When that relationship is sound there is no need for yielding to temptation. Counselors who help build solid marriages are preventing temptation and sexual sin.

It is a serious question asked in verse 16: why should a man **disperse** his semen outside his own legitimate marriage bed? Sexual pleasures should be enjoyed by him and his wife alone (v. 17). One's wife is like a **fountain** who should be **blessed** by his attention to her alone and he should find his pleasure in her. Like a loving, **graceful** animal, he says, let her movements please your eyes and find your **satisfaction** in *her* **breasts, intoxicated** (ravished) by your love for her and hers for you

19 She is a loving chamois and a graceful ibix.
Let her breasts satisfy you at all times;
may you always be ravished by her love.
20 My son, why should you be ravished by an alien woman
and embrace the bosom of a foreigner?
21 A man's ways are before Yahweh
and He considers all his tracks.
22 The wicked will be caught in his own iniquities;
he will be held fast by the ropes of his sin.
23 He will die without discipline,
and by the greatness of his stupidity he will go astray.

(v. 19). Counselors may find it necessary to help couples discover the delights they can have in each other: delights through marriage intimacy that are not possible outside of marriage commitments. The question in verse 16 is repeated in a different form in verse 20, where Solomon emphasizes the cultural, non-covenantal aspect of going to bed with a pagan.

Now for the conclusion: first, remember that **Yahweh**, your God, knows all about the sin in your heart and in your acts (v. 21). Secondly, you will end up ensnared, trapped, imprisoned by your sinful habits from which you will find it more and more difficult to extricate yourself. Last, you will **die** in this **undisciplined** life, having gone astray because of the **stupidity** you will ultimately need to confess (as the ruined person of vv. 12-14 does).

What a powerful appeal this is. In using it, don't tone down the verses that deal with sexual pleasure. They are important. In a carefully-measured way (so as not to become titillating to others or yourself) picture the delights of innocent, sexual love between a man and his wife. Contrast that with what you read of the sin and misery found in illicit sex. Make the most of verses 18 and 19; don't let a man avoid their impact. If he protests that it is not possible for him to be **ravished** by his wife (or she by him), explain that it *is* possible if they will only set their hearts right toward God and one another, and determine prayerfully to see that it happens. Take no excuses. Every command of God means at least two things: 1) there is hope; God never commands His children to do anything He doesn't provide all that it is necessary to accomplish; 2) there is no excuse for disobedience.

This chapter is very useful in marital counseling, not only in cases of adultery but also in those where sexual relations have grown cold and insipid.

CHAPTER 6

1 My son, if you guarantee a loan for a friend,
if you have struck palms with a stranger,
2 you are trapped by the words of your mouth,
captured by the words of your mouth.
3 My son, since you have fallen into your neighbor's hand,
do this and free yourself:
go, humble yourself and be bold with your friend:
4 don't close an eye in sleep
or let your eyelids slumber.
5 Free yourself like a gazelle from the hand that holds you,
like a bird from the hand of a fowler.

The writer now turns mostly to other matters (though in the next chapter he will return to the matter of sexual sin, teaching God's will in the matter through a brief, but powerful scenario in which he reveals the process of the seduction and fall of a man through temptation. But more of that then). At the end of this present chapter, however, there is a transitional section that enters into the matter once more.

Verses 1 through 5 abruptly change from sex to business transactions. This is a theme that will repeatedly be mentioned later on in Proverbs. A warning is issued at the outset: **My son, if you guarantee a loan for a friend, if you have struck palms with a stranger, you are trapped by the words of your mouth** (vv. 1, 2). In the enthusiasm of the moment it is easy for one who operates on the basis of feelings rather than principle and good judgment to **strike palms with a stranger** and **guarantee a loan for a friend**. Don't do it, says Solomon. Otherwise, you will find yourself **trapped** by the words of your own **mouth**. Counselees present this very problem from time to time. Instead of allowing a child or relative (sometimes even a close friend) to wait to buy that new car or that house, they co-sign a document that obligates them to make payments if the primary purchaser defaults. What should they do?

First, they should never get into the situation; here is clear direction about the matter (vv. 1, 2). Those who know and follow the Proverbs related to the subject will never enter into such an agreement. But what if a counselee comes, with one foot already in the trap that is about to be sprung? There is but one answer: get out of the obligation before it is too late (vv. 3-5). How important it is to do so is indicated by the extreme to

6 Go to the ant, lazy man:
observe her ways and become wise.
7 She, with no leader, overseer or ruler
8 lays up supplies of food during summer
and gathers stores at harvest.
9 How long will you lie there, lazy man?
When are you going to arise out of your sleep?
10 "A little slumber,
a little folding of the hands to rest . . ."

---

which he is advised to go: **humble yourself and be bold with your friend** (that is, beg him to let you out of the arrangement).

But what if that is not possible? What if the trap has closed? Later on, he indicates that you may lose everything—even your bed (the last possession an Israelite could hold on to). Even at that late date, you should make every legitimate effort to free yourself.

There is great urgency in the passage: one should not hesitate over the matter. Rather, he should **immediately** take action: **don't close an eye in sleep or let your eyelids slumber** (v. 4). This is not one of those matters that you ought to sleep on! The issue is clear. Do everything you can to get out of the obligation *right away*. Otherwise, things will get worse. Like a gazelle, shake loose **from the hand that holds you** and go bounding swiftly away. Like a bird, fly rapidly **from the hand of the fowler**. These warnings are explicit. They allow of no qualifications. And they have helped many a counselee who was wise enough to consult a biblical counselor before **striking palms** (sealing the agreement). You should be prepared at all times to refer counselees to this passage.

Another theme to which the writer will return over and over again throughout the Book is the contrast between industry and laziness. Verses 6 through 11 raise the issue initially. Usually, there is a note of humor (or sarcasm) that Solomon uses to embarrass and prod the sluggard into action. Here, we meet the first note of that sort (though it is milder than others we shall encounter later) in verses 9 and 10: **A little slumber, a little folding of the hands to rest**. . . . Those words depict the lazy man justifying his laziness as only temporary: "just a little more wouldn't do any harm." (every instance mentioned in Proverbs shows some way in which the sluggard excuses himself by rationalization. Take note of that fact and watch for it in counselees).

But first, Solomon commends planning and effort expended now, in lieu of future need by citing the example of the ant. **Go to the ant**, he tells

11 and poverty will come to you like a bandit
and your need like an armed man.
12 A worthless person
practices deceit with his mouth.
13 He winks with his eyes,
scrapes with his feet,
points with his fingers.
14 Perverse plans are in his heart;
he is constantly plotting evil.
He spreads strife.
15 Therefore, suddenly disaster will come;
suddenly he will be broken—beyond remedy.

---

the **lazy man**. That he directs him to take a look at this small creature, scores of which we unknowingly crush under our feet every time we walk abroad, in itself is humiliating. Everything about his dealings with laziness seems to involve a humbling element. Obviously, then, that is the way to handle the problem. Learn to shame lazy persons into action. By means of dialog, in an altogether apposite manner, he does this by picturing him lying there, convincing himself that all he is doing is taking a little nap (vv. 9, 10). But when this is a scene repeated over and over he develops habits that lead to **poverty**. He fails to (or won't) see this, but one day (too late) he will recognize it as it overtakes him unexpectedly, as a thief in the night.

Learn to use all of these powerful means in counseling: the vignette, dialog, humor and sarcasm, pointing to lowly creatures which, like the ant, do by instinct what the counselee needs to do by choice (vv. 6-8). Note also, he does not mince words: the lazy man is called such. No excuses are made for his sloth; he is not diagnosed as having "low energy," a "mid-life crisis" or "chronic fatigue syndrome." He is simply called lazy!

Now, of course, there are genuine physical conditions that do sap energy or create fatigue. One must be careful not to accuse a counselee of laziness when true sickness is the problem. But where laziness is present (and a faithful examination of all the passages in Proverbs will help you to decide if a given case is such) it should be labeled for what it is and dealt with accordingly.

Again, a gloomy future is forecast for the **worthless**, **perverted deceiver** who, by words and signs, works his evil **plans** to **spread strife** and dissension among God's people (v. 12ff.). Every church has people like this. They are trouble-*makers*; they produce trouble when there is

16 Yahweh hates six things;
indeed, there are seven that He detests:
17 haughty eyes, a lying tongue,
hands that shed innocent blood,
18 a heart that plans wicked schemes,
feet that rush quickly into evil,
19 a false witness who breathes lies,
and one who spreads strife among brothers.

---

none. These **worthless** people will **suddenly** experience **irremediable disaster** (v. 15).

In Titus 3:10 the schismatic is mentioned and the solution to the problems he causes is given: if after one or two counseling sessions he fails to respond, get rid of him. Otherwise the trouble that he is trying to hatch may get loose among the members of the congregation and split it. In other words, abandon your normal counseling procedure in which you may spend as many as 8 or 10 sessions working with a counselee, if after one or two, it becomes apparent that he is a **worthless person** bent on **plotting** and executing evil **plans**. Instead, put him out of the congregation so that he can cause no more harm. Church discipline is necessary in such cases. Those who have hesitated to follow Paul's directive about this have learned (too late again) that they can not be kinder than God. While they are dragging on the process, thinking they might change the **worthless one**, they subject the rest of the congregation to his nefarious ways. There is no lack of concern in treating him this way; the concern is simply focused on those who most need it. Incidentally, the description "worthless" (v. 12) is a designation to show to the self-esteem crowd.

Verses 17 through 19 contain a list of seven things that God **hates**. In verses 18 and 19 the man just described in the previous verses is included. This shows how strongly God despises those whose heart is wicked. There is little question about the referents of the seven items on the list; they are all plainly set forth. Perhaps the only one that might need some explanation is the sixth: **a false witness who breathes lies**. To what does this image of **breathing lies** refer? It means that as automatically, regularly and unconsciously as one breathes (you don't make a conscious decision to do so), the habitual liar gives false witness. The expression is akin to William Safire's characterization of Hillary Clinton as "a congenital liar." Lying has become second nature to such a person.

The seventh item on the list, the person who spread strife in order to set brothers against one another, I have already mentioned. The man of

20 My son, keep your father's commands
and don't forsake your mother's law.
21 Fasten them on your heart where they will be with you always;
tie them around your neck.
22 When you walk, they will lead you;
when you lie down they will protect you.
And when you awaken they will talk to you.

---

haughty eyes (the proud, arrogant boaster who *looks down on others* from his self-made perch), whose **tongue** is filled with **lies**, about his own prowess, and who lies about others in an attempt to rise above them by bringing them down, is equally detestable to God. To **plan wickedness** (person number three on the list falls into that category) is even worse than falling inadvertently into it. Note, like person number four, to **rush quickly** to become involved in **evil** whenever there is an opportunity to do so, is every bit as heinous in God's sight. Whereas the former loves to **plot and plan wickedness**, the latter loves to perpetrate and participate in it. And it is probably unnecessary to mention person number three: the murderer. Of him, perhaps two facts may be noted: 1) murder, the shedding of **innocent blood**, is what is forbidden: not killing. Execution, causing death in a just war, are exempted. 2) What makes murder sin is not some supposed "sanctity of life," but the fact that it is an attack on God. Man is made in God's image; therefore to attack a man is to attack God (cf. Genesis 9:6 in which that reason is given for executing the murderer).

There is one remaining section (vv. 20-22) to consider before returning to a further discussion of sexual sin. It is a further admonition interjected to urge obedience to God's law mediated to children through the family. The operative verbs in verses 20 and 21 are **keep, don't forsake, fasten, tie**. The ideas they inculcate were set forth earlier in the Book of Proverbs. But verse 22 advances the thought a bit: **When you walk, they will lead you; when you lie down they will protect you. And when you awaken they will talk to you.** In these lines, a counselor is introduced to the effects of attaching God's Word to himself, **on the heart, around the neck**. This **fastening and tying** has as its purpose fixing God's teachings **where they will be with one always**, in every circumstance. Doing that, in turn, enables him to be divinely **led** as he goes about living life (N.B., one is led not by some other revelational means, but by biblical commands mediated through one's father and mother) and protected and addressed about his lifestyle (**they will talk to you**).

23 The command is a lamp and the law is a light;
and the reproofs of discipline are a way of life
24 to protect you from the evil woman,
from the alien woman's smooth tongue.

It is important for counselors to stress the commandment-led life over against the feeling-led one propagated by some today who advocate following hunches and promptings, looking for signs and sensing God's will. If a Christian is **led** in those ways, there is no need to go to the trouble of attaching commandments to his **heart** or **neck**!

To what does this **tying and fastening** refer? The learning of the truths of God in such a manner that they are always at hand for use *in the milieu*. But how does one attach Scripture to himself? One simple answer is by learning proverbs—especially those that appear in easily-memorized couplet form, that appear from chapter 10 on. They may easily become, as I have said, *Portable Truth*. Even if one does not memorize them all as such, he can learn their substance and their locations (to read more about the importance of locational knowledge, etc., see my book *What to Do on Thursday* which is a handbook of Bible usage in the milieu). The commands of the Bible, Solomon says, **talk** to one in the decision-making situations of life. No still, small voice is promised to do this, but the Scriptures will! "But that requires work," someone protests. Yes, exactly so. Explain that fact to counselees. Living properly for God demands time and effort; wisdom does not come automatically along with conversion or through some semi-mystical experience or formula.

Now, Solomon turns once more to the ever-present problem of sexual sin (v. 23). Following this discussion, in the next chapter he will present a trenchant scenario approximating anything you will find elsewhere in the finest literature. But in these thirteen verses, Solomon makes the case against sexual license. Blow after blow is struck in rapid succession.

God's Word gives all the **light** necessary to discern the truth about the matter if anyone will accept it, along with the **reproofs** that accompany **discipline** designed to enable him both to attach these commands to his heart and to learn how to put them into practice on a daily basis. The **way of life** (v. 23^{b}) pleasing to God, is to walk in the **light** shed on one's path by the **lamp** of His Word. D. L. Moody wrote on the inside cover of his Bible "Either this Book will keep me from sin or sin will keep me from this Book." That is the scriptural view of living righteously: it is a matter of commandment-oriented living over against the feeling-oriented

25 Don't lust after her beauty in your heart;
don't let her catch you with her eyelids.
26 Because of a prostitute a man is reduced to a piece of bread;
but another man's wife hunts for his precious life.
27 Can a man clasp fire to his chest
and his clothes not be burned?
28 Can a man walk on hot coals
and not scorch his feet?
29 That's the way that it is with one who goes in to his neighbor's wife;
whoever touches her will not go unpunished.

---

living so dominant in the church today that has brought about so much confusion and heartache, and has occasioned so much need for counseling. It might be wise to print out Moody's line for distribution to your counselees!

Biblical teaching **protects** one from **evil women** with their **smooth tongues** (v. 24). How? By both prohibitions and warnings. By pointing to the true source of sexual happiness (cf. 5:18ff.). By setting forth God's order of things over against that which is "against nature" (*kata phusin;* cf. Romans 1:27ff.).

There is the attraction of the eye to **beauty**, and as one retains what he saw and thinks sinfully about it in his **heart** (v. 25), he transforms appreciation of beauty into lust. Doubtless, it is in the heart that sin begins (cf. James 1:14ff.; Matthew 5:27ff.). If it can be cut off at the pass, it may never go any further. The way to do so is to **guard** the heart with all diligence, as Solomon previously indicated (4:23). To guard against lust is to guard against supplying it with material that will stimulate desire or having failed to do that which perpetuates it.

It is by her looks (**beauty, eyelids**) that she attracts. Beware of such fatal attraction (v. 25). When a counselee is tempted to indulge in lustful thoughts, he may bring the warnings of verses 26 through 28 into the picture. They ought to cool him off quickly! He must stop thinking of the momentary illicit pleasure he might have; rather, he should think of the long-term consequences to which that will lead—poverty, dissipation, possible death. "It won't happen to me," you say? Well, read verses 27 and 28. In one way or another, sexual evil will turn back on you. You *will* be burned by it. Incidentally, these two verses would be ideal for counselees to memorize as portable truth to use in the hour of temptation. At that time they will **talk** to them, speaking volumes!

30 People don't despise a thief
if he steals to satisfy himself when he is hungry.
31 But if he is caught, he has to pay back seven times;
he has to give up all the goods in his house.
32 He who commits adultery with a woman lacks sense;
he who does it destroys his own life.
33 He gets a wound and disgrace;
and his shame will not be wiped away.
34 Jealousy enrages a man
and he won't spare you in the day of vengeance;
35 he won't accept any ransom
and he won't rest content even if you multiply bribes.

Now, in verse 29, the matter of adultery, mentioned in verse 26, comes to the fore. For a man to **touch a neighbor's wife** is to place himself in great jeopardy. In one way or another, he will be **punished** for doing so. As verse 26 indicates, her husband may **hunt** for his **life**. Verses 32 and following also emphasize the danger. If that doesn't occur, he may be bled dry financially—even a **thief** must make ruinous restitution (vv. 30-31). But the adulterer shouldn't count on getting off that easily (cf. vv. 34-35). To commit adultery, then, just doesn't make sense (v. 32). The risks simply aren't worth it. That is one way to present it to a counselee.

CHAPTER 7

1 My son, guard my words
and store up my commands within you.
2 Guard my commands and live;
and my teachings as the pupil of your eye.
3 Tie them on your fingers;
write them on the tablet of your heart.
4 Say to wisdom, "My sister!"
and call understanding "kinsman,"
5 to guard you from the alien woman,
the foreigner with her smooth words.
6 I looked through the lattice
in the window of my house,
7 and I saw a senseless young man
among the naive youth
8 passing through the street near her corner,
making his way to her house
9 at twilight, in the evening,
in the blackness and darkness of the night.
10 Now look! Here comes a woman, dressed like a prostitute, to meet him.
She has secret plans in her heart.

The words of 6:23-25 lead naturally to the scenario so ably set forth in chapter seven. Let's take a look at it. I say, "take a look," rather than "explain it," because there is so little to explain. The chapter ably speaks for itself. To **guard** biblical teachings **as** one would **guard the pupil of his eye** (v. 1) is to do so with the great care and concern we have to protect our eyes from danger. To regard the elements of wisdom as a **sister or kinsman** is to become closely attached, related, to them. The scenario that begins with verse 6 is a prime example of how intimacy with scriptural teaching can protect one from sin and misery, in this case, **from the alien woman with her smooth words** (v. 5).

The words of verses 6 through 27, as I indicated, speak eloquently for themselves. I won't exegete them verse by verse, but I do want to comment on them—especially about their use in counseling.

First, in all cases involving sexual temptation (either by a woman tempting the man, or the man as the subject of her temptation), the passage has potency. It would be wise to print it out in full, ready to hand out.

11 She is loud and unruly;
her feet never stay at home.
12 Now she is outside, now in the streets;
she lies in wait at every corner.
13 She seizes him and kisses him;
she hardens her face and says to him:
14 "I have the sacrifices of peace offerings;
today I have paid my vows.
15 That's why I came to meet you.
I have looked for you earnestly, and I have found you.
16 I have spread my couch with coverings,
with striped linen from Egypt.
17 I have sprinkled my bed with myrrh,
aloes and cinnamon.
18 Come, let's drink our fill of love all night long;
let's enjoy making love.
19 My husband isn't home;
he's on the road—far off somewhere.
20 He took a bag of silver in his hand;
he'll return on the day of the full moon."

To the counselee-temptress, show that God is on to her ways. Here He reveals his explicit knowledge of her aims and approach. Tell her to read the description of her wiles and seductive moves and warn against her continuing of them. Call her to repentance and change. Hand out a copy to any man foolish enough to contemplate adultery, suggesting that as he reads he should take all to heart, but in particular, that he should never forget Solomon's dramatic, concluding description of the prostitute's bedroom as a **bedroom of death**.

Secondly, call on the one tempted to notice how God through Solomon sets forth the process of temptation. The temptress is crude (v. 11). That very fact may be enticing to some. She is out to catch anyone she can (v. 12), but lies when she lays hold of someone, telling him that he was in her thoughts all the while (v. 15). Following flattery and lies, she uses tactile means to seduce him to fall (v. 13). To avert any scriptural objections he might have, she assures him (falsely) that all is OK before God. After all, isn't she religious—see verse 14? She lures him with promises of pleasantness and pleasure (vv. 16-18) and, then, seeks to assure him there is no danger (vv. 19, 20).

He hesitates, but he goes on listening to her; that is his mistake, since it is **by many such words she causes him to yield** (v. 21). He should

21 By many such words she causes him to yield;
with her smooth lips she leads him astray.
22 All at once he goes after her—
like an ox going to slaughter,
like a stupid fool in chains goes for punishment,
23 like a bird hurrying into a trap,
and not knowing his life is at stake—
until an arrow pierces his liver!
24 Now then, my sons, listen to me.
Pay attention to the words of my mouth.
25 Don't let your heart turn aside to her ways;
don't stray into her paths.
26 Many are the victims that she has felled,
and those she has killed are numerous.
27 Her house is the way to the unseen world;
it leads down to the bedrooms of death!

---

have turned away, gotten out of hearing, before her **smooth** talk **led him astray**.

At length, he suddenly gives in (v. 22), but as **he goes after her**, he plunges headlong into a trap (v. 23). In the end, his few moments of pleasure cost him his life (23ff.). He is caught and taken **like an ox to the slaughter**. He doesn't know it, but he isn't the first (vv. 26, 27). He is just the *latest* victim.

Going through the process this way, after reading the scenario, makes it even more vivid. Do so, then hand it to the counselee. Surely, you can expect the Holy Spirit to work through this vital Word of His if He has plowed the ground to receive the seed.

I cannot commend the use of this chapter too strongly in cases of sexual temptation. You should be not only familiar with it, but ready to point out the steps in the process by which a tempted man may fall. With women who are involved in tempting men into adultery, by reading it you may also make a strong case for God knowing all about her sinful ways—and His concern to guard others against them by supplying this scenario. God has her pegged. How does she think then that she can escape His judgment?

CHAPTER 8

1 Doesn't wisdom call?
Doesn't she raise her voice?
2 On the high places along the way,
at the crossroads, she takes her stand.
3 At the side of the gates,
in the front of the city,
at its entrance she shouts:
4 "I call to you men;
I raise my voice to the sons of men.
5 Understand prudence, naive ones;
have an understanding heart.

From the sinful temptress and the weak youth that we have been considering, we turn in this chapter to the other woman who seeks the life of the reader: **wisdom** personified. She too seeks his **love**; but what she offers is pure, sincere and life-giving. Rather than **the ways of death**, hers are **the ways of life**. It is a pleasure to turn from the sordidness to which we are introduced in chapter seven to this fine description of holiness.

In this chapter, **wisdom** calls to all (v. 4), but especially to the **naive**, those who may be tottering on the brink of making a decision to respond favorably to the **alien** prostitute (v. 5). If they listen to wisdom as she calls, there is hope—even for them.

Now, it isn't as if **wisdom** were hiding, hard to find, difficult to discover. Exactly the opposite is true. That is a welcome fact for counselees. Solomon asks, **Doesn't wisdom call? Doesn't she raise her voice?** The answer is "Of course she does!" God doesn't whisper truth; he doesn't act in a dark corner. He **shouts to the sons of men** (vv. 1, 4). It isn't as if wisdom were lurking in some remote place; she **calls** to all who pass her way. Indeed, she calls from the **high places**, places where she is easily seen and heard. She may be found at **the crossroads** and in the **city gates**, where most people travel or assemble. She invites all sorts to come to her for **prudence and understanding** (v. 5). So, if counselees protest that wisdom is hard to come by, refer to these verses and show them that that simply isn't true. Nip every such excuse in the bud. All one needs to do is to seek the **prudence** she offers **with an understanding heart** (v. 5). For more detail on the matter of listening, hearing and appropriating truth from God with **understanding**, see my book *Teaching to Observe: The Counselor as Teacher.*

6 Listen! I will speak important things,
and from the opening of my lips will come right things.
7 My mouth will speak truth
and wickedness is hateful to my lips.
8 All the words of my mouth are spoken in righteousness,
and there isn't a twisted or crooked thing in them.
9 All of them are straight to the discerning
and upright to those who find knowledge.
10 Accept my discipline rather than silver,
and knowledge rather than choice gold,
11 because wisdom is better than jewels
and nothing that you desire can be compared with her.
12 I, wisdom, live with prudence,
and I have discovered proper practices.

Wisdom continues to speak in verses 6 through 9. Wisdom describes her **instruction as important** (v. 6). What could be more so than God's own words of wisdom? They are **important** for all of life.

What wisdom says is dependable. She describes her words as things that are **right**. They conform to God's standards, the only rule of that which is right. Not only that; what wisdom teaches is accurate: **My mouth will speak truth** (cf. John 17:17). There isn't a deceitful or lying word in the lot (v. 7). Wisdom is the antithesis to all such things: **wickedness is hateful to me**. In different words, verse 8 reiterates the fact. When a **discerning and upright person** is asked about wisdom, he testifies that she is **straight**. After all, it is such a person who ought to know, since he has been walking with her along her **ways**. Verse 8^b says that there is no catch about wisdom, no fine print that takes away much of that which is presented in a larger font size. What you see is what you get. All is straightforward; a person who walks with wisdom finds that she is all she ever claimed to be.

Once more the *value* of wisdom is emphasized in words already familiar to the reader (vv. 10, 11; cf. 2:4; 3:14, 15). What sorts of things may be found associated with **wisdom**? **Prudence**, for one, is a very close companion of hers. Appropriateness and **proper** actions, also may be found at her side (v. 12).

But how does one get **wisdom**? By **fearing Yahweh**, which, negatively considered, leads to **hating evil, arrogance, pride, evil ways and perverted speech**. All of these are incompatible with wisdom. On the other hand, positively speaking, having **wisdom** means possessing **coun-**

13 The fear of Yahweh is to hate evil;
I hate arrogance, pride, evil ways and a perverse mouth.
14 Counsel and sound wisdom are mine.
I am understanding. I have power.
15 By me kings reign
and rulers decree righteousness.
16 By me princes and nobles rule,
and all the judges of the land.
17 I love those who love me,
and those who seek me early find me.
18 Riches and honor are with me,
enduring wealth and righteousness.
19 My fruit is better than gold—even pure gold—
and my yield is better than choice silver.
20 I walk in the way of righteousness,
among the paths of justice,

---

sel, sound thinking, understanding and power. Those are some of the sterling qualities that, together, constitute wisdom.

Power? How so? Well, as Solomon writes, **by wisdom kings reign and rulers issue righteous decrees** (v. 15). That is but one indication of wisdom's **power**. Rule is affected for good, thus becoming a great force for righteousness (v. 16).

Wisdom shows **love to those who love her by seeking her early**. That is, earnestly, and before all else. What does wisdom provide for those **who love her**? **Riches, honor, lasting wealth and righteousness**. What she offers is **better** than purest **gold** or the choicest **silver** (v. 19).

Counselor, doesn't wisdom sound like the very thing that many of your counselees lack? Wouldn't it solve most of their problems? Certainly. But they must not focus on what wisdom *provides*, but on wisdom *herself.* True, the two go hand-in-hand, but the by-products associated with wisdom (e.g., **wealth** and **honor**) are just that—by-products. You must marry her for *herself*! Solomon calls these by-products **fruit** in verse 19. **Fruit** is not the plant itself, but only what the plant produces. Wisdom is what must be sought—and fundamentally in order to please God. **Wisdom** is the correct **knowledge** and skillful application and implementation of biblical truths and directives in practical ways. But it takes **early seeking** of these things to acquire her. When they are yours—properly cultivated and cared for—they will abundantly produce **fruit**.

To **walk** with wisdom, therefore, one must **walk in the way of righteousness** (v. 20). That is because that is the path wisdom takes. Wisdom,

21 to enable my lovers to inherit wealth,
and I fill their storerooms.
22 Yahweh possessed me at the beginning of His ways,
before His works of old;
23 I was set up from eternity, from the beginning,
from before earth's earliest ages.
24 When there were no oceans,
when there were no springs full of water,
I was brought forth.
25 Before the mountains were sunk in place,
before the hills,
I was brought forth.
26 When He had not made the land,
the fields and the topsoil of the earth,
27 when He prepared the heavens,
and when He inscribed a circle on the face of the deep,
I was there.
28 When He established the clouds above,
when He fixed the springs of the deep,
29 when He set the boundaries for the sea
that the waters should not pass beyond His command,
when He decreed the foundations of the earth,
30 then I was at His side.
I was a master workman day by day,

---

herself, says so because she wants those she loves to **inherit wealth** and **fill their storehouses**.

Wisdom goes way back to creation, even before. That is, she is the eternal companion of **Yahweh**. So, to walk with wisdom is to walk with Him (vv. 22-31). According to verse 30, it was by **wisdom** that all the **works** of creation (many of which are mentioned in the previous eight verses) were brought into being. She says, **I was a master workman day by day**. God's works of creation were wisely executed according to His prudent and righteous will. All the amazing intricacies of the world that we know (and much more) are the work of her hands. And amidst all else, wisdom has always had good will toward **man** (v. 31). With such facts explained and urged upon counselees, how can they fail to seek her **early**? Only a **fool** would turn his back on **wisdom**.

Concluding the personification of wisdom and her **call** to the reader, Solomon writes the poignant words found in verses 32 through 36. Wis-

rejoicing before Him at all times;
31 rejoicing in the world, His earth,
and my delights were with the sons of men."
32 So now, my sons, listen to me:
they are happy who keep my ways.
33 Heed discipline and be wise;
don't ignore it.
34 Happy is the person who listens to me,
who watches at my gates day by day;
who guards the posts of my doors.
35 Whoever finds me finds life,
and he will obtain favor from Yahweh.
36 But he who sins against me harms himself;
all who hate me love death.

---

dom leads to **happiness** (v. 32) when **discipline** is **heeded** and **not ignored** (v. 33). But it takes effort and diligence to retain it in a world oriented in the opposite direction (v. 34). Two antithetical options, then, are open to all who hear wisdom **call**. These are set forth plainly in verses 35 and 36. They are: **life and death** (God's **favor** or His wrath).

Notice throughout the eight chapters studied so far the antithetical nature of Solomon's teaching. There is little of that sort of teaching today—even in the church. Yet, the Bible, and all of the proverbs, are heavily antithetical. God's ways are regularly set over against all others. And, as we move into chapters 10 and following, we discover not less, but more antithesis. Indeed, the majority of the couplets that begin there are simple antitheses. Counseling that is true to the spirit of the Scriptures (and the Spirit under Whose aegis they were written) will always present truth antithetically. Those who hold back from this method misrepresent God and His Word. As a result, their counseling will prove harmful to counselees who conclude that there may be many ways to go. The Scriptures are not gray; they are black and white.

CHAPTER 9

1 Wisdom has built her house;
she has carved out her seven pillars.
2 She has butchered her meat;
she has mixed her wine;
she has also set her table.
3 She has sent her maidens out;
she calls on the top of the city heights:
4 "Whoever is naive and lacks sense,
let him turn in here."
She says to him,
5 "Come, eat of my bread
and drink of the wine I have mixed.
6 Forsake the naive and live;
walk in the way of understanding.

With this chapter we end our commentary on Part One of the Book of Proverbs. There will be six more parts to this multifaceted Book. This ninth chapter opens with an additional description of **wisdom** together with a second opportunity to hear what **wisdom** says, especially to the **naive** (v. 4). Wisdom is represented as having built a magnificent palace (v. 1) and in it has prepared and readied a sumptuous feast (v. 2). Now, by her **maidens** (teachers) she invites all who will to come and enjoy it (vv. 3, 4). In her name, at the most prominent places, where all can hear (v. 3), they urge those in need of her food to **turn in** to her palace and eat (vv. 4-6).

A new element is introduced into the description of wisdom: to befriend her, past associations must be abandoned. One can no longer hang around with the crowd, and a new **way** must be taken (v. 6). Counselors will find this emphasis made over and over in subsequent sections of the Book of Proverbs, but it is first introduced here. Don't miss this point in using Proverbs in counseling; many counselees think they can have it both ways. That is impossible; along with antithesis (mentioned in the discussion of chapter eight) goes a repentance in which one turns his back on his old life and his old ways—including his old associates (if they will not hear his plea for them to accompany him along the path of wisdom).

But though some of the naive will respond positively to wisdom's gracious invitation, others, who are in the process of becoming **scorners**

7 Whoever reproves a mocker gets insulted,
and whoever corrects a wicked person invites bruises.
8 Don't correct a mocker or he will hate you;
correct a wise man and he will love you.
9 Give correction to a wise man and he will be wiser still;
inform a just man and he will increase in learning.
10 The fear of Yahweh is the beginning of wisdom,
and the knowledge of the Holy One is understanding.
11 By me, your days will be increased,
and years will be added to your life.
12 If you are wise, you will help yourself by it,
and if you mock you will have no one to blame but yourself."
13 A stubborn fool is loud;
she is naive and knows nothing at all.
14 She sits at the door of her house
on a seat in the city heights
15 to call to those who pass along the way,
who are going straight on their paths:

(mockers), will return **insults** for the well-meant **reproof** and **correction** of their converted friends. Indeed, in some instances, they may even become physical about it (v. 7)! When one recognizes that another is a **scorner**, he should refrain from counseling him; there is no sense in casting pearls before swine (cf. Matthew 7:6). That means there are persons with whom it is futile for counselors to work. But **wise** people, in contrast, not only accept helpful criticism well; they profit from it (v. 9). They, of course, make ideal counselees. Every counselor will face his share of both over the years.

Wisdom begins by coming to faith in **Yahweh** through Jesus Christ, His Son. Such saving **knowledge** leads to **understanding** (v. 10). Once more, wisdom (personified) speaks directly: **By me your days will be increased, and years will be added to your life. If you are wise, you will help yourself by it; and if you mock you will have no one to blame but yourself** (vv. 11, 12). No excuses are accepted; all responsibility is placed squarely on the shoulders of the mocker.

Part one (chapters 1-9) concludes on Solomon's most dominant theme in this section of the Proverbs: sexual sin (vv. 13-18). The only place where a woman is called a *kesil* (**stubborn fool**) in the book is in verse 13. She thinks herself **wise**, but is uncouth, course and very **ignorant**. She appeals to people like herself, men who are **naive and who have no sense** (v. 16). Listen to her come on: **Stolen waters are sweet,**

16 "You who are naive—turn in here,"
and to the one who has no sense she says,
17 "Stolen waters are sweet,
and bread eaten in secret is pleasant."
18 But he doesn't know that the dead are there,
and that her guests are in the depths of the unseen world.

---

and bread eaten in secret is pleasant (v. 17). But the pleasure is short-lived; it quickly passes only to give way to misery and **death**.

This chapter presents little that is new, but its compactness, and some of the dialog, are very useful for reading to counselees or handing out in printed form. I suggest that you rely on the Book of Proverbs heavily. Especially, use the sections on sexual sin, adulterers, violence, theft. They are some of the most powerful in the Bible on these subjects and you need them in your counseling repertoire.

NOTE: In verses 2 and 5 of this chapter we read of **wine**. Some wonder about the matter of wine in the Bible. Note that the wine is said to be **mixed**. In both Old and New Testament times wine was a staple of the average person's diet along with **bread** (cf. v. 5). Water alone was not always safe to drink. But the ordinary wine table drink was diluted by *mixing* it with water. The alcohol killed harmful bacteria. And the wine that was taken from day to day, so diluted, was not intoxicating. The ***unmixed*** **wrath of God** is mentioned in the Book of Revelation (cf. 14:10). The idea there is that wrath *in full strength* was poured out. Certainly, the wine of the Bible is intoxicating if used immoderately and in full strength. But, as it was used in ordinary eating and drinking in the home, it was not. The solution to the problem of wine in Scripture, therefore, is simple and straightforward; it needs no eisegesis to solve.

CHAPTER 10

Part Two: Chapters 10-22:16

1 A wise son makes his father glad,
but a stubborn, foolish son grieves his mother.
2 Wickedly acquired treasures don't profit,
but righteousness delivers from death.

The **wise son brings joy** to his family; the **stubborn foolish** one, **grief**. Father and mother are mentioned separately to indicate that the entire family is affected either for good or for ill, according to the way that a son acts (the idea is not that happiness is more likely associated with the **father** and grief with the **mother**). Verse one is a fitting introduction to the entire chapter since it concerns the matters that make the difference. In counseling, regularly, you see the effects of wayward children on a family. If you have the opportunity to do so, show this verse to the child that has gone astray. Make it clear to him when he says, "What I do is my business," that it is the business of the whole family. His actions cannot but have a strong impact on everyone. He also is responsible for happiness or grief. In doing so, you want to get him to assume some responsibility for the welfare of the family; he is not simply a single individual, living on his own, apart from the love and concern of others. Yet, a family, in spite of his failure, may rise above the sorrow and heartache that he brings to it by committing themselves to Christ and going on in His strength. Ultimately, their hope and peace and joy is in Him, not in the **son**.

There are many ways of getting rich, some of which are wrong. Solomon says that, in the long run, riches (**treasures** = wealth, land, etc.) **acquired** unjustly do not bring the satisfaction that the one who acquires them believes they will. The problem, as every counselor must realize, doesn't begin with theft, cheating and the like. Rather, it starts with a wrong *goal* in life: the desire to become wealthy (cf. I Timothy 6:9). In that letter, Paul says that those who set their heart on becoming rich will be caught in a trap because they will fall into all sorts of temptations. Money and property aren't the problem; it is the *love* of money, etc., that is the root of all sorts of sin (I Timothy 6:10). Putting the acquisition of money or things first in life—as one's goal for living—is to make them his god. Whatever one lives for is his god. But to do so brings ruin (I Timothy 6:9). Indeed, it can even lead to death, as Proverbs 2 indicates. The

3 Yahweh doesn't allow the righteous to go hungry,
but He thwarts the wicked's desire.
4 Whoever works with a negligent hand will be poor,
but a diligent hand makes one rich.

---

truth of this verse is applicable today: every day we hear of the death of some of those who are involved in gambling, robbery and the illicit drug traffic. This proverb warns of becoming involved in such a lifestyle. Counselors will find the verse helpful when dealing with those who have set the possession of money and things before them as their life goal.

There is a wonderful promise for God's children in verse 3: **Yahweh doesn't allow the righteous to go hungry.** It corresponds to Jesus' words in Matthew 6:25-34. In times of economic upheaval like ours, many Christians tend to worry about finances (even leading to questions about whether they will have enough food to eat); in this verse there is a promise that counselors may use to alleviate such fears. But there is also a warning that the **desires** of **wicked** persons will be **thwarted**. That may not mean what one wishes for by way of wealth or food will be withheld (though in some instances it might) but, more often, it will mean that there is no satisfaction or good outcome in obtaining a desire. Ultimately, the **desire** is not for the thing itself but for the pleasure, peace and satisfaction that one believes having it will produce. Rarely, will he find that **desire** fulfilled for very long. As Solomon says, the **desire** will be **thwarted**.

In verse 4 it is clear that **riches**, properly acquired (through diligent, honest labor) are not a curse (cf. v. 2) but a blessing. So in counseling you must never condemn wealth *per se* (see also I Timothy 6:17). God often provides **riches** "to enjoy." Indeed, as this proverb indicates, God may bless **diligent** Christians with **riches**. Many counselees who are in financial distress, however, have brought that condition upon themselves by indolence, foolish spending and the like. They too need to hear the words of this verse.

When a counselee complains that he has worked **diligently**, but has never been blessed with **riches**, you need to make it clear that this doesn't say that all who work hard will become rich, but only that when it does happen it is through **diligence**. God may have reasons for withholding wealth in such cases. Also, one's definition of **riches** may vary from His. Moreover, **diligence** is not the only condition for obtaining riches.

Continuing the theme of the wise son and the diligent worker, Solomon commends the son who **stores in summer** and condemns the one

5 A wise son stores in summer,
but one that snores at harvest time causes shame.
6 Happiness is on the head of the righteous,
but the wicked's mouth covers violence.
7 The righteous is happily remembered,
but the name of the wicked will rot.
8 One who has a wise heart accepts commands,
but one with foolish lips will be thrown down.
9 One who walks in integrity walks securely,
but one who takes a crooked path will be found out.

---

who **snores at harvest** (v. 5). Literally, the Hebrew says **stores** and **snores. Summer** is the time to store up food for the winter. But, because it is easy to come by it in **summer**, unless one shows forethought for the lean season ahead, he may slack off. The **shame** mentioned means that he has nothing when needed and is forced to beg. How important the two-part principle in this verse is for counselors! On the one hand, the need for **diligent work** when there is opportunity to gather and store is stressed, while on the other hand foresight and planning is encouraged. Many counselees need to develop one or the other of these vital traits—or both!

Happiness is the fruit of quiet, **righteous** living (cf. I Thessalonians 4:11) according to verse 6. The turmoil of a **violent** lifestyle brings heartache. The wicked may **cover** up his trouble by his false boasts, but there is no true **happiness** or peace in such living. Here is an insight that takes counselors beyond the bragging and boasting of the world to what **wicked** living actually is like.

People **remember** and say good things about those whose **righteousness** made some segment of society better, more peaceful, etc. (v. 7). But the name of the one who disturbed others by his life leaves only the stench of **rot**. Though it may not matter to some what others say once they are gone, to some it is quite important and, therefore, an additional incentive to live righteously.

Verse 8 speaks of how one acts toward duly-appointed authority. The one with a **wise heart** obeys all legitimate commands (wherever they may originate). But by his **foolish** responses (surely, sarcastic talk) he may literally **be thrown down** (by a policeman, for instance). One way or another, his attitude will lead him to forced humiliation. This is a warning that counselees, from whose mouths there drips acid as they talk, should be made to face.

10 One who winks with his eye causes trouble,
and one with foolish lips will fall down.
11 The mouth of the righteous is a fountain of life,
but the wicked's mouth conceals violence.
12 Hatred stirs up strife,
but love covers all sorts of transgressions.

To **walk in integrity**, as the Hebrew word *tam* in verse 9 means, is to pursue a lifestyle in which one is growing well spiritually in all aspects of his life. In the term there is the idea of *having it all together* (cf. James 1:4, 5). James' *teleios* man is the exact equivalent. While not sinless, of course, the person with integrity has no hidden area of deep sin to which he clings. The one traveling the **crooked** path of unrighteousness, however, does (perhaps even many such). In time, these **will be found out**. Sin cannot be covered up forever—except in Christ. It is often your unpleasant task, counselor, to be the one who ferrets out this sin. The verse is an encouragement to you in the sense that you know that no matter how cleverly he hides his sin, it may be discovered. Often the **finding out** of sin is the prelude to change. One of your tasks is to help bring counselees to confession of sin and repentance.

In verse 10 we meet the person who, while saying one thing to someone, through bodily action indicates to others that he doesn't mean what he says. In the end this liar, who deliberately causes **trouble** for others, finds that the very **trouble** he initiated will return to bring him down. What he says is pure **foolishness** and will not withstand the test of time.

The first half of verse 11 should be important to every counselor. His stock-in-trade is speech. Counsel is, by definition, verbal advice. God recognizes that when a **righteous** person gives wise counsel his words can bring healing, refreshment and abundant **life** to those who hear and heed. Isn't that what you want your counseling room to become—a **fountain of life**? What more apt description could there be for biblical counseling, from which flows the words of eternal life? No other sort of counseling can even begin to provide life—let alone abundant life! That flows only from the **fountain** of Scripture ministered in the power of the Spirit. For comment on the second half of verse 11, see notes on verse 6. Here, it seems, he is covering up the miseries violent living brings by speech intended to lead others into thinking that violence is good, thereby leading them astray.

13 Wisdom is found on the lips of a discerning person,
but a rod is for the back of a senseless person.
14 Wise persons store up knowledge,
but the foolish person's mouth is a present destruction.
15 The rich man's wealth is his strong city;
the ruin of the poor is their poverty.

Verse 12 is quoted in 17:9; 19:11; James 5:20 and I Peter 4:8. The first half of the proverb reveals a truth to be remembered and brought into every counseling equation: **hatred stirs up strife**. It is inevitable. Where **strife** occurs, therefore, look for **hatred**. Where **hatred** is evident, look for **strife**.

Contrary to all of that, one who doesn't develop a hostile attitude but shows **love, covers all sorts of transgressions**. That does not mean that he engages in a cover up of some nefarious sort; it means that rather than stir up **strife** by how he responds to the words and actions of another, out of **love**, he lets the transgression pass and makes no more of it. Those offenses that **separate** Christians (throw the cover off), however, must be dealt with according to Matthew 18:15ff. As one grows in his love he will learn not to be affected so often by what other sinners do, recognizing how many of their sins and failures **he ought to cover in love**.

Verse 13 is straightforward enough; if, in our society, we were to use the rod as a punishment, there would be less **senseless** action.

It is interesting to note, as verse 14 clearly says, that a person who has already become **wise** never rests on his laurels. That is part of his wisdom. He goes on **storing up** more **knowledge**. He loves to acquire it; he knows that he will need it, so he goes on getting it. Paul was a wise man and—at the very end of his life—we see him asking Timothy to bring his books (II Timothy 4:13), even though he had been sentenced to death. A good counselor is like that. He is never satisfied with what he knows. He must know more and more of God; to understand more of His Word is his delight. The wise counselor who **stores** knowledge, like the well-instructed scribe of Matthew 13:52, is able to bring out just what is needed in every counseling situation. In contrast, the fool's advice brings only immediate devastation to those who follow it. How many counselees ruined by poor advice have you helped during the last year?

An observation (v. 15): that which gives protection to some people is their wealth; equally true is the fact that the poverty of others brings them down. No exhortation is appended, but previous comments on riches (cf.

16 The wages of the righteous is life,
but the wicked's payment is punishment.
17 He who heeds discipline is on the path of life,
but he who rejects reproof goes astray.
18 He has lying lips who conceals hatred,
and he who spreads slander is a stubborn fool.
19 With a multitude of words comes transgression,
but he who restrains his words is wise.

---

v. 4), in addition to others that will follow, indicate that often one is responsible for these conditions. It is clear that wealth will not ultimately protect from the wrath to come; it is equally clear that the poor person may find refuge and help in God—if he will. So, in both cases, it is *trust* in wealth that causes the ruin.

Verse 16 probably speaks of eternity. Romans 6:23 may even be an allusion to it. At any rate, both verses teach the same fact.

The **heeding of discipline** (v. 17) is evidence that one is walking the right road. How a counselee receives well-meant reproof and correction is important for determining this fact. Indeed, failure in this regard may lead to discipline that, in turn, may show that the person involved gives no indication of salvation. To reject biblical counsel, properly given by a pastoral counselor, (as the second half of the couplet implies) leads to even further sin: the rejecter goes **astray**. This verse also shows the importance of good counseling; it can help people remain on the **path** that leads to **life**.

When one **conceals hatred**, he does so by **lying** (v. 18), usually through flattery and smooth talk. But if he opens his mouth to speak anything else, it is only to **spread slander**. He is a **stubborn fool**. He will not receive correction, but goes on in his obstinate ways.

Some counselees get into trouble because they won't keep quiet (v. 19). They babble on, whether they know what they are talking about or not. Then, when they make absurd statements and are called on them, they may tend to defend themselves with more questionable talk. They are soon found out; people no longer believe them, and don't wish to confide in them any more than in the slanderer mentioned in the previous verse. It is wise to **speak** only about what one knows for sure and, even then, to **speak** less than one might be inclined to.

An incessant bore, whom people avoid, is also a person of many words—almost all of which concern himself. Again, when focusing on

20 The tongue of the righteous is like choice silver,
but the wicked person's heart is worth little.
21 The lips of the righteous feed many,
but stupid fools die for their senselessness.
22 It is the Lord's blessing that makes one rich,
and He adds no sorrow to it.
23 To devise evil schemes is like play to the stubborn fool,
just as wisdom is to the person with understanding.

---

that usually uninteresting subject, this loquacious person tends to exaggerate his good traits and conceal the rest—often in ways that are sinful.

So counselor, as a man of words, take heed to your own speech. Learn when to restrain **speech** and how to advise and train others to do so.

Verse 20 can be added to the list of verses that encourage counselors (and others) to recognize how valuable helpful speech can be (it is like **choice silver**). Behind such speech is a **heart** for God that is of even greater value since it is what generates good action as well as speech. The opposite is true of the **wicked person's heart**. In contrast to the **heart** and **tongue** that is **choice silver**, his **heart** is **worth little**. Self-esteem advocates are not happy with such statements, but God is the One Who guided Solomon to pen them! It is time they changed their belief in the worth of persons generally, and begin to think biblically. Self-esteem dogma hinders good counsel because it gives people false notions of man's condition.

Verse 21 continues to address the matter of speech. The chapter, with its many vital verses on the subject, is of great help to counselors, who ought to read it frequently. He should knead the statements he reads into the dough of counseling. In this verse, a counselor can see how his advice may sustain a counselee in time of trouble or need as food sustains his physical life: it may **feed many**. What a good way to think of counseling! It is feeding people on the words that come out of God's mouth; it is a recognition that "man cannot live by bread alone." **Stupid fools** refuse the bread that you hold out to them and **die** for their **senselessness**.

Verse 22 is a reiteration of verses found earlier in the chapter—with this significant addition: **and He adds no sorrow to it**. Think of that: God gives riches and so blesses them that their recipients will thoroughly *enjoy* them! That is the picture of true *Shalom*: peace and prosperity.

When you find a person who enjoys cooking up evil schemes as another would enjoy watching a baseball game, you are dealing with a **fool** (v. 23). When you find one who enjoys soaking up wisdom in like

24 What the wicked fears is what will come upon him,
but what the righteous desires is granted.
25 When the storm passes the wicked is not,
but the righteous has an enduring foundation.
26 To those who send him,
a lazy person is like vinegar to the teeth and smoke to the eyes.
27 The fear of Yahweh prolongs days,
but the wicked's years will be shortened.
28 The righteous person's hope leads to joyful fulfillment,
but the wicked's expectation will perish.

---

manner, you are dealing with a person of **understanding**. The observation by Solomon carries obvious implications—too obvious for further comment.

Verse 24 contrasts **what the wicked fears** with **what the righteous desires** and says each will receive it. Neither outcome may be immediate, however, as David indicates in Psalm 73:3ff. And as he says, he nearly slipped into sin at seeing the *temporary* prosperity of the **wicked**. This verse shows that the **wicked** have hidden fears, the greatest of which is death, and unless they repent their worst fears will be realized.

The way in which God brings judgment on evildoers is addressed in verse 25. Under the image of physical disaster the **wicked** are shown falling and the **righteous** standing. The one has the **foundation** that the other does not have (cf. Jesus' story of the two houses in Matthew 7). The foundation here is biblical **wisdom**, something unknown to unbelievers. Counselors must often build from scratch, starting with the foundation of their counselee's lives. If trials sweep Christians from their foundations, they have not been trusting in Scripture as they should. Show them there is no need for this to happen (cf. I Corinthians 10:13).

The point of verse 26 is that the **lazy person**, like **vinegar on teeth** or **smoke in the eyes** is irritating to the one who sent him. If an assignment is given to someone, but he takes his time getting around to fulfilling it because of laziness, he becomes a vexation rather than a help. So? So, it is better not to entrust a task to him. Better still, let the lazy person wake up to the fact and become dependable.

We have met previously the thought in verse 27 concerning longevity. See previous discussions. A healthy, safe, quiet lifestyle, along with a clear conscience, promotes it. The opposite tends to shorten one's lifespan.

Verse 28 is of similar import to that which is taught in verse 24.

29 Yahweh's way means strength for the upright,
but ruin for all evil doers.
30 The righteous will never be shaken,
but the wicked will not dwell in the land.
31 The righteous person's mouth sprouts with wisdom,
but the perverse tongue will be rooted out.
32 The lips of the righteous know what is acceptable,
but the mouth of the wicked knows only perversities.

There is **strength** in righteousness. Those who live lives of integrity, where the Spirit is at work in all areas, know the spiritual **strength** that this provides. Where there is no Achilles heel, there is no place of weakness. The wicked are vulnerable on all sides; this weakness leads to ruin.

In verse 30 there is an echo of verse 25. One, because of his foundation, remains after trial (**shaking**); the other does not. He is removed from the land. Counselees need to hear this over and over from various perspectives, said in numerous ways; otherwise, the repetition in Proverbs would be superfluous.

Under an agricultural figure, the **mouth** of the **righteous** is described as producing living plants of **wisdom**, while the **tongue** that produces the **fruit** of wickedness will be **uprooted** (v. 31). God will not allow such speech to continue indefinitely. Wisdom will prosper and multiply; perversity will die out since its source is uprooted.

What are we to make of chapter ten? Certainly, because of its many references to the tongue and to speech it is surely a principal source of counseling material on that subject. The antithetical nature of the couplets is also instructive about how to convey truth. The use of the many figures employed should encourage us to put truth in such form when teaching counselees. While the righteous do not escape the storm, they are kept in it. And the ultimate ruin of the wicked or the blessing of the righteous is the subject of many of the verses.

CHAPTER 11

1 A false balance is an abomination to Yahweh,
but an accurate weight delights Him.
2 Comes arrogance—comes shame,
but wisdom is with the humble.
3 The integrity of the upright leads them,
but the deceit of hypocrites destroys them.
4 Wealth will not help in the day of wrath,
but righteousness delivers from death.

God is concerned about business practices. He knows whose **balance** is deliberately off and whose **weights** are inaccurate (v. 1). Some counselees engage (or have engaged) in shoddy business ethics. God uses very strong language (an **abomination** = something He detests) when speaking of those who cheat in business. Counselors should not water down His Words when dealing with the problem. On the other hand, He declares that He is **delighted** with honest business practices. Here is material to be used when confronting those who are considering shady business transactions. Of course, though scales and weights may not be the exact problem in a given case, the principle involved extends to all attempts to cheat a customer.

Pride and **arrogance** lead to **shame** (v. 2). Sooner or later (in God's perfect timing) someone will knock the proud off the lofty perch he has erected for himself. Pride is bad; arrogant attitudes that often accompany it are even worse. If one won't humble himself, God has ways of humbling him. Humble persons recognize that all they are and all they have that is good comes from God. They have nothing to brag or act arrogant about, but everything to be thankful for. Grace accounts for everything that is fine and worthwhile. How can one be arrogant about that which he received when he deserved nothing but the opposite? Teaching counselees the truths of grace is the antidote to **arrogance**.

The fact that one has it together (is a person of **integrity**) is helpful **in leading** people along the paths of life since such people seek to serve **Yahweh**. They are genuine through and through (v. 3). Counselors must strive to be such people (for more on this, see comments in the commentary on James 1 in this series). **Hypocrisy**, in contrast, leads one into ruin and **destruction**. The **deceits of hypocrites** come back to haunt them (e.g., people eventually stop believing them, trusting and depending on

5 The righteousness of a person with integrity makes his way straight,
but the wicked person falls by his own wickedness.
6 The righteousness of the upright delivers them,
but hypocrites will be trapped by their own desire.
7 When a wicked person dies his expectation will perish,
and the unjust person's hope of wealth will be lost.
8 The righteous is delivered from distress,
and the wicked takes his place.

---

them). The problems they have caused others become problems for them as well. In the short term deceit may gain an advantage; tell counselees that in the long run it will not, but will prove ruinous to them.

The teaching of verse 5 has already been discussed in previous verses. Ezekiel 7:19 refers the sentiments of verse 4 to God's **day** of judgment. What it is saying in that context is that those who depend on money to buy their way out of trouble will find that, when they most need deliverance, money will fail. The tendency is to think that since money paid off with sinful men, it will also pay off with God; nothing could be farther from the truth. Though others may be, God is not impressed with one's **wealth**.

Evil complicates life; because hypocrites pretend to be something that they are not, at length, their deception **traps** them (vv. 5, 6; cf. v. 3). For instance, a man may pretend to be a Christian in order to win a Christian girl for his wife. Later, he discovers that this pretense brings nothing but agony to them both. But **uprightness**, willingness to be what God wants, simplifies life. The **person with integrity** is **delivered** from many of the problems that **wicked**, complex living brings on one's self (v. 6). The **desire**-oriented living of the **wicked**, in contrast to the commandment-oriented living of the **righteous** is what makes the difference (for more on the nature of desire as it relates to counseling, see comments in the *Christian Counselor's Commentary on II Peter*).

At **death** the **wicked** person can take nothing with him. All he lived for is lost. The **wealth** he spends his life seeking and accumulating will vanish from his grasp, along with every good thing—forever (v. 7). Many counselees need to be reminded of this fact. When money and things glitter in their eyes, they tend to be blinded to truth. That is when someone else must bring them up short.

Verse 8 makes it clear that God sees to it that **wicked** men take the **place** of the **righteous** when He **delivers** the latter **from distress**. Often that comes in the form of turning the tables. Warn against confidence that

9 With his mouth the ungodly person corrupts his friend,
but the righteous is delivered by knowledge.
10 When things go well for the righteous the city rejoices,
and at the perishing of the wicked there is shouting.
11 A city is lifted up by the blessing of the upright,
but by the mouth of the wicked it is torn down.
12 One who shows contempt for his friend is senseless,
but an understanding person is silent.

---

another is taking it in the neck; it may be that this will reverse itself in no time if a counselee persists in such thinking.

Verse 9 is crucial. Too many counseling sessions fail because someone outside counseling is advising all the wrong things. And your counselee is listening. The **ungodly person** can give only **the counsel of the ungodly** (Psalm 1:1) which will **corrupt** your counselee. It is, therefore, essential for counselors to be sure that there is no outside influence tugging in the wrong direction. If your investigation reveals the existence of such influence, you must eliminate it. "How?" you ask. The best way I know is to be open and frank about the matter, as Proverbs itself is whenever it discusses the influence of bad associations (a theme we shall encounter frequently in this book as well as in I Corinthians 15:33). When I detect such a problem, I say something like this, "You cannot go East and West at the same time without injury to yourself. You must choose: will you receive God's counsel or someone else's?" If a person is allowed to burn the candle from both ends while attempting to hold it, he will be burned. What he needs is not **ungodly** counsel but biblical **knowledge**.

Verses 10 and 11 speak about the reaction of the populace to **righteous** and wicked rulers. Everyone is adversely affected by the rise of **wicked** rulers and blessed when the **righteous** take control. There is **shouting and rejoicing** when the wicked are overthrown. The verse, along with the Book of Judges, teaches that leadership is important. That is true in a city or a country of course, but it is true also in a church, a home or any other organization.

A **neighbor** is to be cultivated, not despised (v. 12). To speak, or otherwise show **contempt** for him, is **senseless**. Such words and actions will estrange him. If nothing good can be said, then, says Solomon, be **silent**. Silence is always better than saying the wrong thing. How often a counselee would profit from the simple advice to "shut up!"

Similar to the previous proverbs is verse 13. The **gossip** is the person who doesn't keep quiet when he should. He **reveals secrets** that should

13 A gossip goes about revealing secrets,
but a trustworthy person conceals a matter.
14 Without guidance the people fall,
but there is safety in many counselors.
15 Whoever guarantees a loan for a foreigner will suffer for it,
but the one who hates striking hands is safe.
16 A gracious woman acquires honor,
and vigorous persons acquire riches.
17 A merciful person benefits himself,
but the cruel person hurts himself.

---

never be told. A **trustworthy person conceals** them. Gossip is not only a matter of spreading *false* information, as some seem to think. Rather, it is the spreading of any information—true or false—that it is unnecessary to reveal. A husband and wife engage in a shouting match. Later, they quietly, lovingly resolve their differences in a biblical manner. Their next door neighbor hears the shouting but he fails to hear the quiet, endearing words of forgiveness. If he spreads the facts about what he heard, he has spoken only half of the truth. He has no right to talk to others about what he heard; the only ones to whom he might speak are the quarreling couple—and then, only to offer help in the spirit of Galatians 6:1.

A nation needs multiple **counselors** to whom a leader may turn. It is unwise to make great decisions involving war, etc., on the advice of only one person (v. 14). Wise rulers will listen to more than those who agree with them. Note: against all that Carl Rogers taught, **counsel** is explained as giving **guidance**.

The ideas in verse 15 are not new. See previous expositions.

According to verse 16, **women** who conduct themselves **gracefully** will be **honored** for it. They are not honored for aggressive, masculine manners. On the other hand, **wealth** is obtained by **men** who are **vigorous** in their approach rather than effeminate. In other words, in spite of the feminist mentality of many today, which tends to reverse (or, at best mix) sex roles, Solomon sets forth God's fundamental role for each. Each role when followed, in turn, produces **honor** or **wealth**.

Verse 17 makes it clear that to show **mercy** is **beneficial** to one's self because of the sort of person this helps him become. He extends himself beyond self-interests and softens his heart toward the plight of others. And the grateful response that he receives from merciful acts is encouraging as well. His reputation is enhanced. But, if you turn all of that inside out, you can refer it to the one who is **cruel**.

18 A wicked person earns false wages,
but one who sows righteousness reaps a true reward.
19 Genuine righteousness leads to life,
but one who pursues evil will die.
20 The crooked in heart are an abomination to Yahweh,
but His delight is in those who take integrity's way.
21 Take my hand on it—the evil will not be acquitted,
but the descendent of the righteous will escape.
22 Like a gold ring in a swine's snout
is a beautiful woman who lacks good taste.

A sentiment that, in different form, has already been expressed is found in verse 18: money gained in sinful ways (lying, cheating) is what **wicked** people delight in—to their own detriment. It is interesting to listen to the wicked speak; they think it is great to get away with such dealings (they even boast about it). But the one **who sows righteousness will reap a true reward** (cf. 10:22). In God's order of things, people simply do not get away with unrighteousness. In one way or another, in His time, the day of reckoning arrives and the **wages** of the **wicked**, which for a time seemed great, turn to ashes. The **reward of the righteous**, conversely, that seemed so meager, in the end turns out to be the **true** riches.

Verse 19 follows hard on the previous verse, setting forth the ultimate fruit of both **righteousness** and **evil**: **life** and **death**. Help counselees to look beyond the immediate effects of their behavior which, as in the verse above, may be the very opposite of the eternal outcomes.

In verse 20 **Yahweh** speaks of those whose **hearts** are **crooked** as an **abomination** to Himself. Again, the source of the action (the heart) is the subject of concern. He detests crooked**, twisted ways.** God **delights** in persons who are open and honest, whose ways are straight. Counselees who change, must change to please God; not merely to gain some desired end.

According to verse 21, though it may take a generation to work out (we are all too much tied to our short lifespans), God's righteous government will see to it that evil **and integrity** will receive their own proper rewards. Many counselees forget that their actions have long-standing consequences—especially for their children and children's children. Here is a point that is too infrequently mentioned in counseling.

The gross inappropriateness of the image in verse 22 gives it its power. The proverb speaks for itself. Use such strong contrasts in counsel-

23 The desire of the righteous leads only to good,
but the expectation of the wicked to wrath.
24 There is a sort of person who scatters and yet further increases,
but one who withholds what should be given comes to poverty.
25 A generous person will be enriched;
one who waters also will drink fully.
26 People curse the one who withholds grain,
but there will be a blessing on the head of the one who sells grain.
27 He who early seeks good finds favor,
but evil comes to the one who searches for it.
28 One who trusts in his riches will fall,
but the righteous will flourish like a green leaf.

---

ing to drive points home. They cause shock or laughter and, thereby, become memorable. Don't hesitate to quote this proverb as is, when useful.

Right and wrong **desires** result in good or bad outcomes according to verse 23. Once more, the heart (which is the seat of desire) should be brought into focus. What one desires, if righteous, can **only** result in **good**, whereas, what he desires, if **wicked**, can only result in God's **wrath**. Because of the contrast between **good** and **wrath**, it would seem to mean that God does good to the one whose desires are right.

In verses 24 through 26, the blessings of **giving** and the **curses** of **withholding** are plainly set forth. Paul alludes to these verses in II Corinthians 8 and 9. "God," said the old southern preacher, "shovels back to you as you shovel from your **gain** to Him. The difference is that God has a bigger shovel!" How many counselees, suffering from financial problems, find themselves in that situation because of a niggardly attitude toward giving? When financial difficulties are presented in counseling, always check out the giving habits of the counselees. You may have to teach them the truth of these verses.

To **seek early** (v. 27) is an expression that means to put something first on your agenda, and not to drag your feet in getting to it. It means that you are serious about what you are doing: serious enough to give it priority. Some are quick and earnest about doing **good**; others **search** hard for **evil**. Counselees will get in return what they place first and foremost in life.

Riches will dry up and fade like leaves in fall and the one who **trusts** in them rather than in **Yahweh** will come fluttering to the ground as well. The righteous, on the other hand, will **flourish** like a fresh, green leaf of spring (v. 28; see Psalm 1).

29 Whoever stirs up trouble for his household will inherit the wind,
and the stupid fool becomes servant to the wise-hearted.
30 The fruit of the righteous is a tree of life,
and he who wins people is wise.
31 See! If the righteous will be repaid on the earth
how much more the wicked and the sinner!

Probably verse 29 is as powerful a verse for those who are engaged in marital difficulties as any in the Book of Proverbs. It sets forth the utter stupidity of those who continue to **stir up trouble** in a family rather than seek to quiet and resolve it. As verses 15:6 and 27 indicate, there are many ways of **troubling** one's **household**. To what does it lead? Absolutely nothing worthwhile: the **wind**. Stirring up trouble results only in emptiness. All the energy that is expended in doing so achieves nothing. Indeed, to tear down one's home means that the fool who does so will be reduced to slavery, **serving** those who are **wise**.

Righteous living makes one a **tree of life** (v. 30; i.e., one who is a blessing and help to others. They may find healing in his leaves; cf. Revelation 22:2). Every counselor should become such a tree. Indeed, one who **wins** others to God's way of life is **wise**. The idea in the second half of the verse is similar to James 5:19, which may allude to this verse.

Though, as we have seen, the wages of righteousness and sin may not be fully paid in this world (v. 19) or even in this generation (v. 21), some of what is coming *is* received in one's lifetime. But if the **righteous** experience a measure of retribution in this world (cf. I Corinthians 11:30-32), **how much more** will unsaved **sinners** and **wicked** persons (v. 31)! Though your counselee may not see this righteous recompense occurring as fully or as quickly as he would like, he really knows nothing of what is happening in the heart and soul of a wicked person. He usually is unaware of the many heartaches and other difficulties sin has already occasioned, or the problems that his family experiences.

CHAPTER 12

1 Whoever loves discipline loves knowledge,
but he who hates reproof is like a dumb animal.
2 A good man brings forth approval from Yahweh,
but He will condemn a schemer.
3 A person will not be established by wickedness,
but the root of the righteous is unshakable.

There is no other way to gain **knowledge** than through **disciplined** effort (v. 1). That is why, in addition to other matters, biblical counselors find themselves teaching and structuring for **discipline** (see my book *Teaching to Observe: The Counselor as Teacher*). Discipline involves regularity, consistency, effort, planning, time. When undisciplined counselees (just about two-thirds of your counselees will be undisciplined) attempt to develop new patterns at first they will be inconsistent, irregular, etc. They will need **reproof** for this—especially if they have not really tried. You must insist on the structure that you have helped them create. Those who heed the mild **reproofs** (actually used as encouragement) you give, in time *will* change. Those who learn to **hate** reproof and refuse to do those things that lead to change will fail to learn what they should and, as a result, like a **dumb**, unreasoning **animal**, will go on following feelings instead of following the commands of God.

What really counts, you must convince your counselees, is **Yahweh's approval** (v. 2). It really doesn't matter what others may say so long as He expresses approval of their lifestyle. The man whose life conforms to His Word will find God's favor beaming down upon him. On the other hand, nothing is more to be feared than God's **condemnation**. A **schemer** is detested by Yahweh, Who wants people to be straightforward and honest. Scheming is not on God's agenda for your counselees. The one plans to do good to others; the other hatches schemes for exploiting or working wrong toward them. There is nothing more important than receiving God's **approval**.

Wickedness is never firmly **rooted**; it **establishes** itself only temporarily (v. 3). Soon, it dries up, withers and blows away. The **root of the righteous**, on the contrary, cannot be **shaken**. Let the winds of adversity test both and the results of each will be clear! To be **unshakable**, as the Hebrew indicates, is to be unable to be pulled up. When God truly plants a vine in His kingdom, it sends down roots deeply into the soil. The believer

4 An able wife is her husband's crown,
but one who causes shame is like rottenness in the bones.
5 The thoughts of the righteous are just,
but the counsels of the wicked are deceitful.
6 The words of the wicked are a bloody ambush,
but the mouth of the upright delivers them.

---

will not be uprooted; indeed, he will grow and prosper and bear fruit. The temporary nature of the seeming prosperity of the **wicked** is misleading. Check out their final end.

Most men who are successful have **able wives** as helpers (cf. Genesis 2:18). As the one who wears a crown is conspicuous, so too are the achievements of the wife of a successful man. To him she is an honor as well as a helper. He is proud of her in a godly way (grateful for what the Lord has done in giving him such a worthy partner). But a wife to be **ashamed** of is the one who causes deep misery. Like a body in which the very **bones are rotting**, she is a drag on him; she holds him back in all he attempts to do. She is as much a hinderance as a dread, debilitating disease. This is a good verse to use in dealing with marital difficulties! Ask the nagging, complaining, self-centered wife who is always causing trouble in her home "Are you a crown on your husband's head or rottenness in his bones?" Let her think about that for a while. If she asks "Why, what does that mean?" Say, "tell me what *you* think it means." If she gets near the target in her explanation, well and good; reinforce what she says. If she doesn't get anywhere near it (or fails to offer any explanation whatever) then explain how a wife helps or hinders the success of her husband. But, reading the verse and then asking the question makes her think about the matter—something she needs to do.

In verse 5 the inner life is before us. It is in the "heart" that all of one's **thoughts** and intents originate (Hebrews 4:12). From the heart come **just** and **deceitful thoughts** and **counsels**. Again, counselors are encouraged to stress the need for inner change of heart—not mere outward conformity to commands. The need is for the inner goals, aspirations, loyalties and intentions to be changed; apart from such change, all is temporary, unapproved by God and worse than worthless since it deceives both the counselee and others. Self-deception is the worst form of deception.

According to verse 6, a counselor should see as part of his task rescuing counselees from the plots and schemes of those who seek to harm

7 Overthrow the wicked and they are not,
but the house of the righteous will stand.
8 A person is praised for good sense,
but a person with a twisted heart will be despised.
9 It is better to be insignificant and have a servant
than to honor one's self and lack bread.
10 A righteous person cares about the life of his animal,
but the compassions of the wicked are cruel.

---

him; a not too pleasant task, but an important and eminently rewarding one. Though the **words of the wicked** may not always lead to murder or bloodshed, their plans to trap the righteous are every bit as nefarious as if they physically **ambushed** them. By his helpful guidance, in the form of biblical advice, the counselor can steer his counselee around many of the traps his enemies set for him. **Upright** counsel is what is called for in such situations.

The sad truth taught in verse 7 is that **wicked** persons have no staying power; indeed, by their wicked ways, they bring down their entire household with them. Nevertheless, the great encouragement is that righteous persons establish families that **will stand**. Usually, it is adversity that brings out the truths of these two statements. The great hope in this verse is that there is resiliency in righteousness. When wicked persons turn from their ways in repentance, they too can enjoy the solidity that righteousness adds to living.

The teaching in verse 8 is but an observation that includes, first, encouragement and, secondly, warning. The verse should be used for both purposes.

Pride, and its effects, is dealt with in verse 9. It shows where self-esteem thinking leads. To brag about **one's self** (bragging is claiming what one cannot deliver) is of no real value. To not put one's self forward at all, but to genuinely possess what the braggart only talks about, is far preferable. To **honor one's self** is to toot his own horn. Few people can endure a self-made man who continually tells you that he is. Someone has said that the smallest package in the world is a person all wrapped up in himself. In effect, the verse says, "Put up or shut up."

Even one's livestock experience whether their owner is **righteous** or **wicked**. In every area of life—even in how he cares for his animals—a person reveals his basic inner self. By their works will you know them! Observing **care** and **compassion** (or its lack) for a helpless animal on the part of a parishioner is one way a pastor can learn much about him. To

11 He who slaves over his land will find his fill of bread,
but he who pursues emptiness lacks sense.
12 The wicked desires what evil people net,
but the righteous root gives.
13 An evil person is trapped by the transgression of his lips,
but the righteous will emerge from trouble.
14 By the fruit of his mouth will a person be satisfied with good things,
and the results of his hands will return to him.

---

observe cruelty to one's pet, for instance, is to recognize the hardened nature of the member of his congregation. Compassion on the weak and helpless is a good sign of genuineness in a person (v. 10). Sometimes, counselor, just to inquire about one's pets or livestock, and getting him to talk about them, will give you the insight into a counselee that you need. Steer the conversation around to this area and get him talking about them. You may be surprised about what you learn.

In verse 11, diligence is contrasted with laziness once again. The effects of each are set forth: to work hard (**slave**) produces much; to pursue **empty,** worthless activities instead, is **senseless** because it produces nothing. God expects those that He has created in His image to use their heads; there is no reason for senseless living and decision-making. Watching TV, hours spent playing video (or computer) games and the like are the sorts of things to which Solomon refers.

Verse 12 contrasts those who **desire** the evil things that **evil people** catch in their **nets** with the **righteous** who **give** of the fruit of their firmly **rooted** lives. A good question to ask yourself about a counselee when assessing his lifestyle is whether he is basically a *giver* or a *taker*? And if the latter, in addition to all else, that fact tells you to ask, "What is it that he seeks?"

When one is caught in a lie, he becomes untrustworthy in the eyes of others. So when trouble comes, even if he has done no wrong, people won't believe him. However, if a person's word is known to be dependable in the past, during a doubtful time of **trouble** he will be believed and supported. He will **emerge** from the **trouble** unscathed. Verse 13 says that one's reputation for trustworthiness is vital. Many counselees need to hear this fact and act upon it.

All preachers and counselors, whose tasks involve speech, know that it is through speech that they earn their living. And what one accomplishes by his efforts will reap rewards (v. 14). I guess the verse says to all of us that we had better do well in this regard—or else!

15 The way of a stupid fool is right in his own eyes,
but one who listens to counsel is wise.
16 A stupid fool's irritation is known immediately,
but the prudent man ignores an insult.
17 He who speaks truth reveals righteousness,
but a false witness deceit.
18 There is a kind of careless speaking that is like sword thrusts,
but the tongue of wise men heals.
19 Truthful lips are established forever,
but a lying tongue lasts only for the wink of an eye.

Verse 15 is vital for use in counseling. There come points when one must **listen to counsel** or persist in his own **foolish** way. Often, as a last hope, one may have to dismiss a counselee who is unwilling to do what God requires with a reading of this verse. Learn it and its location for such use. Indeed, it might even be helpful to memorize it.

The **stupid fool** gets **irritated** easily and lets everyone **know** it. A **prudent man**, on the other hand, does not consider every **insult** a challenge he must take up. Rather, he simply considers the source, prays for the person leveling the insult and refuses to become upset over it. Many counselees could profit from learning and regularly applying the verse to their situations. Restraint of inappropriate emotion is something that many psychiatrists think is unhealthy; they advocate ventilation. God teaches otherwise. Who will you follow?

A person is known as **righteous** or as a **deceiver** according to whether he **speaks truth** or bears **false witness**. His words, therefore, **reveal** the kind of person he is (v. 17). It is important, then, for a counselor to examine carefully how reliable a counselee's words may be. In checking these out, one can tell much about his basic character (note other verses in this chapter which say virtually the same thing).

Verse 18 pinpoints a problem various counselees have: **careless speech**. When one speaks before he thinks about the consequences that his words will have, what he says is likely to hurt others. To speak carelessly—and who hasn't at times—is like **thrusting** a **sword** at another. On the contrary, the **wise** counselor speaks words of **healing**. What a marvellous opportunity the counselor has to heal others by means of the wise use of his **tongue**.

It is true, as we have seen in the Proverbs, that when one gets a reputation for **lying** it will not be long (only **a wink of an eye**) before he is dismissed. People will stop believing him even when he tells the truth (v. 19).

20 There is deceit in the heart of those who plan evil,
but to the counselors of peace there is joy.
21 No harm can come to the righteous,
but the wicked will be full of trouble.
22 Lying lips are an abomination to Yahweh,
but those who act truthfully are His delight.
23 A prudent person covers knowledge,
but the hearts of stubborn fools shout stupidity.
24 The hand of hard workers will control,
but laziness leads to forced labor.
25 Worry in a person's heart makes it sink,
but a good word makes it glad.

Make it clear to counselees that if they seek to have an **established** reputation for truthtelling, so that people go on trusting their words, they must not allow error or lies to fall from their lips.

Verse 20 seems to indicate that the **deceitful** person is an unhappy person. There can be little true **joy** in **planning evil** (or, as this word may be translated: *trouble*). But there is much joy in giving **counsel** that brings **peace**. Jesus said, "Happy are the peacemakers." Troublemakers make trouble not only for others, but also for themselves.

Verse 21 seems to be the sequel to the previous verse. Again, the lives of **wicked** persons are said to be **full of trouble**. On the other hand, the **righteous** are set free from these inner **troubles**. Such troubles issue from malevolent attitudes.

Verse 22 is repetitive of previous verses.

The **stubborn fool** mentioned in verse 23 lets everyone know how stupid he is by **shouting** out his foolish ideas. The **prudent person**, however, doesn't let all and sundry know how knowledgable he is. Scratch the surface and you will soon learn of his knowledge. But he will not trumpet it abroad. Many need to learn to act **prudently** (cf. 17:28).

Diligence and **laziness** are once again contrasted in verse 24. But this time the contrast is between those who rise to places of leadership and those who fail to do so. **Hard work** is that which separates the two. Places of prominence and power are appropriate to those who have proven they can be responsible (cf. 22:29). A lazy person is not dependable.

The effects of **worry** upon the inner man are serious; literally, one can **worry** himself sick (v. 25). But your words of encouragement and hope bring joy. The picture is of one **sinking** down into the depths; perhaps this is referring to the kind of fatigue that often accompanies those

26 The righteous guides his friends,
but the wicked misleads them.
27 A lazy person doesn't start out after his prey,
but the wealth of a hard working man is valuable.
28 In the path of righteousness is life,
and in that pathway is no death.

---

who **worry**. Don't forget to bring in Philippians 4 and Matthew 6 when discussing worry.

Righteous people guide their friends into the paths of righteousness (v. 26). This they do both by precept and example (cf. Philippians 4:9). **Wicked persons mislead** them in the same two ways. The writer seems to be saying that one should follow only those who set a godly example and give good counsel. If you are counseling another, you must lead him wisely *in both ways*.

Verse 27 once more introduces us to the **lazy** man who is so lazy that he fails to go out and retrieve the game he has caught in his trap. But, contrariwise, to a diligent person everything he gets is **valuable**. He would no more squander even the **wealth** of a single catch than he would fail to appropriate a million dollars.

Finally, the chapter ends in a summary statement about the destination to which the righteous **path** leads: **life**. In it there is neither spiritual nor eternal **death**.

CHAPTER 13

1 A wise son profits from his father's discipline,
but a scoffer does not listen to reproof.
2 From the fruit of a man's mouth he eats well,
but the treacherous person eats violence.
3 He who guards his mouth keeps his life;
he who opens wide his lips ruins himself.
4 The lazy person craves and doesn't receive,
but a hard working person will be made fat.

There is little new in the introductory verse of chapter thirteen. But notice, as in other places, **discipline** and **reproof** occur together. There is no way to teach discipline to those who need it apart from correction. But some people—**stubborn fools** and **stupid fools** alike—will not listen to reproof. Here, the new element is the addition of the **scoffer** (*les*) to the list. All three sorts of fools are foolish in this regard. Counselors who discover that reproof (correction) is rejected will eventually classify those who reject it in one of the three categories.

According to verse 2, a man's words have much to do with his livelihood (cf. v. 14 in the previous chapter). Truthful, helpful words pay off—if not immediately, eventually. As preachers and counselors know, they earn their daily bread largely by the use of speech. But what is the **fruit** (result) of **treachery** and **violence**? The words of those who advocate deceit and traitorous action produce nothing but violence—both toward others and themselves (cf. James 3:6). Accordingly, the one who carefully **guards his mouth** preserves **his life** (v. 3). The one with a loose tongue, on the other hand, by careless speaking brings **ruin** to **himself**. Over and over the writer stresses the importance of speech in life. How often do you discuss the matter with your counselees? Often enough?

Verse 4 deals with laziness. **Laziness** on one's part does not exclude desire. Indeed, **lazy persons crave** things like the rest of us. But because of their lack of industry, they don't get what they want. The **hard working person** is the one who **will be made fat**. **Fat** had quite a different connotation in Hebrew society; it meant *prosperous*. That is, he will get all he wants—and more! In using this verse with counselees, you'd better explain how the word fat was used.

People abhor that which **stinks**. According to verse 5 the **wicked stink** and, therefore, are to be abhorred (**hated**) by the **righteous** for their

5 The righteous hates falsehood,
but the wicked stinks and acts shamefully.
6 Righteousness guards the way of the person of integrity,
but wickedness overthrows the sinner.
7 There is a person who acts rich but has nothing at all;
a person who acts poor but has much wealth.
8 A man ransoms himself by his riches,
but the poor person has no means of redemption.

---

falsehoods. Their **shameful** lies and behavior are loathsome to anyone with biblical standards—or ought to be (cf. Lot). Surely this approach to sin in another person does not allow for a non-judgmental "acceptance" of him or his behavior in counseling. But while biblical counselors call shameful acts what they are—stinking and hateful ones in God's sight—in spite of that fact, they are willing to help people who want to extricate themselves from such a lifestyle. They are too kind to unbelievers and Christians who indulge in shameful acts to accept them without judging them for what they are according to biblical standards—a stinking mess (cf. John 7:24). Jesus never approves of sinful people; He regularly told them to "go, sin no more." But He also died for sinners—precisely *because* of their shameful acts. And we must minister to them too.

Verse 6 is not merely a reiteration of previous verses. It personifies both **righteousness** and **wickedness** as those who affect their followers in opposite ways. One **guards** the **way** of the person of **integrity**, whereas the other **overthrows** the way of its followers. The result is that one follower is called a **person of integrity** whereas the other is called a **sinner**. The results of following each, therefore, are twofold: what the person becomes and what happens to him. Counselors ought to be aware of this twofold development in dealing with counselees. They must minister to them not only to help rectify the happenings but also to reorient the person.

Verse 7 offers an insight into human character. People are not always what they represent themselves to be. Don't be deceived. Many will poor mouth you, whereas others will boast of possessions they really don't have. Reasons why each does so may vary (fear that people will expect things from them; desire to impress others, etc.). In each case where you discover such deception, probe to see what is behind it.

The observation in verse 8 simply states a fact. Perhaps, one is supposed to infer from it that he should work diligently so that he is always in a position to meet such a need. Others read the proverb in the opposite

9 The righteous man's light shines brightly,
but the wicked's lamp will be put out.
10 Strife comes only by pride,
but those who receive counsel promote wisdom.
11 Wealth that comes from nothing will dwindle,
but he who gathers by the work of his hand will increase it.
12 Hope deferred makes the heart sick,
but desire fulfilled is a tree of life.
13 He who arrogantly condemns the Word will be held responsible,
but he who fears the command will be rewarded.

---

way: the lives of poor people are not held for **ransom** since others know that they have nothing to give. Both facts are true. But since the proverb itself makes no application, it is possible to reach either (or both) of the constructions.

There is a strong warning in verse 9. The **righteous man's light** will go on **shining** brightly throughout the night. The **wicked's lamp will be** extinguished early. The verse is a figurative restatement of the principle already articulated more didactically—righteousness prolongs life.

The next verse (v. 10) is a very important one for counselors: where there is **strife**, look for **pride**. People may deny that they are proud, but this verse indicates otherwise. Counselors, therefore, will seek to **promote wisdom**, since those who are wise generally will not allow themselves to become proud, and will do all they can to allay strife. There is both insight into the problem and direction for solving it: inculcate biblical wisdom in situations involving strife.

Those who receive **wealth** in some way other than by **working** for it **find that it dwindles** (v. 11). Large inheritances usually dwindle over the succeeding generations. Money that comes from gambling, theft and other nefarious enterprises also dwindles even more rapidly. But **hard work** (especially over succeeding generations) makes **wealth** grow.

You will encounter counselees who are, literally, **sick at heart** (despondent, crushed, etc.) because they have not attained to various expectations. **Desire fulfilled**, on the other hand, brings happiness, health and good feelings (it is a tree of life). This verse should alert the counselor to the importance of giving counselees hope (see my *Christian Counselor's Manual* for details).

The attitudes and words of those counselors who castigate biblical teaching, scoff at biblical counseling and prefer some man-made approach to human problems over a biblical one, indicate that they are in

14 The law of the wise is a fountain of life
to escape from death traps.
15 Good sense wins favor,
but the way of transgressors is hard.
16 Every cautious person acts out of knowledge,
but a stubborn fool exposes his folly.
17 An unreliable messenger falls into trouble,
but a faithful envoy brings healing.

---

danger (v. 13). Their **arrogance** in thinking that they know better than God will not be overlooked: they **will be held responsible**. Biblical counselors who **fear** Yahweh's commands can take heart over the fact that, in His time, God will **reward** them. Here is an important encouragement for biblical counselors.

The teachings of **wise** persons and the directions that they give others are like pure, thirst-quenching, life-giving water from a **fountain**. These teachings enable those who drink deeply of them to **escape** many deadly **traps** into which those without such help step (v. 14). Counselors ought to become such fountains.

Often, I use verse 15^b as a warning to those who reject God's truth, stringing it out over a final session by repeating it as many as eight or ten times. I may say, "Scripture teaches that 'the way of the transgressor is hard.' Now, when you leave here, having rejected God's way, you will soon discover that 'the. . . is hard.' And when you find that 'the. . . is hard,' I hope you say to yourself, 'You know, the Bible is right; "the. . . is hard."'" Of course, I intersperse other thoughts between each of these quotations. One who deliberately sets out to go his way rather than rely on Scripture, isn't using **good sense**. In the long run, he will **win favor** from neither God nor man.

Cautious persons are **careful** to be accurate about facts in order to regulate their **acts**. They want as much knowledge as possible before they move ahead. But, by plunging ahead without such knowledge, the **stubborn fool** (who seeks autonomy) quickly **exposes his folly**. He will obviously get into all sorts of trouble for his lack of caution (v. 16). Warn about hasty actions taken without adequate research about the facts involved in them.

In one way or another (because of laziness, lack of truthfulness, etc.) a **messenger** may become **unreliable** (v. 17). Regardless of the reason behind this unreliability, he is headed for **trouble.** That is for sure! One who is **faithful** brings an accurate message, on time, and thus brings a

18 Poverty and shame come to the one who ignores discipline,
but the one who heeds correction will be honored.
19 Desire gratified is sweet to a person,
but stubborn fools hate to turn away from trouble.
20 He who walks with wise persons will become wise,
but an associate of stubborn fools will become evil.
21 Trouble pursues sinners,
but the righteous will be rewarded with good.

---

word of **healing** for those who receive it. Can you think of three ways in which this verse may apply to a counselee?

There is no lasting **honor** to those who **ignore discipline**; that comes only to those who **heed correction** (v. 18). All the undisciplined person may expect is **poverty and shame**. These are the natural, inevitable consequences of the lack of discipline. Counselees who reject correction (without which discipline is not possible) must be warned of the results of their rejection.

Why are the two parts of verse 19 conjoined? The idea seems to be that everyone—fool or wise—likes to have his **desires gratified** (it is **sweet** to have it so), but those **fools who stubbornly** continue causing **trouble** and will not **turn away** from doing so, will never realize the satisfaction of their desires.

Proverbs emphasizes the importance of proper **associations**; one becomes like those with whom he regularly associates (cf. 14:7). Counselors often discover that one segment of the solution to a counselee's problems is a change of those with whom he spends time (cf. also I Corinthians 15:33). In Luke 6:40 Jesus taught something similar to what verse 20 teaches.

Verse 21 again makes use of a strong figure of speech: like a hunter (or predator bent on overtaking its prey), **trouble** is pictured as chasing **sinners** until it captures them. **Sinners** here means those who persist in sinning, unrepentant. It isn't an image far from actuality as counselees themselves sometimes express it: "I feel hunted," or "Trouble seems to stalk my path," etc. If they don't express it in so many words, you might even suggest it: "I guess what you're telling me is that it is as if trouble is dogging your tracks." Either way, it might provide the entrée into this verse as you both consider why this is so.

Those who care for more than themselves build up their estate for future generations (v. 22). Those who care only for themselves are actu-

22 A good person leaves an inheritance for his son's sons,
but the sinner's wealth is stored up for the righteous.
23 The fallow land of the poor yields much food,
but it is swept away when there is injustice.
24 He who holds back his rod hates his son,
but the one who loves him chastens him right away.
25 The righteous eats to his satisfaction,
but the wicked one's belly is empty.

---

ally **storing up** their **wealth** for a **righteous** person other than a member of their family, and for someone else's heirs.

Even a poor man's **fallow land** has the potential of producing **much food** (v. 23), but the potential is never realized because of his **injustice** (expressed in various acts that lead to **poverty** rather than to wealth). The Book of Proverbs mentions a number of these.

Swift punishment of a child is an act of love; to **hold back chastisement** is evidence of hatred **for or the** despising **of him**. Many counselees since Spock don't realize this.

Righteousness leads to prosperity (it is pictured as **eating to one's satisfaction**) while **wickedness** leads to poverty (it is pictured as doing the opposite).

There are many verses in this chapter that teach similar truths. As an exercise that I believe you will find profitable, take the chapter as a whole, and attempt to bring it into a consistent running commentary on the ways of righteousness and wickedness, showing causes, results and effects of each that may be of great benefit to you and your counselees in the future.

CHAPTER 14

1 A wise woman builds her house,
but a foolish one pulls it down with her own hands.
2 He who walks uprightly fears Yahweh,
but he whose ways are perverted despises Him.
3 In the mouth of a stupid fool is a rod of pride,
but the lips of the wise will preserve him.

How **foolish** many **women** prove to be! By their own acts they **pull down** everything they and others have spent years building up. Perhaps this is an even far more common occurrence today than in Solomon's time because of the greater freedom accorded to everyone, and to women in particular. But it is not new. Foolish actions (overspending, resentful deeds, lack of submissiveness, rebellious attitudes, unwillingness to discipline children, separation, divorce and adultery are among the most common) ruin their families. When you talk to them years later many of these women wonder why life is so hard. Some even blame God for what was plainly the work of their **own hands**. Verse 1 contrasts the wise woman whose interest is in building her family (**house**).

An **upright** lifestyle is impossible apart from **fear of Yahweh** (v. 2). And those who *are* upright will fear Him. How is that true? To be **upright** is, by biblical definition, to **walk** (conduct one's life) according to God's ways, which are found in the Bible. His will, in His Word, is the Standard by which one's ways are judged to be either **upright** or **perverted**. **Perverted** (literally, "crooked") **ways** are evidence of one's fundamental antipathy toward God (he **despises Him**; and, therefore, His **ways**). It is interesting that, as you probe for information when you discover one abhors God's ways, you see that his life history is a record of twisted, crooked turns. Righteousness leads to simplicity; sin to unnecessary complexity.

In verse 3 the question is "What does Solomon mean by **the rod of pride in the stupid fool's mouth** as over against the **lips of the wise that preserve him**?" Probably, the idea in view is the **rod** that others will use to beat the **fool** who speaks proudly, just as the words that the **wise** speak bring protection from others. Clearly, in one way or another, the contrast is between punishment and protection, the former arising from proud words and the latter from wise words. Training a counselee to use his **lips** wisely is one of the prime tasks of the counselor. While he has no **rod**

4 Where there are no cattle the stall is empty
but by the strength of an ox comes much increase.
5 A faithful witness will not lie,
but a false witness breathes them.
6 A scorner seeks wisdom and doesn't obtain it,
but knowledge comes swiftly to the discerning.

---

with which to instruct the fool, he may warn against the many rodlike punishments that will come to the one who cannot control his mouth (lost confidence, being let go from jobs, broken marriages and the like).

Of course it is easier to keep the **stall** clean (**empty**) when there is no animal present to foul it. But without the animal there is **no increase** (wealth). You can't have the one without the other. Added advantages increase responsibilities. If you want to have a good harvest (and the prosperity that it brings), you must assume the responsibilities that go with it. How many counselees fail because they want what the "ox" can provide without having to provide for the ox! A whole generation has grown up expecting all their parents have—and more—apart from the years of effort and struggle that it cost their parents to obtain it. When you encounter the problem, counselor (and you will; so look for it), verse 4 is the verse to use to counter it!

The **faithful witness**, in the courtroom or in the counseling room, can be depended on to give you a reliable account of the facts so far as he knows them (v. 5). To do so, for him, is as much a part of him as the ability to eat. On the other hand, telling **lies** is as natural to the **false witness** as **breathing**. When one becomes so accomplished a liar as that, it is difficult for a counselor to detect the fact that he is lying as he speaks. Probably, in most cases, it will take a couple of weeks and some failed homework assignments to do so. You will discover this from those assignments if they are built on previous information gleaned from him. If that information is incorrect, he will not be able to accomplish the assignments. If he cannot do so, when you investigate the reasons for the failure, at length, you will uncover the lies. A house built on a shaky foundation will begin to show cracks in the plaster, etc. At length, if something is not done to correct the problem, it will gradually fall apart—or simply collapse!

Verse 6 observes that the **scorner's** attitude inhibits him; his cynical, arrogant views militate against the acquisition of **wisdom**, though he may **seek** it. Because he assumes a stance above others, critical of all they say,

7 Leave the presence of a stubborn fool
when you hear no knowledge from his lips.
8 The wisdom of the cautious leads him to discern his way,
but the folly of stubborn fools leads them to deceive.

---

his pride prohibits him learning anything from them. What he wants he will never get because he always "knows better." How can he gain wisdom when he acts as if he were the fountain of it? On the other hand, a **discerning** person finds that **knowledge comes swiftly**. His love of truth and desire to learn make him humble in the presence of others from whom he may learn. Counselors who try (in vain) to teach **scorners** (know-it-alls who scoff at what you say) soon learn to bring counseling to a screeching halt. Until a scorner's attitude changes, it is hopeless to try to help. The **discerning person**, in contrast, eats up any and all help you can give him. He is a joy and a delight to counsel. Because he is anxious to attain **knowledge**, he catches on **swiftly**, puts knowledge to work immediately, and (as a result) does not need to remain in counseling for very long. The scorner, in most instances, turns out to be an unbeliever. Hope for him, if that is true, will come only from repentance and faith in Jesus Christ as Savior. If a counselee asks how long counseling will be, you can turn him to this verse, read it, and explain "Not very long either way!"

Verse 7 is one of the many verses in Proverbs in which the reader is told to avoid close associations with **stubborn fools**. Counselors meet those who are influenced by **fools** all the time. It is amazing what foolishness comes from their lips. When you hear it, try to discover if it is the product of the counselee or if he is merely mouthing what he has heard another say. If you can show him that the one influencing him lacks true spiritual **knowledge**, you may then show him from this verse that he must break off any deep association with him since, as the verse implies, he has begun to think and act like him. The trouble is, many show up in counseling precisely because they have failed to make such a break. Strong advice in this direction is in order. This verse should afford the help needed to convince them.

Caution is a significant element of **wisdom** (v. 8). In life, the wise person chooses the right direction because he uses **discernment** in doing so. That is, he has learned to *distinguish between* what is good and what is bad: what is true and what is false. In short, he has become adept in discerning God's will by contrasting it with all other ways. **Stubborn fools**, however, exhibit their folly not only by falling for error, but by allowing it

9 Stupid fools mock at guilt,
but among the righteous is favor.
10 The heart knows its own bitterness
and a stranger doesn't share its joy.

---

to lead them into **deceiving** others. It is sad to note that many **foolish** persons plunge headlong into bad decisions, get involved in sinful ways and pursue empty dreams simply because they lack **caution**. Caution, or prudence, is a quality to inculcate in counseling. Most counselees need it. It causes one to stop and think before moving ahead. In doing so, he must use the Bible to help him to investigate, to contrast and to compare various options. In driving them to the Bible, caution will often bring them to Romans 14:22 and 23 in which is found the "holding principle" (One must not move ahead until he is certain that it is right to do so). But you can't tell **stubborn fools** anything. They will persist in their ruinous ways. And, of equal import in some cases, what you say will be used to bolster their wrong views making them think that their choices are superior.

Verse 9 is well-known. And it is of great value to the Christian counselor. The **stupid fool** thinks he can make light of his sin: he **mocks at guilt** ("Oh, come on now, I was only having a little fun. You're too serious about such things. Get a life!"). To treat one's conscience in that way is to sear it. Thus, he decreases its sensibility to future wrongdoing. That is dangerous; it will lead to greater sin and more severe consequences. Warn counselees about this whenever you see the mocking tendency at work. If they do not repent and change they will reap the fruit of unholy levity. Sin is against a holy God; it is always disobedience to Him. That is nothing to make light of. The **righteous** person knows the seriousness of sin; he doesn't laugh about it. He grieves over it. He seeks forgiveness for it. He tries to avoid it in the future. At the same time, he knows what to laugh about—things that do not offend God. His way brings **favor** from God and other **righteous** persons. Mocking cannot incite anything less than disfavor from God.

How true of sorrowing counselees are the words in verse 10! Only the one who undergoes trial and suffering knows fully what it is like. It is useless—not to say harmful—for you to assure a counselee that you "understand," as some counselors advise you to do. You don't! You know only in part. Rather, tell counselees that though you might not, *God* understands. That's really what counts. Jesus endured all sorts of temptations and trials so that He, and He alone, as a man, *does* know and is able

11 The house of wicked people will be destroyed,
but the tent of upright people will be strong.
12 There is a way that seems right to a man,
but at its end are the ways of death.

---

to sympathize rightly. That is why the counselee (and counselor) can depend upon His Word in the Bible to have the correct answer. Other counselors have no one to whom they may turn for that kind of empathetic help! What you do know, as an individual (and therefore as a counselor) is God's comfort and assistance that you have experienced (see comments on II Corinthians 1). And, of course, you can never enter fully into another's joy either. Emotions are highly *personal*; they can be shared only to a limited extent. That is another reason for not focusing on emotions in counseling.

In verse 11, **house** is set over against **tent**. Usually, a house is considered a permanent, sturdy dwelling, and a tent the opposite. In this verse, however, the reverse is said to be true. The seeming strength of the **wicked** is only apparent; the seeming weakness of the **upright** is but an illusion. The facts are the reverse of what they appear to be. What makes the difference is the relationship of the persons involved to God. The blessing of the Lord on the one, and His curse on the other is the determining factor. This important insight is one that every counselor should find useful when dealing with either type of person. He may need not only to know the difference—a fact that will guide him in how to proceed in giving biblical advice—but also in pointing out that appearances do not always reveal the truth.

First occurring here in verse 12 (see also 16:25), this significant saying goes to the heart of the problem of many counselees: they *think* wrongly. Many **ways** that may **seem right**, in the end, turn out to be roads leading to **death**! That is true concerning both physical and spiritual death. The notion that it doesn't matter what a person believes or thinks, so long as he is sincere, is smashed to smithereens by this proverb. Thinking has consequences! Biblical thinking is what one needs (cf. Isaiah 55: 7-9). Truth matters. Indeed, it matters *eternally*! You can count on it: what **seems right** to a rebellious, sinful person *is not right*. It is important to help counselees bring their thinking into line with God's thinking so as to think His thoughts after Him.

Every counselor knows about the thin veneer of **laughter** that conceals an **aching heart** (v. 13). He sees the happy face that grieving per-

13 Even in laughter the heart may ache
and the end of joy may be grief.
14 The one who draws back from God in his heart
will be filled with his own ways.
15 The naive person believes every word,
but the prudent man considers his step.
16 The wise person fears and avoids evil,
but the stupid fool passes on and is reckless.

---

sons may wear in public, but discard in the counseling room. Ultimately, however, the grief that dwells within—if not assuaged—will break out, putting an end to the false, insupportable **joy** that he has exhibited. True grief may not be covered for long. That is a warning counselors may give those who, instead of finding their place of comfort in Christ, think they can face life with a stiff upper lip.

The message of proverb 14 in this chapter is that one who **draws back** from God's help into himself will soon find himself **filled with his own ways**. That is to say, he will discover that his own "solutions" to problems only add to them. Unlike God's ways, they **fill** him with more misery than before. Here is another strong warning for those who try to "go it alone" without God and His Word. Pretty soon, as we say, he will have "had it—up to here!"

The **naive** person (of v. 15) is the one who is open to all influences, good or bad. The first half of the couplet is, perhaps, the clearest description of the fault of such naiveté to be found in Proverbs. He fails to investigate the facts. He is too trusting of others; he **believes every word** they speak. He has no powers of discrimination. His senses are not trained to discern between good and evil (cf. Hebrews 5). Someone has said, "An open mind is like an open window: you have to put screens in to keep the bugs out." The screen of the mind is the Scriptures. Counselors should teach counselees to judge all things by the Word of God—even their own teaching. See my book *Teaching to Observe* for more information about this matter. A **prudent**, discerning person knows the world is full of error. Therefore, he considers carefully, prayerfully and scripturally what courses he will follow. The Christian who is true to his Lord is no sucker for ideas that *sound* good but prove otherwise (cf. v. 12). He is able to see through them by looking at them through the lens of the Bible.

Once again, in line with previous proverbs in this chapter, but with a slightly different twist, we are told that a **wise person** has a **fear** of displeasing God that helps him **avoid evil**. Here, the word **evil** may have both

17 He who has a quick temper acts foolishly,
but a man of discretion is patient.
18 The naive inherit foolishness,
but the prudent are surrounded with knowledge.
19 Evil people will bow down to the good
and the wicked at the gates of the just.

---

of its meanings: sin and trouble. After all, they both accompany one another. But others **stupidly** stumble into one problem after another because of their **reckless**, unthinking ways. The **fool** in question fails to stop and consider whether or not his actions will please God; he simply **passes on**—beyond the point of no return—and ends up in trouble with God and man (v. 16).

In verse 17 we meet another who fails to use **discretion**: one whose problem is haste. He lacks the **patience** he needs to avoid **foolish** behavior. Before checking facts, before summoning up needed self-control, before thinking about God's commandments, he blurts out whatever comes to mind. He has a **quick temper**. Counselors will find that almost every person with a quick temper will act foolishly. Such counselees must be taught the **patience** that is born of developing **discretion** and trust in God.

In verse 18 we meet the **naive** person again. He **inherits**, as his lot, only more **foolishness**. There is an abundance of it in the world left to those who are "open" (cf. v. 15). It is more than available to all those who will receive it. Counselors must teach, in contrast, that **prudent** people soon are **surrounded with knowledge**. That is, one inherits what he is open to. The naive is open to everything; prudent persons only to the knowledge of truth and righteousness. Teach both true openness and true narrowness: few counselees have learned either.

In doesn't always take place in this life, but now or later the promise of verse 19 will be fulfilled. Those whom God has made **good** in Christ will rise to ascendancy; **evil and wicked** persons will **bow down** to them and recognize the prominent place to which God will bring them for Christ's sake. As all will confess "Jesus is Lord" (Philippians 2), so too will they confess that the **just** (those justified by faith) were right. They will be vindicated. Even in this life, there is often a grudging acknowledgment (sometimes inward only) that **good** people are (at least) a cut above the average. There is something admirable about them that, even while they attempt to destroy or tempt them, many will concede.

20 The poor is looked down upon even by his neighbor,
but there are many who curry favor with the rich.
21 He who despises his neighbor sins,
but he who favors the poor is happy.
22 Don't those who devise evil go astray?
But mercy and truth are for those who plan good.
23 In all toil is profit,
but mere talk leads to poverty.

In verse 20 is an observation: even **neighbors look down on** the poor (sometimes with the attitude, "There goes the neighborhood!"), while all sorts of persons do whatever they can to **curry favor from the rich**. Want an example? Check out what happens to the person who wins the multi-million dollar lottery! On the other hand, watch what happens to someone who is suddenly reduced to penury. Expose both of these wrong attitudes in counselees.

In concert with the previous verse, the Lord condemns those who **despise** their **neighbors** (v. 21). It is **sin**. Counselors must not excuse such attitudes expressed by counselees as anything less than **sin**. But, instead, they must encourage concern for the **poor**. To help them is one way to find **happiness**. Some counselees have missed entirely this means of attaining peace and joy from God. And remember, as Jesus taught, one's neighbor is not only one who lives nearby; it is everyone you know who has a need you can meet.

To **devise evil**, in the original, means both to plan and to execute it. But those who do, end up only devising trouble for themselves. They are not able to attain their end; they **go astray** (v. 22). In contrast to their failure, **those who plan good** receive, in return, **mercy and truth** from God. There are counselees who, you will discover, are not only devising ways to harm others, but who want to use you as the means to achieve this end. The verse under consideration may be used as a powerful deterrent. It is God's warning to cease and desist.

Verse 23 contrasts **toil** with **talk**. Too many are all **talk** and no action. God blesses toil exerted in His honor. This is a great verse to counter those who incessantly tell you about all their plans, but never get around to doing anything. The double contrast of the words **toil** and **talk** along with **profit** and **poverty** makes the proverb easy to memorize in English. Teach it to those who need to learn its message.

What **crowns** a **wise** person is his wisdom—which is the **riches** he possesses. Like a crown, resplendent in beauty, wealth and poise, **wisdom**

24 The crown of the wise is their riches,
but the folly of stubborn fools is foolishness.
25 A truthful witness delivers people
but a deceitful one breathes lies.
26 By the fear of Yahweh one has strong confidence,
and his children will have a refuge.
27 In the fear of Yahweh is a fountain of life
to turn one from death traps.

---

is what beautifies him in the sight of others. But it is true, as well, that **riches** come to the **wise** to crown him (v. 24). Obviously, only **foolishness** accrues to those who work foolishness; in both cases, there is more of the same. Folly is what is conspicuous about the fool. What you do leads to what you get (the sowing/reaping dynamic); and, in such cases, *what you get indicates what you have done.*

Verse 25 has to do with testimony before a court of law. **Truthful witnesses deliver** those who are falsely accused (cf. v. 5 for the interpretation of breathing lies). When a **deceitful** person takes the stand one can expect **lies** to be spoken as easily as he breathes. Counselors should take this into consideration when they have discovered that one has lied before. A history of lies or truth is an important factor. Courts should do likewise.

The fear of Yahweh (v. 26) gives a person **confidence**. Trusting in the One Who has power to destroy (and, therefore, is to be feared) means also that He is able to defend those who do so and destroy all their enemies. The very idea of the **fear of Yahweh** leads, by a *seeming* paradox, to **confidence**. He will do what He plans; of that there can be no doubt. **Children** born and raised to this fear, from early days, have the same **refuge**. This verse shows how important one's beliefs are to the welfare of his children. In this world of violence and danger it is important for children to have a safe **refuge**. To counselees who protest that their lives are their own and that what they do is but their own business, you may point out that this is not true; apart from the Lord, their children are in jeopardy. How important, then, to bring children into a covenant relationship to Him. But parents, whose faith is weak, who are self-centered in their living, will fail to do so.

In verse 27 the benefits of **fearing Yahweh** are enlarged upon. That **fear** (trust in the powerful, holy God of Scripture) is like a **fountain** from which flows the waters that tend to **life** (cf. 13:14. In both proverbs the life-giving properties of the Christian faith are contrasted with the dangers of **death** that, like **traps**, lie on every hand). In other words, the way of

28 In the multitude of people is a king's splendor,
but in the lack of people is a prince's ruin.
29 One who is slow to anger is of great discernment,
but one who is short tempered exalts folly.
30 A healthy heart is the life of the flesh,
but envy leads to the rottenness of one's bones.
31 He who oppresses the poor insults his Maker,
but one who is kind to the needy honors Him.

Christ preserves a believer from many unnecessary dangers by promoting those things that prolong and preserve life. Many counselees think the opposite. Assure them that they are wrong and that the proverb is correct.

What makes a **king's** reign **splendid** (v. 28) is the fact that he governs many **people**. A **lack of people** ruins it (think of how we refer to a small, insignificant country as a "banana republic.") A wise ruler, therefore, will do whatever is legitimately possible to increase the size of his population and maintain the health and welfare of his people.

In verse 29 once again Solomon deals with **anger** (cf. v. 17). The **discerning** person is **slow to anger**; unnecessary trouble comes from short-tempered words and actions. Indeed, failure to control anger **exalts folly** (i.e., one who refuses to control anger by such behavior unwittingly makes folly his goal). Raising foolishness to a place of prominence in his life, he calls everyone's attention to the fact.

Verse 30 shows that the effect of the mind on the body was clearly known in biblical times; it is not a modern discovery. The **healthy** (sound) **heart** is peaceful, calm. Such attitudes as those commended in Scripture promote physical health and strength. A **heart** agitated by **envy**, on the other hand, leads to **rottenness of one's bones**. That means physical detriment to the entire body of the one who allows such things to disturb and trouble him. Counselees with ill-defined physical ailments may be suffering from a problem along these lines.

In verse 21 we saw that **happiness** comes to the one who **favors the poor**, while one who **despises** his impoverished neighbor **sins**. Why is this sin? In verse 31 we are told that **oppressing the poor** is an **insult** to God, his **Maker**. The one who is kind to the poor, **honors God**. Man—poor or rich—is made in God's image. As when one murders another, in effect, it is as if he murders God; so too, when one **oppresses** the **poor** it is as if he were oppressing God. Make this clear to wealthy counselees who care not a lick for the effect of their actions on the poor.

Verse 32 may have to do with what happens to the **wicked** and the **just** at death; some think so. But it may also have to do with membership

32 The wicked person is thrust out because of his evildoing,
but the righteous person has refuge in his integrity.
33 Wisdom rests in the heart of the discerning,
but in the stubborn fool's it is not made known.
34 Righteousness exalts a nation,
but sin is a disgrace to any people.
35 The king shows his favor to a servant who acts wisely,
but his wrath is upon the one who acts shamefully.

---

in the covenant community. Indeed, while including one or both of these applications, the verse may be general enough to speak of various situations where danger overtakes one. Those who provide **refuge** in times of trouble and danger will include only the **righteous**. That may be the general import of the proverb. The warning then would be, if one wants help in time of trouble, he had better be the kind of person to whom others are most likely to extend help. The wicked are not admitted into the place of refuge, but, when attempting to enter, are **thrust out**. Of course, the flood is the prime example, And that will be true some day when Christ comes again.

What makes the difference, as I have observed elsewhere, is what **is in the heart** (v. 33). If wisdom lives there, one becomes a **discerning** person; if in his **stubborn foolishness** he refuses to learn and live according to God's wisdom, one's heart (and, as a result, his life) will lack discernment. When he needs it, he will have nothing within to fall back upon. The error of Carl Rogers—that each person comes prepackaged with his own solutions to problems—will become painfully apparent to all involved. **Wisdom** comes from God: not from within. It must take up residence in a person's heart; it is not innate.

Verse 34 is well-known. History has demonstrated many times that its teaching is true. The thrust of the passage transcends Judaism; what it says is pertinent to any and all **nations**, but it is most fully exemplified in the history of Israel. When counselees complain about various governmental inequities, this is the verse to turn to. Then, having read it, you may wish to observe: "You may become a part of the solution to our country's failings by becoming a part of the **righteous** group who **exalt a nation**."

Finally, in verse 35, an obvious truth is stated. Yet, it needs repeating. The treatment that you receive from a superior at work usually reflects how you have served him. To **act** in an upright manner is to act **wisely**. But that is only a part of the picture. Check out the other matters Proverbs mentions that are also elements of wise action.

CHAPTER 15

1 A soft answer turns away wrath,
but a foolish word stirs up anger.
2 The tongue of the wise makes knowledge seem good,
but the mouth of stubborn fools pours out foolishness.
3 The eyes of Yahweh are in every place
watching the evil and the good.

I always think of Ping-Pong when I read verse 1. If someone slams a Ping-Pong ball at you, you may respond in one of two ways: slam it back or give it a gentle return by simply holding the paddle in its way and letting the ball hit it, returning by its own force. The first response will drive your opponent back, away from you. The second will move him in closer. The same is true of the way in which one responds to **wrath**. A **soft answer turns away wrath** (there is little fun in punching pillows; unlike a punching bag, they give!). A **foolish** verbal response **stirs up anger**. Thus it drives others farther away from you. This is a wonderful verse to use in a large number of counseling situations.

There is much in this chapter about the use of the **tongue**. Counselors, who must deal with problems of speech, will want to remember that fact. Verse 2 puts an interesting spin on how **knowledge** is presented. It says more than that the **wise person** speaks **knowledge** (that much is assumed). Rather, it adds that when he does so, he speaks in such a way as to exalt that knowledge—i.e., make it **seem good** to others who are thereby attracted to it. He draws others away from foolishness and toward wisdom by *how* he speaks. That is an important insight for counselors to inculcate in counselees. It is not only what one says that God considers important; He is concerned about how he says it. There is a proselytizing element that should not be missing from wise speech. On the other hand, what stubborn fools pour out **of their mouths is not attractive because** they pour out gallons of folly.

God's omniscience (v. 3) means that no behavior, word or attitude escapes Him (cf. v. 11). **Yahweh's eyes** are pictured scanning the world, like a faithful watchman who continually surveys the horizon. He misses nothing—**good or evil**. A counselee may try to hide his sin, and possibly will escape your detection, but he cannot hide from God. Tell him so!

The words of those who speak **soothingly** bring **life**, healing and good to others (v. 4). That is the basic mode for good counseling. But

4 A soothing tongue is a tree of life,
but poverty in it breaks one's spirit.
5 A stupid fool despises his father's discipline,
but the one who heeds his correction is cautious.
6 In the house of the righteous is much treasure,
but the income of the wicked is trouble.
7 The lips of the wise disperse knowledge,
but the heart of stubborn fools scatters valueless things.

---

poverty in it (i.e., the lack of these things) is like hammer blows that crush another's **spirit**. Words can powerfully affect others. Counselor, you are a dealer in words. More than likely, at some point, your counselees will also have to use the proper words to handle the problems they face. Take heed to the importance of using the right words.

To **despise** a **father's** training is to become a **fool** who acts **stupidly** (v. 5). But the child who **heeds his correction** becomes a **cautious** person. Training accepted early in life develops prudent character in a believer. N.B., throughout Proverbs, the responsibility of the child in **heeding discipline** is stressed as strongly as that of the parent in giving it. Indeed, there is probably more about the former than about the latter. When a child goes astray, therefore, it is not always (or even usually?) the parents' fault. That is important in counseling despondent parents who have genuinely attempted to train their children well, but have found that they went astray anyway. Often, of course, in time they will return.

In verse 6 Solomon observes that a **righteous** person has treasures (money and things) that bring joy and satisfaction, but that the opposite is true of the **income of the wicked**. Along with what he acquires, the wicked person also acquires **trouble**. What is a blessing to the one is a curse to the other. Wealth—what many counselees think will solve problems—actually does not. Indeed, it may create new ones. It is not the wealth or the lack of it, however, that makes the difference; it is the person and his attitude toward it.

Speech, again, is the subject of verse 7. **Wise** persons teach others; they **dispense knowledge**. Counselor, if you have acquired wisdom from God, it is your duty (and privilege) to **dispense** it to others. That, of course, runs counter to all ideas of reflective "counseling" (which is not *counseling* at all). **What stubborn fools scatter** far and wide is **valueless things**. The sad truth is that fewer dispense knowledge than others dispense valueless talk. That situation needs to be changed, and you can be one to help change it!

8 Yahweh hates the sacrifice of the wicked,
but the prayer of the upright is his delight.
9 Yahweh hates the way of the wicked,
but He loves the one pursuing righteousness.
10 There is severe discipline for the one who forsakes the path;
he who hates reproof will die.
11 Sheol and Abaddon are known to Yahweh;
how much more the hearts of the sons of man.

Yahweh is not concerned with **sacrifice**; what He loves is **prayer** and **sacrifice** by those who are **upright** (v. 8). The one without the other is worthless. Both, combined, are a **delight**. Again, as in the previous proverb, it is not the thing itself but the person doing it that makes the difference. Make it clear to counselees that true religion consists not of ceremonies or religious acts alone, but these (when done according to the Scriptures) performed by persons whose lives accord with them. Steer counselees away from ritualism.

That **Yahweh hates** is hard for many to accept; yet verse 9 (among many others) teaches just that. God's hatred of the **way of the wicked** (i.e., his lifestyle) is likewise affirmed. Conversely, the proverb says that **Yahweh loves**. Who is the one that He loves? The person who **pursues righteousness**. That hatred and love will be manifested until the end when, despite their religiosity, the former will be turned into hell and the latter will be received into glory.

While God's **discipline** toward those who turn their backs on the faith they once professed is **severe** (in the New Testament it constitutes delivering him to Satan for the destruction of the flesh), the one who goes so far as to **hate** all attempts to reclaim him (by **reproof**) **demonstrates** that his supposed faith never was genuine (v. 10). He will **die** eternally. A strong call is issued here to the one who **forsakes the path** to return to it. Verse 10, then, is quite apropos to cases involving church discipline.

Verse 11 speaks of God's knowledge of all that goes on in the unseen world (*sheol*) and the place of punishment within it (*Abaddon*) as evidence of His knowledge of **men's hearts** (cf. v. 3). If **Yahweh** knows about those things that happen in the other world—about which we know precious little, and that only by revelation—surely He knows all about human beings and their affairs. The **how much more** construction is an argument from the greater to the lesser (a good way to argue in counseling, incidentally). If He knows the greater, He surely knows the lesser as well.

12 A scorner doesn't love the one who corrects him;
He will not go to wise men for counsel.
13 A joyful heart makes one's face pleasant,
but an aching heart breaks his spirit.
14 The heart of a discerning person seeks knowledge,
but the mouth of stubborn fools feeds on folly.
15 All the days of the afflicted are miserable,
but goodness of heart is a continual feast.

As far as the counselor is concerned, verse 12[b] is a benefit. Not many scorners will come for counseling; probably none—on their own. Sometimes they may come, when dragged by someone wise. The reason a **scorner will not** is clearly stated: he wants no **counsel** from those who are **wiser** than he. After all, he may have to admit he is wrong; others may correct him! Because of his pride, he scorns others who know more than he; he will not acknowledge the fact (cf. 14:6). Once you recognize that you have a scorner for a counselee, resolve to dismiss him unless he is willing to humble himself.

Again, verse 13, like 14:30, points out the effects of attitudes on one's physical being. **Joy** in the **heart** shows in the face; **heartache** likewise has powerful outer and inner effects on one by **breaking his spirit** (cheerfulness and hope are replaced by gloom and despair). But the truth of God ministered in the power of the Spirit can restore the former while sweeping away the latter.

Because they eat up **folly**, **stubborn fools** will not **seek knowledge**. **Discerning persons** cannot get enough of it. They are already discerning, yet they **seek** even more **knowledge** to increase their **discernment**. What one enjoys, he will seek more of. That is the point. There is little hope in interesting fools in counseling; until they gain some discernment they will go on **feeding on folly** (v. 14). Whenever you find someone who shows no interest whatsoever in attaining biblical knowledge, you might turn to this verse and, having read it, then ask "Is this your problem?" Sometimes the thoughtful question is all that is needed to shake one out of his lethargy and sin.

Verse 15 is difficult for some to believe and for most to achieve. It means that in **affliction**, though every day there is **misery** from it, nevertheless, those whose **hearts** are filled with **goodness** (toward God and others) will enjoy happy days in spite of the affliction. Indeed, their days will be like an ongoing **feast**. Feasts were happy events. However, they were limited in duration. Solomon here speaks of a feast that lasts as long

16 Better is little accompanied by fear of Yahweh,
than much treasure accompanied by turmoil.
17 Better is a meal of vegetables with love
than a fattened ox where hatred is.
18 A hot headed man stirs up strife,
but one who is slow to anger calms contention.
19 The way of a lazy person is like a road blocked by thorns,
but the path of a righteous person is built up.

---

as the **affliction** (note the words **all the days** and **continual**). It is not mere momentary solace about which he speaks. What he says is that **throughout** the period of **affliction** the **good** person (one who has a good heart) can maintain a joyful, happy attitude. This is the epitome of what a counselor may tell afflicted persons. The verse holds true for all sorts of affliction—physical pain, sorrow, disappointment, etc. Think about this and learn how to distinguish between mere outer happiness and the continual feast of deep-seated joy.

Verse 15 expresses a sentiment that in various forms reoccurs throughout the Proverbs. The poor Christian is better off than the wealthy unbeliever whose life is in **turmoil**. It is intended as an antidote to envy and should be used for countering it. Verse 17 repeats the sentiment in another form. A vegetarian diet **with love** is to be preferred over one that includes steak or roast beef where **hatred** prevails. This, rather than recommending vegetarianism, does just the opposite. If, under conditions where all other things are equal, meat-eating is not to be preferred over vegetarians, then the point of the proverb is lost.

On verse 18, see verse 1. The point is the same: **hotheaded** persons cause problems (**strife**) between people. Those **slow to anger**, by contrast, **calm contention**. A good verse for many counselees to remember! It is probably still principally referring to what one's words lead to. Certainly that is a key area in which to practice the calming note.

In all he attempts, the **lazy person**, who has failed to prepare his way by cutting the thorn bushes down before they grew thick, finds that his former laziness now prevents him from making progress at a later date when he is anxious to do so. He has failed to practice the piano regularly—out of laziness. Now, on an occasion when he wants to play, he is all thumbs. He has not studied the Scriptures faithfully; his laziness has gotten in the way. Now that he needs to know God's will in an important decision, he doesn't know where to turn (v. 19). The **path of the righteous** has been **built** (lit. "thrown") up like a well-maintained road. While

20 A wise son makes his father glad,
but a foolish man despises his mother.
21 Foolishness is a joy to one who lacks sense,
but a discerning man walks straight.
22 Purposes are frustrated without counsel,
but by great counselors they succeed.

---

the results of the lazy man's laziness return to plague him in the future, the results of a righteous man's industry only serve to help him.

Verse 20 closely corresponds to 10:1 and 29:3. The foolish son of 10:1, here, we shall see, has continued his contempt for his **mother** into manhood. That is a sad commentary on many today who, continuing in their **foolish** ways, in order to justify their base behavior, continue to despise their mothers because of their contrary counsel. Indeed, if they fall prey to certain counseling and psychotherapeutic systems, they will justify present sinful behavior by referring to an overly strict parent (usually the **mother**) as its cause. This must not be accepted in biblical counseling. And this verse will go a long way toward refuting the error for those who are willing to take God's Word as true. No matter what she was like, there is no reason for a son to **despise** his **mother**.

Some **lack sense** (lit., "lack heart;" a Hebrew idiom for want of sense), a fact that discloses itself in the pleasure such persons find in **foolishness**. As a consequence, a person who lacks sense will take many wrong turns in life. His steps continually will take him astray. But the man with **discernment** will never be lost. He will **walk straight** toward good goals (v. 21).

The importance of counseling is made clear in verse 22. Without it the **purposes** (goals; see v. 21) of many are **frustrated**. But by **great counselors** (possibly a multitude of counselors) plans **succeed**. The importance of discernment mentioned in the previous verse, combined with the willingness to seek counsel from those who have it, is the factor that saves the godly, humble person many a false start on his way toward achieving goals. And he will turn to godly counsel along the way when he becomes perplexed. Because he possesses biblical discernment, he will know what counsel is correct and what is not; he will be able to choose counselors accordingly and follow counsel that is consonant with biblical principles. He knows how to distinguish that which is biblical from that which is not.

23 A man brings joy by the answer of his mouth
and how good is a word in season!
24 The path of life leads upward for the prudent
that he may turn from Sheol below.
25 Yahweh pulls down the house of the proud,
but He establishes the widow's border.
26 Yahweh hates the thoughts of the wicked,
but the words of the pure are pleasant to Him.

In verse 23, Solomon speaks of the satisfaction (**joy**) that comes to the one who is able to respond to (**answer**) well the questions others ask. Every seasoned biblical counselor should appreciate the verse. Sometimes, however, responses (though true) are not clear enough, bold enough or apropos. At other times answers are inadequate because they do not properly interpret the Scriptures, because they fail to locate, use and apply the most appropriate passages or because they garble up the application, and/or fail to stress implementation. When all of these matters are suitably attended to, the satisfaction comes. The second half of the couplet stresses timing and appropriateness. The **word in season** is the **right word** at the **right time** cogently applied. Here is ample incentive for every counselor to continue growing spiritually in his knowledge of God's Word and in his ability to minister that Word well.

The **path of life** (mentioned in v. 24) is **upward**; it does not lead downward toward the grave and the unseen world of death (**sheol**). Many other proverbs say the same thing in different words. Biblical living is healthier, safer and happier. All of these factors tend toward prolongation of **life**. That is why the righteous person's **path** is called the **path of life**. Why not use such expressions as **the path of life** in counseling? The expression is fresh, not frequently employed, and therefore should be striking and memorable (e.g., "I hope to show you how to walk the path of life, Mary").

God is on the side of the helpless (the widow, orphan, resident alien)—persons without power, protection or many rights (v. 25). Those **proud** persons who think that by their prowess they can maintain their property are mistaken; God Himself will **pull it down**. The land of the weak **widow**, in contrast, will be **established** by Yahweh so that grasping, greedy persons cannot cheat her out of what rightly belongs to her. The **border** (boundary line) of her property will continue inviolate.

Yahweh is concerned not solely with the behavior of **wicked** persons; He is also aware of their **thoughts**—which He **hates** (v. 26). With

27 The one who gets unjust gain troubles his house,
but he who hates bribes will live.
28 The heart of the righteous considers how to answer,
but the mouth of the wicked pours forth evil things.

Jesus, every biblical counselor recognizes that sin begins in the **thoughts**. That is why Satan attacks God's Word (which purifies one's thoughts and directs him in ways pleasing to God) and tempts one to sin by appealing to the ways of the world and of the flesh which are found in the "counsel of the ungodly" (Psalm 1:1). His appeal first receives assent in the mind. But **thoughts** lead to **words**. The good thoughts of those made pure by Christ's blood and now informed by the **pure** Word of God, are **pleasant to Him**. Counselors *also* appeal to the mind. If you can capture a counselee's thinking for Christ, it is likely that you can go on to help him control his entire life biblically.

There is no doubt about it: one who obtains wealth in shady ways **troubles his house** (family). Verse 27 raises the issue; let's discuss it a bit. The fear of discovery, for one thing, drives him. As a result, he makes many unwise moves. This fear may soon permeate everything that he does and says (cf. 28:1). In his mind, he may become a pursued person. Such persons are hard to live with! Many other problems arise from the acquisition of **unjust gain**. The person who **hates bribes** (one form of unjust gain) **will live**. That is, he will live a life worth living! The misery and fear that accompany a shady, corrupt lifestyle do not dog his tracks. The point, of course, is the lasting pleasure and satisfaction that one supposed would result from the **gain unjustly** acquired; it actually turns out to be anything but—one's entire family is upset by it.

In conjunction with verse 23, this verse (28) offers direction to every counselee—a person for whom speech is paramount. While the verses have broader applications than to counselors alone, they do say much to them. **Righteous** people (presumably biblical counselors fall into this lot!) do not **answer** counselees off the tip of their tongues. They first **consider how to answer**. That doesn't mean that if they have thought through matters before they cannot respond immediately. What the writer means is well-thought-through replies, responses from conclusions that have been reached by study and meditation on God's Word. Wicked persons, in contrast, **pour forth** (that is, without due consideration) **evil things** (they can hardly be anything else since they are the product of the thought life of **wicked persons**).

29 Yahweh is far from the wicked,
but He hears the prayer of righteous people.
30 Shining eyes rejoice the heart,
and a good report fattens the bones.
31 The ear that hears a life-giving rebuke
will dwell in the midst of the wise.
32 He who refuses discipline despises himself,
but he who hears reproof gets sense.

"Pray about it." That is the standard, wrong advice given by some counselors. "What, are you against prayer?" No, you misunderstand. **Yahweh** will not listen to the prayer of the wicked. All He will **hear** is a prayer of repentance. Indeed, in many cases, even Christians will not be heard by their heavenly Father when they are disobedient (cf. I Peter 3:7). God **hears** those who are on right terms with Him. That is the message of verse 29. Remember, God is not a machine; He is a Person. You have a relationship to a Person that must be maintained on the proper terms.

Happy feelings lead to **shining eyes** which communicate happiness to others and have a salutary effect on the body (**fatten the bones**). While a counselor should take all sin seriously, the joy of the message of forgiveness and cleansing should so permeate his own life and the atmosphere of the counseling room, his very eyes should speak hope and happiness to counselees (v. 30).

Verse 31 is for counselees. From the time when as a child he obeys the command "Stop!" and is spared death by an approaching automobile, to the day when he departs this life, the listening **ear** of the wise man saves him. He has learned to profit from a **rebuke**. Inform counselees that you have no pleasure in **rebuking** them, but only in saving them from sin and misery, injury and death. Those who listen will find themselves **in the midst of wise persons**, dwelling among persons of good **sense** and prudence. One doesn't always choose his friends and associates; often they choose him. Those who were wise enough to respond in **life-giving** ways will congregate together.

But, unwittingly, whoever **refuses** the rebukes of **discipline, despises himself** (v. 32). That is to say, he does harm to himself by depriving himself of wise friends (see v. 31) and all the benefits and blessings that flow from righteousness. Those who hear reproof continue to grow in knowledge and prudence; they more and more **get sense**.

Finally, verse 33, which links up with the two previous verses, makes it clear that salvation (the **fear of Yahweh**) is itself a heeding of

33 The fear of Yahweh is wise discipline,
and before honor is humility.

---

reproof that leads to **wise** instruction. And before one attains to a place of **honor** before God or man, he must **humble** himself enough to submit to the **discipline** that is a prerequisite to it.

CHAPTER 16

1 To man belongs the plans of his heart,
but the response to his tongue comes from Yahweh.
2 All the ways of a man are pure in his own eyes,
but Yahweh weighs his spirit.

What Solomon says in verse 1 should be considered a genuine blessing when a counselee rightly understands it. It does not forbid **planning**. Indeed, God is a God of order who expects His followers to order their lives as well. That means that Christians should **plan** in their **hearts**. That **planning** for the future, of course, should be in accordance with the general principles of the Scriptures and the specific commands that apply directly to one's circumstances. Thus, all planning ought to be either biblically-directed or biblically-derived. Yet, within the framework of biblical principles, often there is latitude in the specific application of principles so that a number of options may all be equally acceptable to God. For instance, a command may be clear enough, but if there is no specific way detailed for fulfilling the command, one may do so in a number of ways. That also means that we cannot always plan in detail and expect to follow those details to the letter. In terms of details, God may have different plans. We say, "tomorrow I will go to such and such a place...etc" (cf. James 4:13ff.). But we don't even know if we will live until then—let alone accomplish all that we planned (cf. 27:1). What should we do then? Plan, but say, "If the Lord wills...." The idea is to plan well, but plan conditionally. It is right here where many counselees fail. They want no changes in their plans. But you see, God must be taken into your planning. Planning that leaves Him out is not biblical planning. Always tell your counselees to submit their plans in prayer to God for His blue-penciling. Then, rejoice in the changes that He may make. His **response** to the words of your **tongue** will always be better than your original plan. Counselees need teaching about planning.

According to verse 2 our self-judgment is untrustworthy. That is because we are always too ready to make excuses for our faulty, sinful ways. Moreover, our outer behavior often is in accord with Scriptural commands, but our motives and inner attitudes may be wrong. **Yahweh weighs the spirit**. Our scales are off the mark; sometimes we weigh the thumb along with the item and distort the **weight** of what we are up to. God's scales are true; they always give an accurate and precise reading.

3 Roll your works on Yahweh
and your thoughts will succeed.
4 Yahweh has made everything for His own purpose;
even the wicked for the day of trouble.
5 Yahweh hates every person who is proud in heart;
though hand join in hand, he will not be acquitted.

Tell counselees that just because they **think** all is well, it may take some probing to discover whether or not the conclusion is correct. But never create problems where none exist (cf. 12:15; 14:12; 21:2; 24:12).

Verse 3 says what James made clear and what I wrote about in verse 2: one's doings (**works**) should be **rolled on Yahweh**. Ask Him to finalize your plans and all your undertakings according to His sovereign will (cf. Psalm 37:5). In no other way can your plans **succeed**.

God **made** everything for some **purpose** that He had in view. God sovereignly works all that happens for His benevolent and holy ends (v. 4). It is comforting to know that fact. Stress it in opportune times when counseling. But sometimes people wonder about the presence of sin in a good God's world. The reason is expressed plainly in Romans 9:22 and 23. For an in-depth discussion of those two verses, and the so-called problem of evil in general, see my book *The Grand Demonstration*. The answer to the question is that even **wickedness,** evil persons, and **trouble** that awaits one on the **day** in which God chooses to inflict it, has a purpose. He is saying that nothing—even sin and its consequences—is outside of God's eternal **purpose**, but that all accords perfectly with His plan and redounds to His glory. And, in the end, it will be seen that this purpose is a good and righteous one.

Have you noticed how often in Proverbs the Lord is said to **hate**? Here again in verse 5 we read, **Yahweh hates every person who is proud in heart**. This time, it is clearly stated that He hates the persons themselves. Too often we are led to believe that God hates the sin but loves the sinner. That is not true. God hates sinners. He does not divorce their sin from their persons. After all, sin is not an entity; it is a relational issue between *persons*. To sin is to disobey God, to arrogantly assert one's own will rather than follow His. It is rebellion against God's holy government of the world. The idea of **hands joined** (cf. 11:21) is an expression that means though one calls others to **join** him in his sinful, proud ways, he will not prevail. He may protest, as some counselees do, "But everyone else is doing it," but that will not avail with God. He must stand before

6 Iniquity is covered by mercy and truth,
and by the fear of Yahweh people turn from evil.
7 When a man's ways please Yahweh
He makes even his enemies to be at peace with him.
8 Better is a little with righteousness
than much income without justice.
9 A man's heart plans his way,
but Yahweh rightly directs his step.

God to answer Him for what *he* does: not for what *others* might believe or do. And he **will not be acquitted**. Here is the answer you will need to reply to all such protests.

The only way one's **iniquity** may be **covered** (lit., atoned for) is by God's **mercy** (or grace) **and truth**: the truth about sin, Christ's death and the way of salvation through faith. The **fear of Yahweh** (i.e., saving faith in God through Christ) is the way that **people turn from evil**. If counselees think that there is some other way to do so that doesn't require the grace of Jesus Christ (through psychology, etc.) show them otherwise from this verse (v. 6).

Verse 7 contains a wonderful promise: God will make one's **enemies to be at peace with him** when **his ways please Him**. Of course, for His purposes, sometimes God brings suffering to the righteous (cf. Hebrews 11). The verse doesn't say that this *always* happens; only that if it is going to happen, this is the way that it comes about.

The sentiment in verse 8 in different form has already been expressed in previous proverbs (cf. 15:16; also Psalm 37:16). **Little** wealth with **righteousness** (and all the peace and joy that it produces) is **better** than **much income without justice** (i.e., unjustly obtained). James amplifies this point in James 5:1 through 5. Many counselees are caught in the error that wealth makes happiness. If anything, it does the opposite—and *always* does when dishonestly obtained. It is hard enough to handle wealth when one seeks to do God's will.

Verse 9 accords with verse 1. The addition that occurs here is the point that when God changes one's plans He does so in order to make them **right**. At best, there is always *something* wrong with the plans that sinful human beings make. That means that counselees should await God's alterations with joyful anticipation. And they should accept them in the same manner—even when they don't fully understand why the change was made. Help them to see that planning one's life is a joint venture between the Christian and God.

10 A divination may be on the lips of a king,
but in judgment his mouth is not traitorous.
11 A scale and balances are Yahweh's,
and the stones of the bag are His work.
12 It is an abomination for kings to do wickedness;
his throne is established by righteousness.
13 Righteous lips are the king's delight,
and he loves the one who speaks uprightly.

Government is from God and what the ruler says is not wholly his own. A **divination is on his lips**. The word **divination** means a communication coming from God. That is to say, God may direct his words when he judges. Though he may lie, make wrong, iniquitous decisions and decrees (cf. v. 12), one need not fear that what he says will overturn the country (**his mouth is not traitorous**); God will see to that (v. 10). Countries outlast poor leaders.

God cares about the business practices of His people (v. 11). He will not overlook false **scales and balances** or the **stones** (weights) that one uses on them. These instruments of business **are His work** (i.e., are of concern to Him. Cf. vv. 11:1; 20:10 and Leviticus 19:36.) Sometimes the guilt of cheating dogs the steps of counselees. It might be well to inquire frequently about their business practices. God is concerned about them; you ought to be too.

Solomon was a **king** and it is good to realize that this is the philosophy under which he attempted to reign (v. 12). Abhorrent to God is **wickedness** in a ruler; the Old Testament record is a sturdy witness to the fact (see the historical books for examples of God's judgment upon them). It is true that God hates **wickedness** in any man, but since the **king** bears responsibility not only for his own welfare, but for the welfare of his people, it is especially heinous in him. But if he persists in evil, his **wickedness** will be his downfall since a **king's throne is established by righteousness**. That is to say it is secured and made to last. For examples of unrighteous rulers whose thrones were taken from them, see the succession of Caesars at Rome. Leaders of all sorts (who bear responsibility for those under them) would do well to heed these words. You will from time to time meet such people in counseling.

In verse 13, Solomon continues to reflect on the king. Speaking of the good **king**, he says that such a man surrounds himself with truthful advisers. If a king is deceived by those on whom he depends for data necessary to decision-making, his reign will suffer greatly for it. He **delights,**

14 A king's fury is a messenger of death,
but a wise man will placate it.
15 When a king's face shines there is life;
his favor is like a spring rain cloud.
16 How much better to get wisdom than gold,
and to get discernment is to be chosen above silver.

---

therefore, in faithful, true, dependable persons and **loves** those he finds to be so. Again, leaders who trust in those whose word cannot be relied upon go astray. Counselors must help those they counsel to understand that no matter how well-meaning they may be, if they depend on the word of others that is shaky, they will make a great mistake. Yet some counselees, even when they are told about the importance of accurate data (cf. Ephesians 4:25), find it hard to dismiss such persons. As a result, they continue to err and sin because of the poor advice that they follow.

Going on with the discussion of kings and rulers (vv. 14, 15), Solomon speaks of how others relate to them and the effects of inciting a ruler's pleasure and his wrath. To raise his **fury** is to court **death**. When you give him occasion to be angry, you can think of his wrath as a messenger (one who announces it) saying, "You are as good as dead." That is why one who is **wise** will be careful never to incite anger in him and will do all he can to **placate** it when he sees anger brewing that could turn into **fury** (cf. 19:12; 20:2). Some consider pacifying others' weakness; God says otherwise. To excite wrath in another is stupidity, no matter who he is—a ruler, a boss or a leader of some other kind. And all stupidity, according to the consistent message of Proverbs, is sin.

In verse 15, the opposite idea is set forth: the **shining face** of the king means that he is happy, pleased and will grant **life** to a subject. The **favor of a king**, moreover, is like the welcome of the spring rain clouds that come in March or April in Palestine. This expression is somewhat foreign to us; we think of a cloud as symbolizing displeasure or wrath. In the Holy Land, where rain was scarce and where farmers depended on these latter rains for a good harvest, clouds were a sign of God's blessing. They were glad to see clouds because that meant rain.

Verse 16 once more compares the worth of **wisdom and discernment**: they are of more value than gold and silver (cf. 8:11, 19; see also I Kings 3:11-13). How many of your counselees, do you think, place that much value on the attainment of these virtues? Don't you find that, given the chance, many would quickly opt for wealth rather than wisdom, for

17 The highway of upright people turns away from evil;
he who guards himself takes heed to his way.
18 Pride precedes destruction,
and a haughty spirit precedes stumbling.
19 It is better to associate with the poor in spirit
than to divide plunder with the proud.
20 He who considers a matter seriously will find good,
and he who trusts in Yahweh is blessed.

---

dollars rather than discernment? Part of good counseling is to help counselees establish and follow proper priorities. Do you take the time to do so? Think back; when was the last time you said something approximating the word mentioned in verse 16? Do you need to reorient your *own* counseling priorities?

According to verse 17, the way of **upright people** is like a **highway** (not a mere trail or bumpy byway). It is raised (above rising water), smooth and good for travel. That is the sort of life (inwardly, if not outwardly) God provides for those who **guard themselves** from sin and **take heed to** stay on that road. Why would one want to depart from it? That is a good question to ask those mired in some sinful path. Often, that about which counselees complain, as if they had found it on God's highway, in reality is found alongside it or far away from it. Check out each instance to see if the roughness of their situation is because they have taken a false turn. The figure of the path (road, way, highway) is a favorite in Proverbs. It is one that you may use profitably in counseling as well. You'd be wise to exploit it to the full in the examples.

Verses 18 and 19, like 14 and 15, teach complementing truths. Since **pride precedes destruction**, it is **better to associate with the** humble (**poor in spirit**: spirit = attitude). The **haughty** attitude, with which a boastful person swaggers and struts himself, is distasteful not only to others, but to God Himself. It is He that will **destroy** and cause him to **stumble**. God so orders His providence that, at length, he will come to a ruinous end. Unless you want to come down with him when he falls, it is better to abandon him, even if it means the loss of wealth or property in doing so (cf. 1:10-19). Often, it is too late when a ruined counselee appears to warn him of coming **destruction**. But when it fits, you may use these verses to explain what has happened and why, and steer him away from future ruinous **associations**.

In verse 20, once again Solomon urges thorough **consideration** of a **matter** (or of the word; the Hebrew term means "thing, matter, word").

21 The wise in heart will be called a discerning person,
and his sweetness of lips increases persuasion.
22 Prudence is a fountain of life to those who have it,
but the training of stupid fools is folly.
23 The wise of heart uses his mouth prudently,
and to his lips he adds persuasion.

Because it is by means of the Word that one should make decisions and chart courses in life, decision-making about matters involves God's commands. For knowledgeable believers, the two are bound up in one another. For many counselees, there is no recognition of the connection.

A **discerning** person will know how to speak to others; the **wisdom** that resides in his **heart** controls his **lips**. That **wisdom** is obtained from God's Word: preeminently from Proverbs, which has more to say about speech (under the words **tongue, lips, mouth**, etc.) than any other book of the Bible. **Sweetness of lips** in a speaker doesn't mean syrupy, sugary talk; it has to do with how the listener receives it. It is agreeableness, talk that commends itself to the auditor. One is **persuaded**, he says, not only by the matter, but also by the manner. That is something gruff, thoughtless counselees must be taught. The objection "But I was right!" needs to be countered with a remark that asks, "Yes, but were you right, *rightly*?"

Verse 22 accords well with 13:14 and 14:27. A **fountain** is a **source** from which **life**-giving properties flow. **Prudent** action—using caution and discernment by applying Scripture to daily decision-making—brings the abundant life to its fruition. On the other hand, the **stupid fool** is trained daily by folly. The former has an ever-increasing joyful and productive life, while the latter goes from bad to worse. The point? Just this: in seeing this (perhaps by experiencing it) one should leave the instruction folly provides and begin drinking at the fountain of **prudence**. A good question to ask from time to time is, "Is the water you drink polluted or fresh? If polluted, no wonder your spiritual life is sickly and weak."

Verses 23 and 21 are very close. **Wisdom** in the **heart** (the place from which all other activities stem) leads to the **prudent use of the mouth**. One speaks wisely about matters that arise, and along with that **wisdom to his lips he adds persuasion** (cf. v. 21). The idea of a counselor teaching God's truth, then leaving it up to the counselee to decide for or against it, with not so much as a hint of warning, apart from exhortation or urging (at times, even pleading), is a concept foreign to the Scriptures. When counseling, always add persuasion as it is needed (cf. II Timothy

24 Pleasant words flowing with honey
are sweetness to the soul and healing to the bones.
25 There is a way that seems right before a man's face,
but at its end are death roads.
26 A worker's appetite works for him
since his mouth urges him on.
27 A worthless man digs up evil,
and on his lips it is like flaming fire.
28 A perverse man spreads strife
and a gossip separates friends.

4:2). As Calvin put it, when commenting on that passage, use "spurs" along with your teaching.

Verses 21 and 13 ought to be combined in the counselor's thinking with verse 24. The present verse has nothing to do with flattery; it is speaking of helpful speech that meets the needs of others. The words are **pleasant** and flow with **sweetness to the soul** and **healing to the bones** of those undergoing affliction and trouble. Here is the picture of a truly biblical counselor who wields God's Word well in the blessing of others.

For verse 25, see 14:12 where the same words occur. Such repetition indicates the importance of the thought.

In verse 26, the **mouth** represents not speech (as it usually does) but hunger (something to put in the mouth). A man works in order to eat, if for no greater end. Having food for himself and his family ought to spur him to work (cf. II Thessalonians 3:10). Unfortunately, in a socialist society this important principle is thwarted by rewarding indolence rather than **work**.

The person who **digs up** dirt to use for **evil** purposes of **gossip is worthless** (something a person enamored with self-worth dogma should consider). The word means, literally, "a man of Belial," and was used of one who is committed wholly to worthless and harmful projects. He, therefore, is considered to be worthless and Satanic himself. On his **lips** the gossip is like a **flaming fire** (cf. James 3:6). Be sure to show clearly what damage gossip can do and what God thinks of it.

Verse 28 continues the discussion of gossip begun in the previous verse. Here, the effects of gossip are revealed. The **flaming fire** of verse 27 spreads, causing strife wherever it goes. In a church, the effects can be devastating, setting former friends against one another. Church splits, which are caused or widened by gossip, always provide scope for the gos-

29 A violent man baits his neighbor
and leads him along a way that isn't good.
30 He who shuts his eyes in order to plan perverse things, pinching his lips,
brings about evil.
31 The gray head is a crown of glory;
it is found on the road of righteousness.
32 Better is the person who is slow to anger than a mighty one,
and he who governs his temper than one who takes a city by force.

---

sip and slanderer. Come down as hard as God does on gossip (cf. Titus 3:10 in this regard).

The **violent man entices his neighbor** (v. 29) as we saw in 1:10-18, where the process is dramatically portrayed. That is the best commentary on this verse. Isn't it interesting how evil persons wish to involve others in their sin? Warn counselees about this tendency so that they will not consent (cf. Romans 1:32). Note also the use of the figure of the **way** (road, path).

In order to think harder about ways of pursuing evil, the inveterate planner of wickedness squints and pinches his lips (v. 30). When an evil person so intently screws up his face to help him think about his nefarious purposes, how much energy should the believer put into planning good? Don't allow counselees to take the tasks given to him in God's Word lightly, without thought and hard planning.

The "if" supplied by the King James translators effectively distorts the meaning of the proverb found in verse 31. The idea is that longevity, signified by the gray head, **is found on the road of righteousness**. That is to say, a righteous lifestyle leads to long life. It is a **glory** to live a long life of integrity. There are, of course, hoary unbelievers, but to them the color of their hair represents God's mercy in common grace, and their stubborn refusal to recognize it. Their **gray heads** are a crown not of glory, but of shame!

According to verse 32 it takes more power, wisdom and strength to control one's **temper** than to storm a **city by force**. Angry counselees must be informed that to rein in their anger will take courage and strength greater than that of a **mighty warrior**. Indeed, they must win the war within (see my book with that very title). Self-control is part of the Spirit's fruit (Galatians 5:23) and must be cultivated by studying and applying His Words in verses such as this one. Counselors are counselors

33 The lot is cast into the lap,
but the decision is entirely from Yahweh.

---

of war, who help counselees plan a frontal attack on this vicious enemy. One hope, implied in the proverb, is that anger *is* governable.

This chapter closes with mentioning one means of decision-making: the use of the lot (v. 33). Though **Yahweh** is said to use it through His providence, as indeed, all that occurs providentially, this is no excuse for looking on the lot as a solution to every decision. There is a lazy, superstitious use of the lot (and other such means) that is not recommended here. The use of the lot (drawing straws, flipping coins) ought never to supersede biblical commandments and the application of scriptural principles. "When should it be used?" you ask? When, having followed biblical injunctions to their limit you are left with several options, all of which are acceptable to God, the lot may be used to decide among them. For instances of its use, see Leviticus 16:8-10 and I Chronicles 25:8-31. One cannot expect God to concur with the lot in some manner that manifests His direct, special providence, unless He has authorized its use (as in the previous citations). All it implies otherwise is that God's general nonrevelatory providence is at work. With such an understanding the lot may prove helpful and one may only say that God is interested in the decision, which is left up to Him. But where there is biblical direction, the lot should never replace obedience to it.

CHAPTER 17

1 Better is a dry crust of bread with peace
than a house full of sacrifices with strife.
2 A prudent servant will rule over a son who acts shamefully,
and he will share the inheritance as one of his brothers.
3 The refining pot is for silver and the furnace is for gold,
but Yahweh assays hearts.

Verse 1 is essentially the same as 15:17. The **dry crust** reference reaches to the greatest extreme, perhaps, showing that at all costs this sentiment is true. The **sacrifices** point to plenty of meat to eat (sacrifices were, in part, eaten. Cf. Psalm 22:25, 26). Little with **peace** is contrasted with plenty and **strife** (fighting, arguing). Many a counselee can testify to the truth of these words! They are of importance to those who are thinking of marriage. If the parties in question are not able to prove that there will be headship and submission, and communication in which they are able to solve problems God's way from God's Word, they are not ready for marriage. This verse may be used properly to delay uncertain marriages or stop those that would be altogether wrong. Often, in marriages, strife occurs over money (or the lack of it) and possessions. It is of importance to use this verse as a warning when such tendencies are beginning to manifest themselves, and as a corrective when they are in full bloom.

Verse 2 is a warning to disobedient **sons**. Blood may not always be thicker than water. Others who act *as* ***sons*** *should* (when the latter fail to do so) in time occupy their places. This was a radical proposal in the light of Hebrew inheritance laws, and meant that the disobedient son was virtually cut off from the family. In view of the seriousness of the warning, counselors may observe the strong measures to which the Bible points in the matter.

As the instruments mentioned in verse 3 purify gold and silver by separating the precious metal from the dross (the worthless residue) through fire, so too does God assay the value of what is in a person's **heart** (that is to say, the value of the person to other human beings). It is by the fires of trials and tribulations that the heart is purified and tested. Counselees should be made aware of the fact that these experiences, though painful, give them an opportunity to evaluate what they are like and thus to purify their lives as well. A trial enables one to see the sort of stuff he is made of. Help counselees to assay the quality of what is left

4 An evil doer heeds false lips;
a liar listens to a tongue that suits his desire.
5 He who mocks the poor insults his Maker;
he who rejoices at tragedy will not be acquitted.
6 Grandchildren are the crown of old men,
and the glory of sons is their fathers.
7 Excellent speech isn't appropriate to a shameless fool;
much less lying lips to a noble.

---

after the dross is removed and they emerge from the trials of the **refining pot** or **furnace**.

"Birds of a feather flock together" is the import of verse 4. The wicked go about deceiving one another and are, as such, bringing retribution upon each other. Run with a crowd like that and you can expect no more. Tell counselees that this is so. Act like that *yourself* and you will attract associates who also act that way. We say, "It takes one to know one," but it also is true that it takes one to attract one. And in God's providential workings, it takes one to deal with one. Become a **liar**, and you will attract liars who will promise to fulfill your **desires**. But they rarely keep these promises. Liars and fulfilled desires are seldom compatible.

Verse 5[a] should be compared with 14:31. There is, however, an additional thought here. Not only is God **insulted** by **mocking** the **poor**, God also will hold him guilty who **rejoices** over another's **tragedy**. He will not be **acquitted**. The temptation is to gloat over the downfall of an enemy or rival rather than to pity him, pray for him, help him, and take heed that you also do not fall (cf. I Corinthians 10:12). Whenever you detect such rejoicing in a counselee, bring this verse to bear upon him. All too often, in the mix of emotions that attend various counseling cases, this tendency is present. All the *good* work that one does in counseling may be spoiled thereby.

Verse 6 sketches a situation where righteousness has prevailed for at least three generations. What a blessing when each exerts a salutary, spiritual influence on those who succeed him! The saying, common among some Christians, that the second generation always goes bad, is false, as is evident from this proverb. Though it may happen, it need not. There is a possibility of passing down faith and salvation through the generations by faithful living and teaching. Challenge counselees to work toward this event.

The ***inappropriateness*** of such qualities as those listed in verse 7, is what the proverb stresses. Indeed, what belongs to each type of person

8 A bribe is a precious stone in the eyes of its owner;
wherever he turns he succeeds.
9 He who covers a transgression promotes love,
but the one who repeats a matter separates friends.
10 A rebuke makes a deeper impression on an understanding person
than a hundred stripes on a stubborn fool.

---

mentioned is here set forth as inappropriate to the other. They are opposites, and what is proper for each is the opposite. A *nabal* (Hebrew for **shameless fool**,) the strongest word used to describe the three types of fools mentioned in Proverbs, is a person who is openly sarcastic, arrogant and crude. You won't find **excellent speech** coming from him! The Proverbs often express right and wrong in terms of appropriateness: what one may expect to find in a particular sort of individual. Note these, and when you discover the trait present in a counselee, you will know what sort of person you are dealing with.

In verse 8 the gift is a **bribe**, a thing forbidden in Exodus 23:8 and Deuteronomy 16:19. Therefore, the intent of the proverb is not to recommend using such "gifts" as a means to win financial **success**. It is an observation to be noted by counselees who fail to understand that "there is no free lunch." When you receive a gift under such circumstances, you open yourself to pressure from the one who gives it to you. In the eyes of the giver it is like a valuable **stone** (gem) that will enable him to attain whatever it is he desires. But what seems to be good **in his eyes** is in God's eyes sinful and must be avoided.

It is a loving act on the part of one person to **cover** (rather than reveal) another's **transgression** (v. 9). The **one who repeats it**, however, may **separate** the dearest **friends** (cf. 10:12; 16:28). This, of course, doesn't mean that there are not times when sin must be disclosed (cf. Matthew 18:15ff.), but refers only to the *unnecessary* disclosure of the facts of another's sin. (For more on this see my books *From Forgiven to Forgiving* and *The Handbook of Church Discipline*.) Every malicious or careless, as well as unnecessary, revelation of another's misbehavior is strictly forbidden. It is gossip, at best; it may be slanderous. Counselors should be thoroughly prepared to discuss the ins and outs of these issues with any counselee. Counselees will need much guidance from the Bible about such matters; you will find a great deal of confusion on their part.

Every parent has noticed that children differ. Some respond to a look, others only to a **rebuke**. Many not till they receive corporal punishment!

11 A rebel seeks only evil,
but a stern messenger will be sent against him.
12 Better for a man to meet a bear robbed of her cubs
than a stubborn fool involved in his foolishness.

But there are some, who are on their way toward becoming **stubborn fools**, who respond to nothing (v. 10). No matter how many times you paddle them, it seems to make little difference. The **understanding person** learns from a **rebuke**. Indeed, such words, coupled with counsel from God, make a **deeper impression** on him than if you should beat him unmercifully. Counselees who appropriate the help that is found in a counselor's **rebuke** are wise and will profit from counseling. Those who do not, who get angry, make excuses or withdraw, probably will not profit until they learn to handle a loving rebuke in the right way. Early on, a counselor may test a counselee's present ability to benefit from counseling, by rebuking him at the first legitimate opportunity and watching how he responds. The counselor, of course, must be sure that the rebuke is warranted. He must neither invent nor incite circumstances leading to it. Since many counselors are reticent to rebuke counselees, especially early on in counseling, the real problem will be for the counselor to change! If the counselee becomes enraged and leaves counseling (presupposing the rebuke *was* loving) that only saves both of you from wasting time and enduring agony. Probably, it would have happened later on anyway. On rebuking, consider Revelation 3:19.

Because he does that which will preserve his kingdom and the welfare of his people, a king **sends a stern messenger** against the **rebel** who incites **evil** (v. 11). This individual wants to overthrow the king or the kingdom. It is the king's obligation, therefore, to **send** someone to deal summarily with him. The same is true in every authority-submission situation—whether it be in the state or in the church. An authority is obligated by God to maintain peace and order. He cannot countenance rebellion. One of the problems with our federal and state governments at present is that enforcement of rules by the authority has broken down. The same is true in the church (see comments on Titus 3:10).

Verse 12 speaks about a **stubborn fool** who is openly involved in some exhibition of his **foolishness**. To come into contact with him under such circumstances is more disagreeable than **meeting a bear robbed of her cubs** (a powerful hyperbolic figure). Solomon plainly thinks such an encounter ought to be avoided if at all possible. Woe to him who doesn't

13 Whoever repays good with evil
will find that evil will not depart from his house.
14 The beginning of strife is like making a hole to release water;
so quit before fighting breaks out.
15 He who justifies the wicked and he who condemns the just
are equally hateful to Yahweh.

---

get out of the way of the foolish she-bear he has in mind! There is a lesson here in the wisdom of avoiding unnecessary trouble when one can. Some counselees have a hard time learning this lesson; no wonder they are full of claw marks and bruises!

It is bad enough to **repay** evil with **evil** (cf. Romans 12:17-21; Proverbs 20:22), but to repay **good** with **evil** is the epitome of wickedness. Yet counselees are often prepared to do just that. And they will even try to enlist you as one who will participate with (or at least justify) them in the perpetration of this crime. Steer clear of all such traps. Moreover, watch out for the **evil** responses some may make to the good you seek to do for them. Warn them of the threat of God in the second half of the couplet; it is a fearful promise! This means that God's judgment will fall on one's entire family, and will remain there for the rest of their days. Urge all such counselees to repent while there is still time to escape this frightening consequence of such sin.

The picture word in verse 14 is clear enough. The little **hole** in the dike, once made, will grow larger and larger, until the ocean is inside. **Strife** and **fighting** (verbal or physical) is exactly like that. **Quitting** quickly is good advice for those who have already become involved in a battle of some sort (see also 15:1). Better still, is to avoid making any hole in the first place—no matter how small. Christians should be **peacemakers**, as Jesus said (cf. also Romans 12:18). If a counselee fails to heed your warning concerning this, he will soon become overwhelmed when, like **water** bursting forth, the opposition he has egged on engulfs him.

It doesn't matter which of the two sins mentioned that one commits, they are equally bad (v. 15). Counselors must be careful to get the facts—all the necessary facts—or they too, like many counselees, will find themselves **justifying the wicked** or **condemning the just**. In the next chapter, several verses instruct counselors in the task of thorough data-gathering (cf. 18:13, 15, 17). In order to heed this verse, you must also diligently follow the advice given there. This is a serious matter; wrong judgment is **hateful** to **Yahweh**.

16 Why is this money in the hand of a stubborn fool to get wisdom
when he has no sense?
17 A friend loves in every situation,
and a brother is born for trouble.
18 A man without sense strikes the palm;
he pledges before a friend.

Put in the form of a question, Solomon makes the point that it is a waste of **money** for a **stubborn fool** to try to pay someone to make him **wise** (v. 16). Until he gains some **sense** and begins to act sensibly, the attempt will be futile. He must leave behind his proud, stubborn, arrogant ways and humble himself before God and others in order to receive and utilize instruction. Here is a warning, counselor, that you will not succeed in your counseling with some people until (or unless) that change is made. There are people to reject. When it is apparent that you have such a person in counseling, bring sessions to a halt.

True **friends** and a true **brother** are there when you need them. How important it is to have some such close associates on whom you can rely when the calamities of life overtake you! Counselors regularly see counselees in distress who have no one like this to whom they may turn. There may be many reasons for this—some legitimate; some not. One may be that the counselee has failed to cultivate friendships, arrogantly thinking that he can go it alone. The counselor can help just so much; he cannot take the place of the missing brother or friend. The best he can do is to help his counselee develop some associations for the future.

Again, Solomon warns against becoming surety for another (v. 18). Only a person with little or no **sense** will do such a thing. For comments see 6:1-5 and 11:15.

There are those who **love** a good fight. They have learned how to provoke a quarrel between others and then stand back and watch the donnybrook. They are people who not only **love strife**; God says that what those with such an attitude *really* **love** is **transgression**! That is why they enjoy fighting. And akin to them is the one **who raises his door** (v. 19). By doing so, **he invites its breach**. What does that mean? A high door to a palace was a matter of pride and pretense. It invited those who were envious to break in. In a home, doors were sometimes built low as a safety factor (one had a harder time getting in unobserved). The high door, therefore, asks for (**invites**) trouble.

19 He who loves transgression loves strife;
he who raises his door invites its breach.
20 He who has a perverse heart doesn't find good,
and he who has a crooked tongue falls into trouble.
21 He who fathers a stubborn fool falls into grief for it;
indeed, the father of a shameless fool has no joy.
22 A joyful heart brings about good healing,
but a crushed spirit saps the bone.
23 The wicked person takes a bribe out of his bosom
to stretch the paths of justice.
24 The discerning person keeps wisdom before him,
but the eyes of a stubborn fool are in the ends of the land.
25 A stubborn fool for a son is a grief to his father
and bitterness to her who gave birth to him.
26 Also it is not good to fine the just:
to strike nobles for being upright.

The **perverse heart** and the **crooked tongue** of the one mentioned in verse 20 go together. They both procure **trouble** for him. They lead to **no good**. The concept is quite simple, but the point is profound. Devious thinking and speaking ultimately mean **trouble** and sorrow. The tongue speaks what is in the heart; the answer to the problem, therefore, is a changed heart.

Verse 21 speaks for itself. Counselors will meet both the **fool** and his **father** in counseling.

On verse 22, see 3:7, 8 and 15:4. Also see Norman Cousin's Book, *The Anatomy of an Illness* for an interesting account of how a human being's body is influenced by his state of mind. Many who are literally sick have made themselves sick by their attitudes. Thus biblical counseling is the way of **healing** them. (Cf. comments on James 5:14ff.)

On verse 23, see comments on verse 8.

To **keep wisdom before** one is to make it his goal; that means to have it always in view, never to forget it. Those who concentrate on **wisdom**, making it a priority, will be the only ones to attain to it. The **stubborn fool** has his **eyes** focused on nothing. Today he wants this; tomorrow that. He is interested in everything and, therefore, really in nothing. He is a jack of all trades, but a master of none. Wisdom requires focus. Help counselees to see this.

Verse 25 is an analog of verse 21.

Verse 26 is akin to verse 15. The principle behind them is the same.

27 He who restrains his words has knowledge,
and a discerning person has a cool spirit.
28 Even a stupid fool who is silent is thought wise;
he who shuts his lips is counted discerning.

How does a **discerning person** obtain a **cool spirit**? One factor is that by learning to exercise self-control, he **restrains his words** (v. 27). It is not necessary for a person to say everything that comes to his mind (counselors must learn this too). That is a part of **knowledge**—knowing when and what to speak.

Finally, verse 28 concludes the chapter. This verse suggests what one may do when he is learning self-control: learn to be quiet. If he practices doing so, he will begin to gain a better reputation: **he will be thought wise, counted discerning**. It is an excellent first step for **stupid fools** to take if they wish to abandon their former practice. And it is a way to wisdom for all who are concerned to attain it.

CHAPTER 18

1 He who separates himself from others seeks to satisfy his own desire;
he rolls headlong against all sound wisdom.
2 A stubborn fool takes no pleasure in discernment
but only in revealing his heart.
3 When the wicked comes, along comes contempt,
and with insult along comes reproach.

Everyone who knows better warns him, but he will not hear. Who is that? The one **who separates himself from others** to pursue his own interest (**desire**). What does he do? He rushes (or **rolls**) **headlong** (that is, thoughtlessly) **against all sound wisdom**. Again, who is this? The recluse, the lone wolf, the person who thinks that he needs no one else. He is so wrapped up in himself and what he is doing that, for all he cares, the world can go hang. Here is the "Christian" who "doesn't need the church." Here is the child who doesn't need his parents. Here is the heresiarch who doesn't need the teachings of the theologians and exegetes. Many such persons believe only in themselves; they think they don't even need a Savior. The self-sufficient person, because of his desire for independence and autonomy, in the end, comes to ruin.

Verse 2 describes one who is similar to the person met in verse 1. He is a **stubborn fool** because he is not at all interested in learning from others who might help him gain **discernment**. His only **pleasure** is in talking—to himself! He likes to give you *his* opinion on every subject, but is not interested in yours. He soon becomes an insufferable bore that everyone tries to avoid. His description? He is never learning but always coming to a knowledge of the truth—or so he thinks! It is unlikely that you will counsel many of those persons who are mentioned in verse 1. If the problem is full-blown, they will avoid you. You will, however, see tendencies of this sort in some that you counsel. And you will often meet those who are mentioned in the present verse. The problem is that they will rarely come for counseling; they will be interested only in **revealing their hearts**. That is to say, a know-it-all like this will attempt to dominate the conversation, direct and run the session, tell you what the problem is and what you should do about it. He will not listen to you or to God's Word as you attempt to present it to him. Incidentally; he usually doesn't come on his own; he is brought by another.

4 The words of a man's mouth are deep waters;
the fountain of wisdom, a flowing stream.
5 To be partial to the wicked isn't good;
or to thrust aside the righteous in judgment.

The **wicked** person appears on the scene (v. 3). Not far behind him **contempt, insult** and **reproach** also will appear. They are his companions who follow him everywhere. He goes nowhere without them; they are inseparable. The only way to remove the last three is to deal effectively with the first. Until a **wicked** person is converted and his life is changed, he will go on spreading contempt, insults and reproaches far and wide. If he is not converted to the gospel of Jesus Christ, he must be removed from the midst. Avoid him like the plague—except to evangelize him. He is not a fit subject for counseling.

In verse 4, the words of a **wise man's mouth** are described as containing **deep waters** (as in a reservoir); it is a **fountain** (source) of **wisdom**; a **flowing stream**. The idea here is that there is substance to such a person; he has much to offer others. He is the opposite of the person referred to in verse 2, who is shallow, self-centered and without resources. This person—and every counselor ought himself to be a prime example of it—has much to offer. Indeed, his depth in truth and life is so great that as you continue to probe him you discover more and more. He rarely tells you all he knows about God's ways because his knowledge is so extensive it would be difficult to do so. It is clear, however, that when he speaks he has but ladled out only a small portion of water from that vast reservoir within. You won't meet many counselees who fit the description; indeed, how many counselors do?

Verse 5 speaks generally about a reversal of God's revealed order, and specifically, as this pertains to courts of law. One reason modern America has such a high crime rate is that laws protect the criminal more than they protect the victim. Many liberal judges, who send murderers and rapists back on to the streets where they perpetuate their crimes, will find out that they will endure God's judgment and wrath for doing so. Proverbs explicitly says that **it is not good to be partial to the wicked**. Counselors, also, must be careful not to fail in this regard; they may not become so sympathetic that they ignore sin. Freudianism—with its failure to place responsibility on the sinner—has permeated our society, and its influence accounts for much of the recidivism we experience today.

6 A stubborn fool's lips cause contention;
his mouth asks for a beating.
7 A stubborn fool's mouth ruins him,
and his lips are a trap for him.
8 A slanderer's words are like tasty morsels;
they go down to the inner parts of the belly.

What comes from the **lips** (*mouth* is what we would say) of the **stubborn fool** brings about trouble for others, usually in the form of **contention** (arguments, dissension, strife) of some sort (v. 6). He cannot spend much time among others without stirring up trouble by what he says. The impact of his words is the opposite of that of the wise person (v. 4). Indeed, as the fool talks, his rash, intemperate, irritating and divisive language virtually **asks for a beating** (and if we didn't live in such a "polite" society, he'd receive it!). Rather than to be listened to, he should be punished for all the trouble he causes. Watch out for him in counseling; unless he repents and allows you to help him change, he will stir up trouble for any other counselees who may be associated with him. It is fruitless—indeed, harmful—to proceed with counseling under such conditions. There will be times when you have to eject him from the counseling room (usually, by verbal means).

The person mentioned in verse 3 and the one described in verse 6 is further described here (v. 7). He speaks, but what he says **ruins him**. The words of his **lips trap him**. How? His lies soon catch up with him; people soon refuse to believe him, even when he tells the truth. His advice is useless, as those who follow it discover; his observations are wrong and his values are all out of kilter. Indeed, his ignorance is profound! People soon recognize him for what he is and either avoid or punish him in some other way. God may also punish as He did in the case of one such woman who for years was bedridden and unable to communicate with others. He effectively silenced her lies!

Continuing to consider speaking and listening, Solomon refers to the **slanderers** (v. 8). Unlike the man who speaks about himself, the **slanderer's** words concern another. And people *will* listen! Why do they want to? Ask yourself, why do people enjoy the front page of a newspaper; why do they read the gossip columns? People gobble up gossip and slander as if they were **tasty morsels**. And they ingest them (**they go down into the innermost parts of the belly**). That is to say, what a man eats is what he becomes. To swallow and assimilate **slander** is dangerous. It influences

9 Also, he who is lax about his work
is a brother to a demolition expert.
10 The Name of Yahweh is a strong tower;
a righteous person runs into it and is high above danger.
11 The rich man's wealth is his strong city;
he imagines it is a high wall of protection.

---

one wrongly toward third parties. In one case, a slanderous person, in God's providence, spent the latter part of her life all by herself, and eventually lost her ability to think and remember. Counselors must not allow gossip or slander in the counseling room. The temptation to do so is great (even counselors like to eat candy!). But see the precaution in verse 17.

One doesn't have to purposely go about destroying something; by becoming **lax about his work** he will do so (v. 9). In a world of sin everything tends toward ruin (your body, your car, your house, your church). Give it time enough, with no effort to reverse the process and, like entropy (the greatest example of which is kudzu), it will creep up on you. Lazy persons truly are **brothers to demolition experts**. Tell lazy counselees about this; they rarely think on the long term. They see only today and live for its pleasure (which, on the short term, means neglect, lounging about and doing only what one *likes* to do).

To speak of **Yahweh's Name** as a **strong tower** in which one may take refuge and find protection from **danger** (v. 10) is difficult for some to comprehend. What does it mean? To us names mean little. But to the Hebrews, names expressed something about the one to whom they were assigned. All that the many names of God mean is what God is. See my book *A Theology of Counseling* for a discussion of the names of God in relation to counseling. **Yahweh**, referring to the God Who is yesterday, today and forever, means that He is always there, always the same, always available for wisdom and help in time of need or danger. Thus He, Himself, like a **strong tower**, is the safe place of refuge—the One to Whom to turn in time of trouble.

In contrast to the previous verse, many **rich men** imagine that, like a **strong city**, their **wealth** will protect them from danger. Of course, they are wrong; wealth can only do so much—as many have found. For some, though it need not be so, it is a choice between God or money. Counselees may find themselves in danger precisely because, faced with a choice, they have chosen poorly. The only safe place to be, in life or in death, is in the shadow of the Almighty One. Some counselees struggle precisely

12 Before everything falls apart a man's heart is haughty,
but before honor is humility.
13 He who answers a matter before he hears
does a stupid and disgraceful thing.
14 A man's spirit will carry him through sickness,
but who can bear the burden of a broken spirit?
15 The discerning heart acquires knowledge,
and the ear of the wise seeks knowledge.

---

with the two alternatives set forth above; help them to opt for the only one that counts. All of society is against them: the ethos of our day—as perhaps also in Solomon's—is that wealth can get you anything. One soon finds that is wrong. The problem is in getting others to believe it *before* they find out—the hard way!

There are counselees who come because they have been riding the crest of the wave only to find that it has suddenly broken and let them down hard (v. 12). Prior to **everything falling apart**, they had been **haughty**, self-sufficient and heedless of warnings in God's Word. At last, amidst the ruin and rubble, they are ready to listen for the first time. Often, that is what it takes to **humble** a person before God. The road to true and lasting **honor** runs—sometimes for miles and miles—through the dark and difficult valleys of humility. It is only those who have traversed these paths on their own successfully who reach the solid heights of honor and fame in a condition to rightly enjoy and appreciate them. There are counselees to whom these facts must be made known. But some will not listen until **everything falls apart**.

Verses 13, 15 and 17 are three vital verses concerning **listening** with which every counselor ought to be familiar. They deal with all sorts of listening, to be sure, but the broad principles advanced in them are of special moment to counselors. I shall consider them together. In verse 13, the counselor is warned never to jump to conclusions about a counselee, or what he tells him. To have predetermined what a person's problem is (or to do so on insufficient data) is to commit the sin of Job's counselors. Job (to some extent) and ultimately God (to a greater extent) proved their approach to be **stupid** and **disgraceful**. Verse 15 shows that good listening is active, not passive. The data-gathering listener ***acquires*** **knowledge** and ***seeks*** **knowledge**. He knows what sort of information he requires and has a method for obtaining it (for help in these matters, see my *Christian Counselor's Manual).* He is in charge of counseling sessions; he does not allow counselees to drone on in a free association manner or repeat the

16 A man's gift makes room for him
and leads him into the presence of the great.
17 The first one to present his case seems right
until another comes and probes him.

---

same thing time and time again. Rather, he directs the conversation toward those data that he must gather in order to help. His probing questions, by which, largely, he obtains such information, are well-thought through and may first be extensive in nature, then intensive (see *The Christian Counselor's Manual* for definitions and explanations of these concepts). Finally, the biblically-trained counselor will be sure to gather data from all the persons involved. He recognizes that there are at least three sides to every issue. These are the side of one person, the side of another—and God's side! He will be certain that he has all the data necessary—including that which constitutes *God's* side.

Verse 14, once again, shows the effect of the inner person on the outer: a hopeful **spirit** (attitude) will **carry** one **through sickness**. If, however, one's **spirit is broken** (he gives up; loses hope) that only adds an additional **burden** to the one he already **bears**. Counselors may not be able to care for the physical illnesses of individuals, but they can help remove the spiritual, inner **burdens** that keep healing from occurring or that enable one to bear those illnesses that are incurable. The importance of such ministry to the sick often goes unrecognized.

In verse 16, a different term is used than that translated "**bribe**" in 17:8. Here it speaks more of the gracious and thoughtful **gift** that opens up pleasant relations between one person and another. The American mind tends to confuse this with a bribe, placing all such things in the same category. But the fact of two diverse terms in the Hebrew expresses a difference. The **gift** is just that—a gift that calls attention to the interest that one has in another. It says something like, "I respect you for what and who you are," and (in general) shows the regard one has for another. Orientals understand the difference. The bribe is designed to obligate the one who receives it; the gift carries no such connotation. The bribe shows disrespect; the gift respect. In a better-than-bribe manner, the gift opens conversation and communication (**makes room for** one, even in **the presence of the great**). In advising counselees, you might suggest the use of the **gift** in certain circumstances, always carefully distinguishing it from the bribe.

18 The lot causes arguments to cease
and keeps strong persons from clashing.
19 An alienated brother is more difficult to win than a strong city
and their disputes than the barred gates of a castle.
20 By the fruit of a man's mouth his stomach will be filled;
with the produce of his lips he will be satisfied.
21 Death and life are in the tongue,
and those who love it will eat its fruit.

Verse 18 adds one element to our discussion of the use of the **lot** in 16:33, though that element may be implied there as well. Under the conditions we noted there, Solomon now says that the lot will preclude **arguments** and **clashes** among **persons** who **strongly** prefer their own ways. There are situations in which counselors might advise the use of the **lot** (but see comments on 16:33 for details).

The **brother** referred to in verse 19 is probably one's literal brother (or sister), though the warning in the verse may refer equally to brothers *in Christ.* The **difficulty** of capturing a **strong city** or of **breaking into a castle** fortified by strongly barred **gates** is compared to the difficulty of reconciling to an **alienated brother**. It can be done, but is hard. Family quarrels tend to be some of the most difficult to resolve. Family members have so much that they can dredge up out of the past to embellish their points that arguments tend to be intensified as they continue. Make this clear. Tell them to scrape off old issues through repentance and forgiveness. Deal with that which precipitated estrangement. But in doing so, be sure to explain clearly the ins and outs of repentance and forgiveness so that they understand the commitments they are making (for further help, see my book *From Forgiven to Forgiving*).

Verse 20 relates to preachers and all who earn their living by means of speech. But as one who sells a product is expected to carry quality merchandise, so too the counselor must be sure that he deals in God's valuable words. Human counsel is worthless. God, Himself, calls it "the counsel of the ungodly," thereby disparaging it (Psalm 1:1). God's counsel is full of wisdom and tends to life. Deal in no inferior product.

The **tongue**, according to verse 21, can lead to **death** or **life**, depending on its use. Those who use it too freely (who **love to use it**) will **eat its fruit** (get what is coming to them). This is a powerful warning. While **life and death** are the extremes to which careless words may lead, all sorts of lesser, but dire, consequences (or, on the other hand, good results) may flow from the tongue. What the proverb says, in effect, is that one must

22 He who finds a wife finds something good
and gets favor from Yahweh.
23 A poor person speaks imploringly,
but a rich one answers roughly.
24 A man with many friends may come to ruin,
but the one who shows love sticks closer than a brother.

---

take care about what he says and how he says it, because *there will be results* (**fruits**) that stem from his speech.

Quite contrary to the words of many of the Rabbis, who deprecated women in general, verse 22 gives proper honor to the **good wife**. She is viewed (rightly) as God's gift (cf. 19:14). There are, naturally, bad wives (today, all too many of them), but the sort of wife to which Solomon refers is the wife described in chapter thirty-one. Tell ungrateful husbands who abuse their wives that they are insulting God Who gave their wives to them (cf. I Peter 3:7).

The observation made in verse 23 is simply that: **poor** people find it necessary to **implore** and beg for what they get—they have no clout. **Rich** persons, on the other hand, may tend to avoid polite manners and ways because they think that their money speaks for them. And all too frequently, this is true to the facts. Because society is largely oriented to expect **right** treatment for such rich persons, they have little incentive to change. Christians, however, should guard against rude, offensive speech to others whether they are **rich** or **poor**. Counselors must never kowtow to anyone because of his money. If they do, their counseling will suffer from it and they will dishonor God.

The chapter closes with an important insight: those who fail to develop deep friendships with a few and have only superficial friendships with many **may come to ruin**. One friend who develops deep loyalty and affection (**love**), in times of trouble, will **stick closer than a brother**.

CHAPTER 19

1 A poor man who walks in his integrity is better
than one who has perverted lips and is a stubborn fool.
2 Also, it isn't good for a person to be without knowledge,
and he who rushes with his feet sins.
3 A man's stupid folly overturns his way,
but his heart rages against Yahweh.

How much money or property one owns says nothing about his lifestyle; that, however, according to verse 1, is more important than his financial profile. To **walk in integrity** is what counts. One who is rich, but has perverted speech (**lips**), and is a **stubborn fool** (cf. 28:6), is not to be preferred over a **poor man of integrity**. Since God places this construction on life, counselors must do so as well.

The importance of gathering the information necessary for any task is emphasized in verse 2. To **rush with one's feet** to accomplish something (apart from obtaining such **knowledge**) leads to **sin** (lit., "missing the mark", which here may mean failure rather than success in the pursuit). How often the problem presented here lies behind a counselee's failure! Don't fail to probe to see if this is the problem, when you can't seem to find another cause. Sometimes you must not only point out that this is the source of a counselee's difficulty, but also show him how to go about determining what sorts of knowledge and skills are necessary to a successful pursuit of the goals he has in mind. While you may not know the precise sources or the technical side of the issue, you can help him with organizational and research skills—all of which ought to be found in the counselor's kit bag.

Blameshifting, which is as old as the Garden of Eden, is frequently encountered in counseling. How utterly important it is, then, to help counselees to accept responsibility for their words and actions, and to recognize the consequences that flow from them. Often a counselee will say, "If only he would do so and so, then I would do thus and thus." You will also hear, "If only she had done her part, then I would have done mine." Such excuses must be met head on: scotch them early in counseling. Explain that a Christian must do that which it is his responsibility to do *to please God*—whether or not any other person assumes his responsibility. This understanding is basic to all successful counseling. You cannot go very far without it. Bring the counselee to an agreement about this principle before

4 Wealth adds many "friends,"
but the poor is deserted by his neighbor.
5 A false witness will not be acquitted,
and he who breathes lies will not escape.
6 Many will curry the favor of a ruler,
and everyone is the friend of a man who gives gifts.
7 All the poor man's brothers despise him and his friends surely leave him;
he pursues them with words but they disappear.
8 Moreover, he who gains sense loves himself;
he who preserves discernment shows regard for good.

---

trying to go further. While such blame-shifting is serious, even more serious is blaming *God* for one's predicament. That is the sort of blameshifting with which verse 3 is concerned. The failures that one encounters are not God's fault; they are the result of the counselee's **stupid folly**. Counselees who are angry with **Yahweh** so that their **hearts rage** against Him must be stopped in their tracks by a reading of this verse. It is the most powerful one on the subject. Learn where it is located and be ready to use it in all such cases.

The kind of "**friends**" mentioned in verse 4, like those of 18:24, are superficial and have become one's friends only because of the **wealth** he has accumulated. They care nothing for him; they are interested only in what he might do for them. They are the sort who **desert a neighbor** when misfortune overtakes him, or when he loses his money. The observation made here is that such persons should not be considered friends at all. Counselors may have to help counselees distinguish true friends from false. This verse provides one criterion that will help in doing so. Warn the person who claims to have many friends that it is usually only a few who can be counted on in the pinch.

The thought in verses 5 and 9 is identical and does not differ from that found in previous verses (cf. 14:5, 25 for further explanation).

Verse 6 differs little from verse 4.

Verse 7 accords with 18:24 and 19:4. The new thought is that, as he pitifully **pursues** others and begs for their help, they go their way (**disappear**) without a thought for him.

One who **gains sense** (as over against those mentioned in 8:36) does that which brings profit to himself (that is the way in which he shows **love** for **himself**). And when he preserves that which he gains, that indicates that he has learned to appreciate (**show regard for**) what is good. Here is

9 A false witness will not be acquitted,
and one who breathes lies will perish.
10 Luxury is not becoming to a stubborn fool,
and it is even worse for a servant to rule over rulers.
11 A man's discretion makes him slow to anger,
and it is his glory to overlook an offense.
12 A king's rage is like a lion's roar,
but his favor is like dew on grass.
13 A foolish son is a ruin to his father,
and the contentions of a wife are a constant dripping.
14 House and riches are the legacy that comes from a father,
but a prudent wife is from Yahweh.

---

an insight counselors may use to determine what a counselee is like: does he **show a regard for good**? And it tells you whether or not he is learning.

On verse 9, see verse 5, etc.

Verse 10, from a different perspective, once more points out the inappropriateness and incongruity of certain factors. **Luxury**, for instance, should not be the lot of a **stubborn fool**. And, what is **even worse** is when a **servant** rises to a place of **rule** and authority over **rulers** (cf. 17:7; 30:21, 22). To a lesser extent, counselors have noted the utter unfitness of what some counselees possess. In observing this, for instance, a counselor might say, "Joe, it isn't fitting for you to have such fine children when you live like you do. Why don't you measure up to your responsibilities to them as God says you should?"

In verse 11 Solomon once more deals with **anger**. He says that it is **discretion** that enables a person to control his anger, and then goes even further, saying, **it is his glory** (that is, to his credit) **to overlook an offense**. Not only should a believer not get angry over every offense, but he may **overlook** it altogether (cf. 15:1; 16:32).

Verse 12 is but another slightly different version of 16:14 and 15.

Two sad disturbances to home life are **foolish** children and **contentious wives** (they are also mothers, remember), as is stated in verse 13. Like a **constant dripping** their **ruinous** effects upon the family will continue until (and unless) they are changed by God's grace. When counselors can help alleviate either or both of these conditions, they do something quite valuable for any home. Nothing short of that kind of change can bring peace to a home disturbed in this way.

It is true that a **father** can leave **house and riches** to his children, but a **prudent wife** comes only from **Yahweh**. Counselors should advise

15 Laziness makes one fall into a deep sleep,
and an idle person will be hungry.
16 Whoever keeps the commandment keeps himself;
whoever is contemptuous of the ways he should go will die.
17 The one who is gracious to the poor lends to Yahweh,
and He will repay what he has done for him.
18 Chasten your son since there is hope in doing so,
but don't determine to let him die.
19 One who has great fury will pay the fine;
if you deliver him, you'll have to do it again.

---

young people to ask Him to give them prudent spouses. After all, what could be more fitting than to ask the One Who is the Source for that which He alone can give?

According to verse 15, **laziness and sleep** go together. When there is too much **sleep**, look for **laziness** as the cause. Idleness leads to hunger (when you meet one who is hungry, always check out his lifestyle in addition to feeding him).

There is a play on the word **keep** in verse 16. To **keep** God's **commandment** is to **keep** one's self from sin and its consequences. But to be **contemptuous** of God's **ways** leads to death (physical and spiritual). Since this concept is frequently mentioned in Proverbs I shall not comment on it.

Giving alms to **the poor** is actually giving to **Yahweh**. Note in verse 17, the gracious person is said to **lend** these alms to Him. Why? Because when one gives to God He repays him for it (cf. comments on 11:24ff.).

Corporal punishment is consistently taught in Proverbs, as it is in verse 18. Such chastisement is *not* child abuse. There is **hope** for a little sinner who has been trained by it. Indeed, if one wants to save him from **death** he will use it (cf. 23:13, 14). Many children in our present society, from which spanking has been all but excluded, have died in childhood as a consequence of wild lifestyles that might have been avoided had parents consistently, carefully and lovingly followed this and other such commands from God.

It is not only once, but again and again, that an angry man must be delivered by **paying a fine**; there is no hope for such a person short of learning to control his temper (v. 19). Such control is the work of God's Spirit through His Word (cf. Galatians 5:23). In other words, unless a counselor helps a counselee overcome the underlying problem by changing his basic habit pattern, his counseling will be in vain. It is not enough (though necessary, of course) to deal with the consequences of the latest

20 Listen to counsel and submit to discipline
that, at length, you may be wise.
21 Many plans are in a man's heart,
but the counsel of Yahweh will prevail.
22 A man's desire [to help] is his charm,
and it is better to be poor than a rich liar.
23 The fear of Yahweh leads to life for one,
and he rests satisfied that he will not be visited by trouble.
24 A lazy person dips his hand into a bowl
and will not even bring it back to his mouth.

---

escapade; there must be a more fundamental alteration of the attitude and habitual set in the counselee of which it is but the most recent instance. Don't settle for anything less.

Verse 20 might be placed on a plaque and posted on the wall of your counseling room. Two prerequisites of **wisdom** are cited: **listening to counsel** and **submitting to discipline**. They go together; both are necessary. And, note as well, the wisdom to which these two lead comes only **at length**. In other words, listening to counsel and submitting to discipline, in putting this counsel into practice, must continue consistently *over a period of time* if it is to become effective. It takes time to habituate new ways. Many counselees will fail only because they gave up too soon. Counselors fail them when they do not keep this in mind and forget to remind their counselees of the fact.

On verse 21, see 16:1.

According to verse 22, a person's **charm**, shown by kind words, is in his **desire to help** those in need. This is often of greater value to the one in need than the promises of money from a **rich liar** who fails to keep his promises.

The Christian who is right with God not only has assurance of eternal life, according to verse 23, but also is able to rest peacefully at night without fear (cf. 3:24; Ecclesiastes 5:12). Often, counselees suffer from the effects of sleep loss that is caused by the disruption of their relationship with God. Such a problem can be remedied only by dealing properly with the disruption.

The humor used to prod a **lazy person** here and elsewhere in Proverbs indicates that the way to handle his laziness is by shaming him into change (v. 24). Counselors should learn from this divine method. Here, the picture is clear, and because of its absurdity, makes the reader smile. Think of someone so lazy that when he goes to the table to eat, he **dips** his

25 Strike a scoffer and the naive will profit,
and reprove a discerning person and he will gain knowledge.
26 He who assaults his father and chases his mother away
is a son who causes shame and brings reproach.
27 My son, stop listening to discipline and you will wander from the ways
of knowledge.
28 A worthless witness scoffs at justice,
and the mouth of the wicked swallows down evil.
29 Penalties are ready for scorners
and blows for the backs of stubborn fools.

---

sop into the **bowl** but is too lazy to **bring** his hand **back** to his mouth to eat! There he sits, hand in bowl, unmoving.

The **scoffer** may not be moved by punishment but **naive** persons, observing it, will (v. 25). Thus, it is important to inflict punishment even on those who don't respond positively to it. It doesn't even take the punishment of another, however, to influence a **discerning person**; mere **reproof** is enough (cf. 17:10).

Verse 26 describes a pathetic scene in which an adult child shamefully **assaults his aged father** and drives his elderly **mother** away in order to take over their property. Akin to this today are legal moves to do the same thing. These may include such things as having them declared incompetent or incarcerating them without cause in a nursing home, etc. A son like this is the **cause of much shame** to them and himself and, when his nefarious ways are found out, he is **reproached** by society.

Verse 27 might be appended to verse 20 as a supplement. If one gives up on **discipline** (will receive it no more) he is sure to **wander from the ways** that lead to **knowledge**. He may be going well but, if he lets up on the pursuit of discipline, he will drift into that which he previously sought to avoid. Either keep rowing against the stream or you will drift with it. Counselors often see counselees in this condition. The answer is repentance, followed by a return to the **ways of knowledge** (that is, those that show one is acting sensibly and that lead, in turn, to further knowledge).

The observation of verse 28 says that a **worthless** person (a "witness of Belial") mocks the idea of rendering **justice**. For money, or for some other desired boon, he will perjure himself, **scoffing at justice**. Rather than feeding on God's Word (cf. Matthew 4:4) his diet consists of **evil** and wickedness.

The chapter closes with this warning: repent and change or else! God will judge with many stripes those who continue in foolishness or become **scorners**.

CHAPTER 20

1 Wine is a mocker; strong drink is noisy.
And each one who is under its influence isn't wise.
2 The fear of a king is like that which a lion's roar inspires;
he who stirs up his anger sins against himself.
3 For a man to cease striving is an honor,
but every stupid fool plunges himself headlong into it.
4 After autumn a lazy man won't plow;
he seeks at harvest but there is nothing for him.
5 Counsel in a man's heart is like deep water,
and a discerning man will draw it out.

Chapter 20 begins with a warning about the abuse of alcohol. By personifying the alcoholic drink, the writer describes the effects it has on the one who is **under its influence** (v. 1). He becomes **noisy** and **mocks** God or His followers—things he would never do otherwise. Drunkenness, therefore, is **not wise**. The flippant words and boisterous acts in which he indulges are due to the foolish act of anesthetizing the control center of his brain.

Compare verse 2 with 16:14 and 15. One should fear a ruler's authority as he fears the **roar** of a wild **lion**. How does he do that? He gets out of the way of the one as he would the other. Fools, however, do not do so. Instead, **by stirring up his anger**, they bring down wrath against themselves.

There is no shame in refusing to fight; as verse 3 says, **to cease striving is an honor**. It is only **stupid fools** who **plunge headlong** into trouble. Some counselees come simply aching for a quarrel—with you or with someone else. When you don't oblige them, they may scorn you. Don't let that bait you into a sinful response. Show them how honorable it can be to back away from quarrels by the grace with which you do so (cf. 15:1). Teach counselees to do the same.

Because it is cold during the winter when one should **plow** (in Palestine), a **lazy** person refuses. He'd rather take it easy in a warm house. All seems OK., but then comes the **harvest** when he looks for food; but because he failed to plow and plant, he has nothing. The verse (v. 4) stresses the importance of helping **lazy** persons plan ahead and work with forethought.

In addition to all that we have read about how people become wise and learn to **discern**, verse 5 depicts the wise man **drawing counsel out**

6 Many a man will proclaim his own lovingkindness,
but who can find a faithful man?
7 The righteous man walks in his integrity—
His sons after him are happy.
8 A king who sits on the throne of judgment
winnows all sorts of evil with his eyes.
9 Who can say, "I have cleansed my heart;
I am free from my sin?"

---

of others. Often, letting down a bucket into the well where wisdom lies **deep** in another's **heart** is the only way to obtain it. How does a counselor do so? By judicious questioning, after having developed a method for doing so (see *The Christian Counselor's Manual* for details). A counselee may learn to draw counsel out of another by the same methods, but usually only after he has become a true friend (cf. John 15:15).

Verse 6 highlights an all-to-obvious trait of sinners: they promise more than they deliver. They talk about all they plan to do, but they fail to follow through. The question with which the couplet ends indicates the sad fact that those are all too few that one can depend upon to come through as they said they would. Such undependability in counselees, then, should surprise no one—least of all a biblically-informed counselor. And as he ponders the problem, he discovers that he has a lot of work to do in rectifying the fact in counselees. The verse deals specifically with kindly deeds one promises to perform but never gets around to doing. I can think of those close to me who have acted this way; can't you recall instances in your own family when this has happened?

In answer to the question with which the previous verse concludes, verse 7 begins with these words, **the righteous man walks in his integrity**. *He* is dependable. That insures a happy life for his children who, if they learn to walk in his ways after him, will be added to the slim ranks of dependable persons in the community.

The wise **king winnows out all sorts of evil** from his kingdom by becoming aware of everything that is going on. He brings perpetrators of crime before **his throne of judgment** and metes out fair and impartial **judgment**. In any country where the government fails to screen out evil by judging and punishing wicked persons, that government is bound to fall (v. 8). That is why many of us fear for our land at the present time.

No man has the power to **cleanse his heart** so as to honestly claim, **I am free from my sin** (v. 9). Only Jesus Christ can do that for a sinner. And even He could not do so apart from going to the cross for His own so

10 Differing stone weights and differing ephah measures—
Yahweh detests them both!
11 Even a child makes himself known by his deeds—
whether his work is clean or upright.
12 The hearing ear and the seeing eye—
indeed, Yahweh has made them both.
13 Don't love sleep or you will be dispossessed;
keep your eyes open and you'll have bread to satisfy you.
14 "No good! No good!" says the buyer,
but when he leaves he boasts.

---

as to render satisfaction to God for their sin. Christ is the only answer to the question of how to free one's self from sin. The problem with pagan and eclectic counseling systems is precisely this: they try to deal with sin and its effects in some other way.

Verse 10 says that false **weights** and **measures** used to cheat customers are an **abomination to Yahweh. He detests both**! Show counselees, whose business practices may be questionable, that God is concerned about the matter. It is not an inconsequential matter to Him; God uses strong language (an **abomination** is something *detestable*) in describing the offense.

The way that any person (**even a child**) **makes known** to others what he is like is **by his deeds** (v. 11). How is that? By discerning **whether** what he does is **clean or upright**. This is done by observing his **deeds** toward others. Hypocrites may fool others for a while, but eventually their actions will betray them.

Verse 12 is difficult to interpret. That **Yahweh made both the hearing ear and the seeing eye** probably means that He made both for their intended purposes: to hear and to see. "Therefore, start using them for those purposes," may be the exhortation intended. There is no reason to think that one cannot obtain all the wisdom and knowledge available to him if he uses these instruments God's way to discern God's truth. Listen and learn; look and see.

Once more, in verse 13, laziness is associated with **sleep** (which he **loves**). But its consequences are loss of property and lack of food (**bread**). (Cf. v. 14.) By staying awake (**keeping the eyes open**) one can solve the problems. He must not indulge himself by yielding to the temptation to **sleep** when he ought to be awake and working.

Verse 14 is but an observation: you cannot believe a person when he haggles. He'll tell you that the item he wants is **no good** (not worth the

15 There is gold and many gems,
but lips of knowledge are a rare vase.
16 Take his garment from one when he becomes surety for an alien,
and take a pledge from him when he gives a guarantee for strangers.
17 Bread gained by deceit tastes sweet to a man,
but afterwards his mouth will be filled with gravel.
18 Plans are laid by means of counsel;
so make war with wise guidance.

---

asking price, which itself is probably too high), but when he buys it at a much lower figure, he then **boasts** to all and sundry what a great bargain he got.

Once more, in verse 15, Solomon compares the ability to communicate (signified by the **lips**) **knowledge** to others with the most expensive products, **gold and gems** aplenty. He finds this ability more valuable than these. Indeed, he says, it is like a **rare vase** (Ming dynasty?). A good preacher or counselor should take note of God's opinion of his ministry. The world may pay huge sums to entertainers and sportsmen and little to those who minister God's Word, but God has a different set of values.

Verse 16 does not present a new thought. **Suretyship** for an **alien**, **pledging** one's **guarantee** for a **stranger**, is like taking all one has from him (the **garment** was the last item a person could retain; cf. Exodus 22:26, 27). Again, this is a warning to heed (see 6:1ff. and comments on those verses).

Sweet in the mouth, but afterwards upsetting to the stomach; that is what food (**bread**) obtained in a **deceitful** way is like (v. 17). Afterwards, when the deceit is detected and the deceiver must face the music, the food that once tasted **so sweet** is now like **gravel filling his mouth**. Help counselees think of future consequences of present actions. It might be well to have those who are prone to precipitously plunge ahead without considering the future ramifications of their actions write out for you at least five possible consequences of taking the action. Doing this will begin to get them thinking seriously about the matter and will give you an opportunity to discuss the issue with them after some consideration on their part (perhaps for the first time).

Plans for **war** ought not be **laid** apart from wise **counsel** and **guidance** (v. 18). Better not to make war if you can't be sure of the outcome beforehand. What is true of making war may be true for the individual going to law against another, etc.

19 One who walks about as a gossip reveals secrets;
so don't associate with him who opens wide his lips.
20 When one curses his father or mother
his lamp will be put out in blackest darkness.
21 An inheritance may be gotten hastily in the beginning
but in the end does not lead to happiness.
22 Don't say, "I will repay evil."
Wait for Yahweh and He will deliver you.
23 Yahweh hates differing stone weights,
and false balances are not good.
24 If a mighty man's steps are from Yahweh
then what can a weak man discern about his way?
25 It is a trap for a man to say rashly, "This is holy,"
and then, after he vows, to reconsider it.

Here is another verse on gossip (v. 19; see also 16:28). There, Solomon speaks of how slander spreads. Here, the counselee is told how to avoid it: by refusing to **associate** with those **who open wide their lips to reveal secrets** that they have no right to speak about. Advise counselees accordingly.

To **put out** one's lamp when he finds himself in **blackest darkness** refers to the ultimate in punishment (hell) which is the dessert of him who **curses his father and mother** (v. 20). He will remain in darkness forever.

The quickly gained fortune rarely blesses; indeed, in the long run, it leads only to **unhappiness** (v. 21).

Verse 22 echoes 17:13 and is related to Romans 12:17 through 21.

Verse 23 contains no new data (see v. 10).

There is in verse 24 an extension of that which is found in previous passages. It is clear that it is not merely *some* whose **steps** are ordered by **Yahweh**; it is true of all alike. Thus, for some common, ordinary person to think that he is exempt from God's providence, when prominent persons are not, is the height of arrogance and foolhardiness. The contrast in the verse is between two words for **man**: the mighty hero and the common man (cf. 21:1).

Verse 25 refers to the custom of declaring something "devoted" to God (or "holy"). It is a warning against **rash vows**. Once made, any legitimate vow must be kept. The idea of rash vows means no Christian may join a secret society. He should not vow to conceal (which is the price of admission) something before knowledge of what it is that he is concealing. Perhaps it ought to be revealed! Consideration of any vow (or promise) ought to be given *before* making it; not afterwards (but contrast 6:1-5).

26 A wise king winnows out wicked persons
and drives the threshing wheel over them.
27 The spirit of man is Yahweh's lamp
searching all the inner paths of his being.
28 Mercy and truth preserve a king,
and his throne is upheld by mercy.
29 The glory of youth is their vigor,
and the honor of the elderly is the gray head.
30 The stripes of a wound cleanse away evil
and strokes, the inward parts of the heart.

The thrust of verse 26 is to show how the **winnowing** process mentioned in verse 8 ought to proceed. Society should be cleansed of crooked and criminal persons. The figure of punishment (**driving the threshing wheel over them**) accords with and grows out of the notion of **winnowing**.

It is the conscience to which Solomon here refers as the **lamp of Yahweh** which goes down into the inner parts of a man, searching out the thoughts and the intents of the heart (v. 27). It is instructive to note that God calls it His lamp; that is to say, one He has designed and uses to bring people to conviction of sin and repentance. Appeal to it; God uses it!

The two qualities mentioned in verse 28 **preserve a king's** reign because, by them, he receives favor from God and from men. The same is true of all who are in places of authority. Just about all that is said about kings in the Book of Proverbs applies equally to such lesser authorities.

What is significant about a **youth** is the **vigor** and strength he has (v. 29). What is good about age is the wisdom and knowledge that the **gray head** symbolizes. These are what give **glory and honor** to each. When a youth will not use his strength to serve and please God, or when the **elderly** wastes his years, learning and imparting little to others for the sake of Christ's kingdom, there is no glory or honor.

Obviously the **stripes** from a whip don't physically **cleanse evil**. The meaning is that punishment helps to prevent it. And **strokes**, in and of themselves, can do nothing to change the inner life of a person. But, because they pose a threat to sinful action, they do curtail it! Our society has failed to appreciate the fact. Parents and society must be reeducated so as to overcome the sickly psychological dictums that now pervade thinking in the West.

Chapter 21

1 The king's heart is like streams of waters in Yahweh's hands;
He directs it as He pleases.
2 Every way of a man is right in his own eyes,
but Yahweh weighs hearts.
3 To practice righteousness and justice for Yahweh
is to be chosen above sacrifice.

Not only does **Yahweh** direct a **mighty man's steps** (20:24), but He directs **the king's heart** as well (v. 1). The irrigation ditches that watered the fields were designed so that water could be turned in any direction the farmer wished. God's sovereign working of all things—even the decrees and actions of kings—is like that. The ditches, made of mud and dirt, were opened or closed by the farmer as he walked along by pushing a pile of dirt aside or by making a hole with his foot. God is in charge. As the Great Farmer, He easily, naturally, conducts the affairs of nations by **directing the hearts of kings**. The **way** in which God providentially works, then, is not through coercion, pressure or driving people against their wills (or heart-desire), but by means of *influencing the heart* from within.

Verse 2 is very close to 16:2 (q.v.). Men are ready to excuse or commend themselves. The only true scales that give accurate weight regarding a person's life are God's. And what He **weighs**, is not the whole man, but the **heart**. That is what truly defines a person; not what he seems to be, but that which only God can see—what he really is in the inner person. Counselors do not have to make a final, heart judgment about counselees; indeed, they dare not do so since they cannot weigh the heart. They help, and do the best that they can, and leave the weighing of the heart to God. They can warn counselees who are prone to boasting and self-righteousness that, as the verse implies, their judgment of themselves is likely to be biased and faulty. That is one reason it is wise to seek counsel from one who is honest and frank: he may be the only one who will give a candid opinion (though not final judgment) of how one comes across to others.

The importance of the genuine living out of one's faith over against mere ritualistic concerns is emphasized in verse 3. This verse is good to remember when confronted with formalism in a counselee. Contrast the previous verse—there, the importance of the heart is set forth; sacrifice

4 Haughty eyes and a proud heart
and the ploughing of the wicked are sin.
5 Plans of the diligent lead only to plenty,
but those of every hasty person lead only to poverty.
6 Treasures obtained by a lying tongue
are a breath expelled by those seeking death.

---

and ritual are not what cuts it. Here, it is the outer working of the inner reality that is in view.

In verse 4 pride is associated, but not equated, with the **ploughing of the wicked**. What does that mean? Well, two items (**haughty eyes and a proud heart**) that are plainly sin are said to be like the wicked going about doing his daily chores (ploughing, planting and reaping as if God were not involved in the process). The godless person is proud of his seeming self-sufficiency. Like all proud persons, he lives daily as if God were not in the picture. He acts as if his crops were merely the product of his own doing. Is God here speaking of a wicked farmer ploughing? Well, yes and no. Yes, the principle embedded in the proverb is attached to the seemingly (but not actually) innocent task of ploughing. But the principle is larger: it applies as well to all one does without thought of God. Seemingly industrious persons who, otherwise, might be commended for their efforts, *cannot* be since in all they do they leave God out. Many counselees, while professing to be Christians, live as if God has no more part in their lives and problems than they give Him by their occasional attendance at church on Sunday. God hates attempts at autonomy; He wants to be given His rightful place in our lives.

Diligent persons *of faith* (v. 5) are not like the man mentioned in the previous proverb. They make **plans** not only *carefully*, but also *prayerfully*! They take the time to think through issues, to study Scripture related to the enterprise and to make decisions that they believe will please God. As a result, their plans come to fruition. **Hasty** people, on the other hand, jump into something without due consideration of the matter involved or thought about God's relationship to it. Consequently, they may expect **poverty** rather than plenty.

Verse 6 speaks of **treasures obtained by a lying tongue**. They are, at the end of the day, no more than a **breath expelled**. That is, by comparison to the *eternal* **death** they **seek** (unwittingly), the enjoyment of these treasures is nothing but a breath because it is so temporary. A breath takes but a second to expel, and it is gone. As the air is driven away, and imme-

7 The violence of wicked people drags them away
because they refuse to do what is right.
8 The way of a guilty man is perverted,
but the work of the pure is right.
9 Better to dwell on the corner of a roof
than to share a house with a quarrelsome woman.
10 A wicked person craves evil;
his neighbor finds no favor in his eyes.

---

diately disappears, so too will the treasures they have obtained. The brief enjoyment of such ill-gotten gain cannot be compared to an eternity of suffering in hell.

Because **they refuse** to repent and change (v. 7), the very same **violence** that **wicked people** inflict on others in time **drags them away** (usually in a body bag!). The message? You can't get away with it. Tell your counselee this in no uncertain terms. Whoever lives by violence will fall by violence. Here is a strong warning for counselees to whom it is appropriate. Because of the violence on TV and in the movies, in counseling, you are likely to encounter more and more violent people.

Verse 8 teaches that unforgiven guilt drives men to do **perverted** (twisted) things. The behavior of such a person is erratic and may tend toward fruitless ways of removing guilt. Counselees who are not on drugs or who do not suffer from significant sleep loss, may very well be involved in bizarre behavior either to throw others off their track (not wanting their sin to be revealed and their guilt exposed) or in vain attempts to rid themselves of that guilt. People adopt many fruitless and weird ways of seeking to atone for sin. They need to hear of God's one way to do so: the only way that brings peace and happiness through His Son.

Verses 9 and 19 are akin. You'd be **better** off with less, in a sparse setting than with plenty and a **quarrelsome**, angry **wife**. No comment, beyond pointing this out to such a woman in counseling, is necessary. There is no need to tell her husband about it!

Because the **wicked person craves evil** (that is, has an appetite for it; enjoys and seeks it), even those who (otherwise) would be his closest friends and associates **find no favor in his eyes** if they do not join in with him (cf. v. 10; I Peter 4:4). As a matter of fact, they may become the very ones toward whom he directs his wickedness. As a counselor, your wisdom and rectitude will not impress such persons; indeed, it is more likely to repel them.

11 When a scorner is punished a naive person gains wisdom,
and when a wise person is instructed he receives knowledge.
12 The Righteous One rightly considers the house of the wicked;
He overthrows a wicked person for his evil.
13 Whoever shuts his ear when the poor cry for help
will himself also call and not be heard.
14 A gift given secretly subdues anger,
and a bribe in the cloak calms strong wrath.
15 It is a joy to a righteous person to do justice,
but ruin comes to those who work at evil.
16 A man who wanders from the way of prudence
will rest in the congregation of the dead.

For verse 11 see comments on 19:25.

In verse 12, the **Righteous One** is Yahweh. In strictest justice and fairness, He evaluates the wicked ways of a **wicked person** and his family **(house)** and judges him accordingly. If God gives consideration to the family of wicked persons, surely your counselee ought to do so too. And if he considers carefully, he will see not only the sin, but also the misery it brings—along with the judgment of God when it finally falls.

James agrees with the idea set forth in verse 13 (cf. James 2:13). The warning is quite clear and concrete. A counselee who is all wrapped up in himself and in his own problems will probably fail to hear the cry of a **poor** person. Another may be the one to whose cry God has **shut His ear** as punishment for having done so to others in the past. In either case, repentance for self-centeredness must precede and lead to a new lifestyle of caring.

Verse 14 contains an observation—not a recommendation. When a **bribe** is given (and received) in full view of others, it is nowhere nearly as effective as if it were given **secretly**. If some, who you expect would be **angered** over a transgression, appear placid and accepting, it is possible that they have been **secretly bribed**. That would explain the otherwise inexplicable lack of **wrath** on their part.

According to verse 15, the blessing is in the *doing* of **justice** (cf. James 1:25), whereas **ruin comes to those who** make an effort to do **evil**. A miserable counselee, whose life is in shambles, may be suffering the results of his own efforts—at wrongdoing. How tragic to work hard at bringing ruin to one's self! There is no lasting **joy** in doing evil, though sin does yield temporary **pleasure** (cf. Hebrews 11:25). If it were not so,

17 A man who loves pleasure will be poor;
he who loves wine and oil will not be rich.
18 The wicked will be a ransom for the just
and the treacherous in place of the upright.
19 It is better to live in a desolate land
than with a quarrelsome and angry woman.
20 A desirable treasure remains in a wise person's home,
but a stubborn fool consumes it.
21 He who pursues righteousness and mercy
finds life, righteousness and honor.
22 A wise person scales the city wall of the mighty
and tears down the stronghold in which they trust.

---

few would choose sin. But it is the long-term effects with which one must be concerned.

Once more, in verse 16, we are told that those who **wander from the way of prudence** will die. In one form or another, this sort of warning occurs throughout the Book of Proverbs. Ought we to give similar warning today? Definitely. In our day of increasing violence, where every night the TV news announces a homicide or two, it is appropriate for many (see also v. 7).

Verse 17 is a reiteration of another theme common to Proverbs: the lazy and **pleasure loving** lifestyle leads to poverty. Certainly, this observation ought to be sounded from the rooftops—or, at least, loudly and frequently in the counseling room and in the pulpit.

The meaning of verse 18 is not immediately plain. The idea seems to be exemplified in the story of Mordecai and Haman, where one takes the place of the other, so that the **wicked, treacherous** person, thereby, **ransoms the just**. He pays the penalty rather than the other. Though this death, of course, is not vicarious; rather, it is deserved.

Verse 19: see verse 9, etc.

Wise persons use sparingly **desirable** (valuable) goods; **fools consume them** (v. 20). They live for the present and afterwards regret it when there is nothing left *but* regrets. This proverb is pertinent to many spendthrift and pleasure loving counselees who sell the day to buy the hour. (See also v. 17.)

Verse 21 is not a new thought. Rather, it is a summary of truths that Solomon has been teaching all along.

Probably in II Corinthians 10:4 Paul alludes to verse 22. Surely, in war, **wisdom** has its place. As one does so in war, so also should he do in

23 He who guards his mouth and his tongue
keeps himself from troubles.
24 "Proud, haughty scoffer" is his name;
he deals in arrogant pride.
25 The desire of the lazy person kills him
since his hands have refused to work.
26 All day long he greedily desires,
but the righteous gives and doesn't withhold.

---

all of life's battles (II Corinthians 10:4 deals with the battle for the mind; capturing men's thoughts for Christ). A wise person knows how to win battles. Physical strength, political clout, superior forces—all these have given way before the wise plans and endeavors of persons with right ideas. Counselees, without other resources, may win battles by becoming wise. There is hope in this verse for those facing obstacles that, at first, seem impregnable.

Again in verse 23, the power of speech in creating problems for one's self is noted. We all know that we say things that get us into **trouble**, but what can be done about it? The key here seems to be to **guard the mouth** and **tongue**. How? First, by thinking before speaking. Then, by not speaking a word you know to be untrue, uncertain, unfair, unkind or unnecessary. These five guidelines might be printed out on a sheet and given to a counselee to carry with him. You might also use the sheet to have him fill in Failures that fit each category. In doing so, not only may he repent of and correct them, but he may learn to **guard** against words of the sort in the future. A guard allows only those who are authorized, to enter a place. In much the same way, the guarding of the **lips** means allowing only that which is divinely authorized to pass through them.

The **scoffer** (*les*) is described in verse 24: he gets a **name** for being **proud**. He is not merely proud; he is **arrogantly** so—he flaunts himself. He is an insufferable companion, one who is always in your face. He has no shame, lacks all decorum.

Verse 25 tells us that the **desire of the lazy person kills him**. What does he **desire**? To be free of work, to be undisturbed, to lounge about, able to shirk all responsibilities. Ever meet anyone like that? Since **he refuses to work**, he will starve from lack of food (cf. II Thessalonians 3:10). Or he will come to ruin from some other result of his sloth.

Verse 26 is a continuation of verse 25. Hunger and lack of other necessities which he **greedily desires** (a play on the previous use of the word **desire**), stalks the lazy person. **All day long** he is plagued by the

27 The sacrifice of the wicked is detestable.
How much more when he brings it with evil intent!
28 A false witness will be cut off,
but the man who listens will go on speaking indefinitely.
29 A wicked person hardens his face,
but an upright person establishes his way.
30 There is no wisdom and there is no discernment
and no counsel that can avail against Yahweh.
31 The horse is made ready for the day of battle
but to Yahweh belongs deliverance.

---

problem. What he wants eludes him. The **righteous** person, in contrast, works diligently, has enough of his own that he is able to **give** to those who are truly in need. And he does so.

Because the **wicked** formally tips his hat to God in a **sacrifice**, he is **detestable** to Him (v. 27). He doesn't mean it. What he offers, therefore, he offers hypocritically. But when he has some ulterior motive for making the offering, that makes his **sacrifice** all the more abominable in God's eyes. Counselees who *use* religion for their own nefarious ends must be informed about God's judgment on them that stems from their **intent**.

When the **falsity** of his testimony is discovered, the lying **witness** is **cut off** (people no longer listen to one who perjures himself—indeed, they may execute him, cutting him off for good!). But **the man who listens** to the facts, and therefore, has truth to tell, will be heard to the very end of his testimony. No one will cut him off!

In verse 29, two persons—opposite in every other particular—are both *firm*. The wicked impudently **hardens his face**. He will not change. He is stubborn and immovable. **Upright persons** also are firm in their righteous lifestyle. They do not waver; temptation does not draw them away from God. The one is a hardened person; the other is a stable one. Help teach counselees the difference.

The wicked may try, but nothing they label **wisdom, discernment or counsel** (wrongly) can avail against **Yahweh** (v. 30). This can be seen in pagan counseling which constantly fails and biblical counseling which growingly is expanding and taking hold.

In a similar vein, verse 31 makes it clear that God always wins His battles. The side that God blesses will win the war, even without superior arms and troops. This is true of all of life's battles. Those who love and serve God, while preparing militarily, must also prepare spiritually.

CHAPTER 22

1 Choose a good name above great riches;
favor is better than silver or gold.
2 Rich and poor people meet together on one thing:
Yahweh is the Maker of them all.
3 A sensible person sees evil and lies low,
but naive persons continue on and suffer for it.
4 The result of humility and the fear of Yahweh
is riches, honor and life.

What Solomon has in mind in verse 1 when he speaks of a **good name** is not fame; nor does he mean that the one who possesses it is well liked generally. A person may be liked (or not) for widely differing reasons. What he has in mind is a good name before God and before His discerning people. Its value here—and certainly hereafter—is **above** wealth. **Favor** with those who love God is **better than silver and gold**. Many counselees are concerned about their reputations before unbelievers (this has been true particularly of academicians, counselors being not the least of these). Help your counselees to focus on a good name before God and His people. While there is a sense in which a believer's reputation before the world should be good (for the right reasons), he must also remember that Jesus said the world would **hate** him (for his faith and good lifestyle). Many counselees need to get these matters straight.

Verse 2 affirms the fact that **rich and poor** alike were made by **Yahweh**, and must some day answer to Him. Differences in wealth or station in life are of no significance to Him. He sees the true riches (or poverty) of heart. A counselee may fool a counselor about his intentions; but he cannot deceive God.

Verse 3 tells you one way to distinguish between the **sensible** and the **naive** person. The first **sees evil** (trouble) and avoids it. That is to say, he has the **sense** to recognize it and to get out of its way. There is no premium on suffering in Christianity (unless it is *necessary* suffering for the sake of Christ). Some have the mistaken idea that all suffering is laudatory. According to this verse, that is a senseless idea! Make this known. The definition of a **naive** person is that he either sees trouble coming and does not avoid it or that he is so dense he doesn't see it until it is upon him. Either way, he will plunge ahead into trouble after trouble. You meet

5 Thorns and traps are along the way of the perverse;
he who guards himself will be far from them.
6 Train a young official after the manner of his task;
even when he is old he will not turn aside from it.
7 The rich rules the poor,
and the borrower is a slave to the lender.
8 He who sows injustice will reap evil,
and the rod of his wrath will fail.

---

quite a few of these sorts of persons in counseling. They need to be taught the truth of this verse.

The fourth verse is but a summary statement of the effects of righteous living (cf. 21:21).

The crooked (**perverse**) person's way is perilous: there are **thorns and traps** all along it (v. 5). But these should make him stop, think and ask why? They should be like barriers, posted to warn him of even more severe conditions up ahead. They should drive him to investigate why he is there and what he should do to change direction. Any such investigation, correctly conducted, would lead him to repentance and faith. The person who does come to faith is able to **guard himself** and remains **far from** those **traps**. You have a wonderful hope to hold before counselees who have come bleeding and torn from trap and thorn encountered on the way of the perverse.

Verse 6 should not lay a burden on the backs of parents whose children go astray. That is not the point of the passage. In a study by Ted Hildebrandt, it seems possible that the verse speaks of the training of a young official (see *Grace Theological Journal*, 9:1 (1988), pp. 3-9). The **manner of his task** means the way he should conduct himself in his office. In F. W. Farrar's *Seekers after God*, he notes the failure of Seneca's tutorship of Nero, and attributes many of his later vices to that failure. Then, he makes the valuable observation that "an education founded on compromise must always necessarily fail" (p. 119). It is that sort of sentiment that is uppermost in the thinking of the writer. Of course, even if this is correct, the verse still holds implications for parental training.

An observation in verse 7 still holds true: the **rich** and the **lender** call the shots in many circles. Those who must depend on them because they are **poor** or because they are in their debt are, to the extent of that dependence, their **slaves**.

The concept of **sowing** and **reaping**, often worked out in the Scriptures to teach God's ways with men, is here invoked to speak of how

9 He who has a generous outlook is happy
because he gives of his bread to the poor.
10 Throw out the scorner and strife will cease;
quarrels and abuse will come to an end.
11 Where there is grace on the lips of the one who loves purity of heart
the king will be his friend.
12 Yahweh's eyes keep watch over knowledge,
and He overthrows the words of the treacherous.

---

injustice sown reaps **trouble**. The **rod of his wrath** (his ability to impose his anger on others) **will fail** (come to an end). This is a warning to the one **sowing injustice** and venting **his wrath** on others. At the same time, the verse holds out hope for the oppressed (v. 8).

The **joy** of **giving** is stressed in verse 9. In the New Testament, we also read "It is more blessed to give than to receive." The **generous outlook** is, literally, "a good eye" (a Hebraic idiom). The idea is of an eye which sees the plight of others and, in compassion, does something to alleviate it. Happiness may (at least in part) elude some counselees because of their failure in this regard.

Verse 10 and Titus 3:10 teach the same principle: church discipline is essential to the unity and the harmony of any congregation. Scorners are cynical about everything. As a result, they keep something going continually. If you want to preserve a congregation whole, and avoid splits, then see to it that a **scorner** (schismatic person), if unrepentant, is put out of the body. Part of counseling is sometimes to make such recommendations.

The winning combination is for one to have both **purity of heart** and **grace on the lips** (v. 11). As always, no one has fully lived up to this ideal but Jesus Christ. But it certainly is the goal that we should hold before us and to which we should seek to attain. **Purity of heart** speaks of the genuineness of the person (he is not a hypocrite; he sincerely seeks to live for God); **grace on the lips** means that he can express himself well (clearly, non-threateningly, etc.). Those who appropriate this ideal to some noticeable extent will attract persons of influence (here, **the king**).

Yahweh is pictured as actively concerned with His creation and with men throughout the Proverbs as, indeed, He is here (v. 12). Solomon was no deist. God is said to **keep watch over** those who possess His **knowledge**. That is an important fact for beleaguered biblical counselors and counselees to know. And for those who speak against them, and whose **words** are treacherous, He promises nothing but ruin. God's truth and His church will prevail.

13 A lazy person says, "There is a lion outside!
I'll be killed in the streets."
14 The mouth of an alien woman is a deep pit;
those Yahweh despises will fall into it.
15 Foolishness is bound up in the heart of a youth;
the rod of discipline will drive it far from him.
16 He who opposes the poor to increase his wealth
and he who gives to the rich for this end will come to poverty.

Lazy persons use **absurd excuses** to avoid work (v. 13). "You certainly wouldn't expect me to go to work under these conditions (with a lion roaming the streets) would you?" Humor, once more, seems to be the method of choice in the Bible to shame the lazy into action.

The prostitute (**alien woman**) is like a **deep pit** from which one who **despises** God will not be able to extricate himself (v. 14). Prostitution, therefore, is judged to be a trap into which many of the wicked **will fall**. When you encounter those who have been caught in this trap, you may find that this verse will bring them to their senses. Use it freely in such instances. Part of the trap today, however, is the possible lethal character of the diseases associated with prostitution. It is dangerous to despise God; He can use the very vices one enjoys to destroy them!

The doctrine of original sin is taught in verse 15. The bent of the **heart** is in the wrong direction. Corporal punishment, as the means of discipline, is recommended as the way to discipline so as to curtail such behavior as a wicked, unregenerate **heart** produces. See other verses that concur with this sentiment.

Similar statements as that found in verse 16 are found throughout the Proverbs. The person in question here is Robin Hood—in reverse! He plunders the **rich** who allow him freedom to fleece the **poor**.

Part Three: Chapters 22:17-24:22

17 Bow down your ear and listen to the words of the wise,
and apply your heart to my knowledge
18 since it will be pleasant if you keep them within you,
and if all of them are on your lips ready to use.
19 That you may trust Yahweh
I have caused you—even you—to know them today.
20 Have I not written excellent sayings for you,
that include counsels and knowledge,
21 to enable you to know the correctness of the words of truth
that you may respond with words of truth to those who question you.

In this section we encounter the **words of the wise**. These, presumably, are the words of others besides Solomon whose proverbs contribute to the whole. One of the characteristics of these proverbs is the negative form in which so many of them are cast ("Don't...").

In verse 17 the reader is invited (or commanded) to humbly (the words used are **bow down** in order to) listen to their words. Having heard, the reader is to **apply his heart** to what the writer has written. That is to say, he is to consider how to put them to work in his life. Verse 18 continues: to **learn** and carry them within is what leads to pleasant living. Proverbs is portable truth, compressed into aphoristic form for ready use. One must have them **ready on his lips** for use in any situation that may arise. The expression is akin to our "on the tip of my tongue."

Verse 19 indicates that the use of proverbs also strengthens faith. One way to foster faith among counselees is to encourage the reading of and meditation on a chapter each day for a month, four months out of a year.

Verse 20 does not refer to "thirty sayings," as some suppose; rather, it speaks of **excellent sayings** (see the Introduction for reasons for this conclusion). The object of this third part of the Book of Proverbs is to establish principles of truth and wisdom in the reader's mind and heart so that (v. 21) he might know that these things are certain and **correct** in order to **respond** properly to those scorners (and others) who might question him (cf. I Peter 3:15).

When you teach a counselee to use a proverb, teach him **how** to use it as well (cf. vv. 19-21):

1. Teach him to internalize it for portable use;
2. Teach him to understand its exact meaning;
3. Teach him to go over it from time to time so that he will not lose it;

22 Don't rob the poor because he is poor,
and don't crush the afflicted in the gate
23 because Yahweh will plead his case
and will plunder the life of those who plunder them.
24 Don't associate with a hot-tempered man
or enter into conversation with an angry man
25 so that you won't learn his ways by association
and get yourself caught in a trap.
26 Don't be one of those who strikes the palm,
who becomes surety for loans.
27 If you can't pay
why should he take your bed from under you?

---

4. Teach him to use it to help others by it;
5. Teach him to use it to meet objections.

The actual words of the wise men who wrote begin with verse 22, a verse that is coupled with verse 23. In it there is a command to which is affixed a reason. It begins by telling the reader that he must never take advantage of the **poor** because he doesn't have the means to retaliate. He must not **crush the afflicted in the gate** (the city hall and courthouse where the elders sat in judgment; cf. 31:23. The city gates were meeting rooms, not mere doors swinging on hinges.). Why? What is the reason? Simply this: **Yahweh** will defend the poor (cf. 23:10, 11) and will do to those who take advantage of them what they have done to the poor (**plunder** them).

The problem of making poor **associations** is highlighted in verses 24 and 25 (cf. 13:20; 14:7; I Corinthians 15:33). The "with Him" method of learning, espoused by Jesus (Mark 3:14; Luke 6:40), works with learning either truth or falsehood, righteousness or wickedness. That is why **associations** are of such importance. Here the association to be avoided is with a **hot-tempered** or **angry man**. The danger is in **learning his ways** and thus **getting caught** in the **traps** laid for such individuals.

Verses 26 and 27, once again, warn against becoming **surety** for others. When all else was gone one's **bed** (usually a cloak) was the last item that remained. So, to take the **bed from under** one is to take *everything* from him (cf. 6:1-5; 11:15; esp., 20:16). That is surely a strong warning.

Verse 28 accords with the mosaic laws (see Deuteronomy 19:14; 27:17; but also Proverbs 23:10). This was not only theft; it was a sacrilege to move the landmark. Because an unscrupulous farmer could easily do so (little by little each year, for instance) the punishment was severe.

28 Don't remove the long-standing boundary marker
that your fathers set up.
29 Do you see a man who is skilled at his work?
He will stand before kings;
he won't stand before unknown persons.

The promise with which this chapter ends is designed to motivate the reader to excellence (v. 29). The **skilled** man is exemplified by Ezra the scribe, who is described by the same Hebrew word that is used here (*mahir*)—see Ezra 7:6 (Ezra became such by determination, practice and teaching). The **skilled** (lit., "quick") person will rise to prominence (**stand before kings**) exerting significant influence. And he will **not stand before unknown** (lit., "obscure") **persons**. Every counselor must make excellence at **his work** (not preeminence; God takes care of that) his goal. But it is clear from this passage that God not only expects skilled work from His people (in whatever they do) but that He also rewards it. A great conclusion to a very interesting section of the Book of Proverbs that we are scarcely beginning to explore.

CHAPTER 23

1 When you sit down to eat with a ruler
consider carefully what is before you
2 and put a knife to your throat
if you have a hearty appetite.
3 Don't desire his delicacies
since they are deceitful food.
4 Don't labor to be rich;
have the discernment to stop.
5 When your eyes light on wealth it is gone.
Surely, like an eagle, it will grow wings
and fly into the heavens.
6 Don't eat a stingy man's food,
and don't desire his delicacies,

The first three verses of this chapter go together. This is not a passage primarily dealing with gluttony (though secondarily it may be used for the purpose of condemning it). The major idea here is that the king is testing his guests. It is a word of caution—especially for those with a **hearty appetite** who are entertained by a superior. The lavish meal is a means for learning about the guests invited. The king wines and dines in order to test one's manners and self-restraint—perhaps before accepting someone into his service. The phrase **deceitful food** is the key: more is at stake here than at first meets the eye (or should I say mouth?). That is why one must **consider carefully what is before** him. Meals are used for the same purpose today. The admonitions, therefore, are still apropos. Another thought is that the host may wish to pry some information out of you. Counselees seeking work, for instance, might be warned about invitations for a job that involve a dinner interview. Another table issue will be taken into consideration in verses 6 through 8 (below).

Verses 4 and 5 accord with I Timothy 6 and many other passages in Proverbs. Wealth is a foolish, sinful goal to pursue, since "money flies" (v. 5). A discerning person knows when he has enough. (Cf. 8:21; 10:2, 4, 22; 11:4, 25; 12:27; 13:11; 14:24; 15:6, 27; 16:8; 20:21; 21:6; 28:6, 8, 11, 22 and especially, 30:8, 9.)

The next unit consists of verses 6 through 8. Verse 7 has been misused by many who carelessly assumed that the KJV rendering set forth a philosophy of life. The context (vv. 6, 8)—and there is one, please note—

7 since he is really what he thinks in himself.
Though he says to you, "Eat, drink,"
his heart isn't with you.
8 The bit you have eaten you will vomit up
and lose your compliments.
9 Don't speak in the ears of a stubborn fool
or he will despise the good sense of your words.
10 Don't move the long-standing boundary marker,
and don't enter the fields of the fatherless,
11 since their Redeemer is formidable;
He will take up their cause against you.

---

makes it clear that the teaching is to not necessarily believe a host who urges more food on you. He is thinking (literally, "counting up") in his mind how much you have eaten. His **heart** (real intention) is **not with you** (he says one thing but thinks another). When you find out—too late—you will feel like **vomiting up** what you have eaten and taking back the **compliments** you wasted on him for his generosity. Why would one urge food when he doesn't mean it? To test you (see verses above) or because he thinks it is the polite thing to do, so that he does so insincerely.

Verse 9 is the Old Testament version of Matthew 7 in which Jesus exhorts us not to cast pearls before pigs. Some counselees do not warrant continued counseling. Why should you waste your time and effort speaking **words** to someone who only **despises** your **good sense**? Learn when enough is enough. All good counselors from time to time find it necessary, however reluctantly, to dismiss certain persons because of this problem. It is right to do so; your time might be more wisely used to help someone who would appreciate and benefit from your counsel.

Verses 10 and 11 are akin to 22:28. Here **Yahweh** sets Himself on the side of the weak (**fatherless**) as their formidable **Redeemer**. When He **takes up their cause against** the would-be thief, the latter doesn't stand a chance. Counselors must warn those who attempt to steal from others by similar practices that they can't win when they go up against God!

The next unit is verses 12 through 14. This unit has to do with family **discipline**. It is almost as if he were speaking of **bringing in** an automobile for inspection (or check up) when the writer says, **Bring in your heart for discipline**. The idea is don't come without a heart set for discipline. If one's heart does not check out, all else he does will be useless. The **words** of verse 12 are important to stress: corporal punishment (cf., vv. 13, 14; also 13:24; 19:18; 22:15; 29:15, 17) is not to be given without

12 Bring in your heart for discipline
and your ears for knowledgeable words.
13 Don't withhold discipline from a boy;
if you strike him with a rod, he won't die.
14 Beat him with a rod
and you will deliver him from Sheol.
15 My son, if your heart is wise
my heart will be glad.
16 And I will rejoice within
when your lips speak rightly.
17 Don't allow your heart to envy sinners,
but only fear Yahweh all the day long
18 since surely there is a future
and your hope will not be cut off.
19 My son, listen and be wise,
and guide your heart along the way.

---

appropriate counsel (cf. Ephesians 6:4: ". . . and counsel"). Rather than killing him, proper physical discipline will keep one's child from death (vv. 13, 14). This biblical truth is not widely accepted today; consequently, many wayward youth come to an early, untimely death.

The next two verses (15, 16) speak of the joy from a child who accepts discipline and grows **wise**. Nothing **gladdens** the **heart** of his parent more than this. And when he hears him say all the **right** things from his heart, he **rejoices within**. There is a place for such an appeal in counseling as well.

A discussion of **envy** follows. Persons here called **sinners** are un*repentant*, un*saved* sinners whose lot seems inconsistent with their lifestyles. Why has not God judged them? How have they been able to prosper beyond others? This is the same problem that David faced and wrote about in a number of places, notably in Psalm 37. The writer here directs the reader to continue to **fear Yahweh**, remembering all that an unbeliever has is what he has now. The believer has eternal life and all that means. So the thing to do when **envy** wells up (as it does in many counselors, not to speak of counselees!) is to think about what God has promised you for the future (cf. I Peter 1:3-5). This **hope** is sure; it will not be terminated (**cut off**).

The **subject of drunkenness** in verses 20 and 21 will be supplemented by the longer discourse in verses 29 through 35. Here, the matters of **drunkenness** and **gluttony** are viewed from the angle of associations.

20 Don't spend time among heavy wine drinkers
or with gluttonous meat eaters
21 since the drunkard and the glutton grow poor,
and sleepiness clothes one with rags.
22 Hear your father who conceived you,
and don't despise your mother when she is old.
23 Buy truth, and don't sell it;
also wisdom, discipline and discernment.
24 The father of righteous sons will rejoice,
and the father of a wise one will delight in him.
25 May your father and mother be glad,
and may the one who bore you rejoice.
26 My son, give me your heart,
and let your eyes watch my ways
27 since a prostitute is a deep pit
and an alien woman is a narrow well.

To be wise, one must be **guided** by the words of verses 20 and 21 (not by feelings, hunches, etc.). These words make it clear that **spending time among heavy wine drinkers** (not the normal beverage of the daily meal: see note at the end of chapter nine) is dangerous and is to be avoided. Drunkenness, gluttony and sloth (the sleepiness that often accompanies these two indulgences) lead to poverty, so that one is likely to end up on skid row in rags.

The admonition to **hear** (pay attention to) the words of one's **father** when he grows to maturity, and to be sure not to **despise** his **mother** when she becomes elderly, is always apropos to every age (v. 22). It does not mean he will always agree with them; but he will always respect them and give full consideration to their words.

Verse 23 is a great one to memorize. It could become the theme of a person's life! At any rate, it might make a good slogan for a counselee to adopt while undergoing counseling. There is a price to pay for **truth** and the accompanying virtues of line two. But they are worth the cost. The price is humility in the assiduous study and application of biblical teaching to life. The danger of **selling** it exists; that is why the warning is given. Any believer may do so to his detriment. So, there is both warning and encouragement in this key verse that will be quoted in most counseling cases at least once.

Verses 24 and 25 contain the same sentiments as verses 15 and 16.

28 Surely she lies in wait for her prey,
and she increases the number of unfaithful men.
29 To whom is woe? To whom is sorrow?
To whom is contentions? To whom is babbling?
To whom are unnecessary wounds? To whom bloodshot eyes?
30 These things belong to those who linger long over wine,
to those who go in to sample mixed wine.
31 Don't look at the wine when it is red,
when it gleams in the cup,
when it goes down smoothly.
32 In the end it will bite like a snake,
and it will sting like a viper.
33 Your eyes will see strange things,
and your heart will speak perverse things.
34 You will be like one who lies down in the heart of the sea,
like one who lies down on the top of a crow's nest.

Once more in verses 26 through 28 the writer warns against sexual sin. He says that the **prostitute and alien woman** are **like a deep pit** (cf. 22:14) or a narrow well. That is to say, the relationship is hard to get out of (also is there an allusion to feminine anatomy in the analogy?) Moreover, verse 28 makes an entirely new point: **prostitution corrupts society**. Those who think it acceptable fail to recognize that it **increases the number of unfaithful men**. That is why any society that encourages (or condones) it harms itself to the extent that it does. The picture of the harlot **lying in wait for her prey** is forcefully enlarged in a dramatic way in chapter seven.

The chapter ends (vv. 29-35) with a vignette on **drunkenness**, largely describing its effects. It brings **sorrow** and **woe**. It causes **contention** and **babbling**. It often ends by **wounding** and causing **eyes** to become **bloodshot** (v. 29). **These things** happen to those who try out various **mixtures** of wine, who **linger** over wine. In other words, those who become enamored with drinking (v. 30) are in view. Verse 31 urges, **Don't** be fascinated by the **gleam** of red wine (the stronger sort of wine) as it **sparkles in the cup** and **goes down smoothly**. Here is the picture of someone who has become so taken up with drink that he is interested not only in its taste, but even in its looks and texture! But the seemingly lovely qualities of wine **in the end** are like the sting of a **snake**—indeed of a **viper** (a deadly snake; v. 32)! Continuing from verse 32, drink is described as deadly, anesthetizing the brain (v. 33), impairing one's ability

35 You'll cry, "They struck me, but I wasn't hurt;
they beat me, but I didn't feel it.
When will I wake up so I can find another drink?"

---

to walk (v. 34), causing injuries that one doesn't even realize until afterwards, and leading to addiction (v. 35). A powerful picture! Read it to a drunkard and ask him to say "yes" every time it strikes a chord.

CHAPTER 24

1 Don't envy evil men
or desire to be with them,
2 since their hearts meditate on violence
and their lips talk about causing trouble.
3 By wisdom a house is built
and it is established by discernment.
4 By knowledge its rooms will be filled
with all precious and pleasant riches.
5 A wise man is strong,
and a knowledgeable man increases his power.

Verses 1 and 2 take up the theme mentioned in 23:17 and 18 (**envy**), adding the note that while **evil** persons may have temporary wealth the reader should check any **desire** to associate **with them**. Why? Because they spend their time thinking about and discussing among themselves **violence** and **trouble-making** (cf. 23:17; 24:19; 3:31; 22:24). Such frequent reference to **envy**, along with the strong warnings against falling into this way of thinking, indicate something of the magnitude of the problem. Counselors must check out every sign of envy in counselees, and when they find that it is part of the problem of a given counselee, they should use the appropriate passages in the Book of Proverbs to address it. They ought, particularly, to look for a counselee's **desire** to be **with** evil persons because of the power and wealth they may have.

Verses 3 and 4, in a fetching picture, sum up much that is said about **wisdom**, stressing its salutary effects on a family of faith. See other passages that teach similar truths. Solid families in secure dwellings are founded and furnished by wisdom. Wisdom is more important than money or possessions; indeed, they are its by-product. N.B., wisdom and wealth are not opposed to, but complement, one another.

Verses 5 and 6 teach that spiritual **power** is mightier than physical prowess. There are two sorts of strength (cf. 21:22; II Corinthians 10:4). Also concerning counsel for war, see 20:18 and 21:31. Seeking wise counsel is strongly recommended; **victory** seems dependent on it in many situations.

The **stupid fool** has nothing worthwhile to say in deliberations that take place in the town hall (gates). He considers the cost of attaining wis-

6 By wise counsel you will wage your war,
and for victory use many counselors.
7 Wisdom is too high for a stupid fool;
he doesn't open his mouth in the gate.
8 He who plans to do evil
will be called a schemer.
9 The planning of evil is sin,
and men detest the scoffer.
10 If you falter in the day of distress
your strength is limited.
11 Deliver those who are taken away to death;
hold back those who are stumbling toward slaughter.
12 You say, "Look, we didn't know this."
Doesn't He who weighs hearts consider it,
and He Who keeps watch over you know it?
Won't He repay a man according to his work?
13 My son, eat honey because it is good,
and the honeycomb is sweet to your palate.

---

dom too great; so he finds it is above his grasp. He may want to, but can contribute nothing to a serious discussion (v. 7).

The name that the one who **plans evil** will acquire is "**schemer**" (cf. vv. 8, 9; Romans 13:14). People who **sin** in this way soon get a reputation. And they will discover that they are despised and **detested** because of their attitudes and their lifestyles.

Verses 10 through 12 have been used to pressure Christians into protests against abortion. The fact of the matter is that the verses have to do with the actions of judges in relation to innocent victims, as the parallel passage in Psalm 82 makes quite clear. The tests of a judge's character come in times of **distress**. God judges the judges. They hold a responsible position before Him. He knows their **hearts**. When they protest ignorance of a matter they may convince others, but they cannot hoodwink God. If a judge caves in under the pressure of sinful men and allows innocent people to be **slaughtered**, all his protests that he did not know the facts are useless in God's sight. God knows! And he will deal with the judge **accordingly**. A verse applicable, in principle, to many situations, but especially, it is also a verse that might be used in a court of law by a Christian lawyer—if he dared! (Cf. also Isaiah 58:6, 7; Psalm 64:3-5; 72:4; 82:3-6.)

Verses 13 and 14 go together. As you **eat honey because it is good** and the **comb tastes sweet**, so too, feast on the **knowledge** that is found in

14 So too is the knowledge of wisdom for you.
If you find it there is a future for you,
and your hope will not be cut off.
15 Don't ambush the dwelling of the righteous
like a wicked person would;
Don't violate his home,
16 Since the righteous person falls seven times and rises again,
but the wicked person will stumble into trouble.
17 Don't gloat when your enemy falls,
and don't allow your heart to be glad when he stumbles.
18 Otherwise, Yahweh will see and be displeased
and withdraw His anger from him.
19 Don't burn in anger because of evildoers,
don't envy the wicked,
20 since there is no future for evil persons
and the lamp of wicked persons will be put out.

God's **wisdom**. When you **find it**, the writer says, you will also discover in it a **future hope** that will not be disappointed (**cut off**). He is speaking of a future *here*, but mostly of the future life with God for *eternity*.

Verses 15 and 16 sound like something out of a lawless era—**ambushing** and **violating** a **home**! It is an age like ours is swiftly becoming; an age in which houses are breached and property is stolen. But it may also refer to an attack on someone's homestead. Temporarily, the wicked person may seem to have achieved his goal; however, yet that is but a *seeming* achievement. God will raise the **righteous person** up from defeat time and time **again** (**seven** is an ideal round number meaning "often"). In contrast to the righteous, the **wicked person** will **stumble** in a full and final (if not fatal) way.

But verses 17 and 18 warn, when your **enemy falls**, you must be careful not to **gloat** over the fact. It is not easy to restrain one's self in this way. Instead, one must pity and pray for him (cf. Matthew 5:44; Luke 6:28). Indeed, if your counselee does rejoice in that event, he may be sure that God **will see this in his heart** (if not in his actions or words) and may **withdraw in anger from** his enemy.

Verses 19 and 20 say the same thing as verses 1 and 2, but in reverse. While the believer has a **future**, the **wicked evildoer** does not. Counselees may fall into the serious double problem of **burning in anger** and **envy** toward **the wicked** who prosper. On the **lamp**, see 13:9.

21 My son, fear Yahweh and the king;
don't associate with those who want change
22 because suddenly calamity will come,
and who knows what ruin both will cause?

A Supplement

23 These also are for the wise:
to have respect of persons in judgment isn't good.
24 He who tells the wicked "You are right,"
peoples will curse him;
nations will despise him.
25 But it will go well with those who rebuke the wicked,
and a good blessing will come upon them.

The final two verses (21, 22) deal with authority, and **association** with those who wish to reject and overthrow it. Such persons will find themselves in a double difficulty: **Yahweh** and the government (**king**) will oppose him. Together, they **will cause ruin** untold.

A Supplement

Following the bulk of part three is a supplement consisting of verses 23 through 34 about which we are told, **these also are for the wise**. The word **also** indicates that they belong with what has preceded. Verse 23[b] warns against playing favorites. All should be treated alike, without bias or favor toward any. That doesn't mean that one may not have special obligations toward some that he doesn't have toward others (cf. Galatians 6:10). What it means is unfair or unloving partiality **in judgment** (i.e., in legal or other situations, as in counseling) where **judgment** must be made between persons (cf. Matthew 7:1ff.; John 7:24).

All the writer says of someone, in general, pertains in particular to counselors (vv. 24, 25). While **nations** or **peoples** won't necessarily **despise** him, a counselee who so distorts God's ways as to make them say the opposite of what He intended, will find that truly fine people will reject him. Never allow yourself as a counselor to side with the **wicked**, telling him that he is **right**. A faithful counselor will **rebuke** the **wicked** and God will **send a good blessing upon** him. Have you not been blessed lately for the counseling you have done? Well, check out how you handle evil and evil persons in counseling. Remember, you may not say so in so many words, but silence in the face of wickedness is often taken for con-

26 He who gives a right response
is like one who kisses the lips.
27 Prepare your work outside
and make it fit for yourself in the field;
then, afterwards, build your house.
28 Don't be a witness against your neighbor without cause,
or deceive with your lips.
29 Don't say, "I'll do to him what he did to me;
I'll pay him back for what he did."

---

sent. If you fail to **rebuke** when it is called for, in some instances that is tantamount to saying "**You are right**," to evil persons.

According to verse 26, counselors will gain approval and bless others (**kiss** them) when they **give** counselees **a right response**. Note especially that they are to respond. No Rogerian dodging here! Rogerian evasion is more like a slap in the face than a **kiss** on the **lips**. The loving thing to do (symbolized by the kiss) is to give God's answer to one who needs it. Directive counseling blesses others; non-directive "counseling" curses them.

Verse 27 stresses priorities, and fits many situations. The principle embedded in the particular situation is to put first things first. It is important, as it stands, for marriage counseling: one should be **prepared** for marriage by achieving those things that will enable a marriage to succeed. Too many rush into marriage; then seek to establish those things that will support it. That is doing things in the wrong order. When your counselees have done so, you must help them to go back and now attempt to establish what should have been established from the beginning.

Verses 28 and 29 warn about **testifying** against another when one knows that he has done nothing wrong. It is not sufficient justification to say, "Well, he did it to me first." Indeed, if what he did was so wrong, one only perpetuates evil that way. Romans 12:19 and 20 is apropos. Retaliation is sin; it has no place in the Christian's life. Many counselees have a revengeful attitude toward others. It must be countered. The verses here, and the realistic dialog of verse 29, especially, are a powerful restraint to the vigilante thinking of some counselees.

The remaining verses (30-34) present a striking scenario concerning the **lazy man**. The *results* of his sloth are featured. Read it in full to counselees whenever appropriate, so you will not miss any of the delightful nuances and humor of the passage (v. 33)—into which verse 34 cuts like a sword! One thing the perspective of the scenario teaches is the importance

30 I passed by the field of the lazy man,
by the vineyard of the man who lacks good sense:
31 and look—it was all overgrown with thorns,
weeds covered the ground
and its stone wall was broken down.
32 So I observed. I focused my heart on it.
I looked and was disciplined by it.
33 "Yet, a little sleep, a little slumber,
a little folding of the hands to rest . . ."
34 and your poverty and want
will come upon you like an armed man.

---

for both counselors and counselees to learn from the failure of others. Study what you encounter in the counseling room and take heed, counselor. You, too, might be able to piece together several other similar scenarios resulting from sinful living of various sorts that you encounter to present to other counselees if you do. The effect of such scenarios is powerful. Learn from the use in this passage and profit (and don't forget to add dialog—dialog is what gives life and reality to what you say).

CHAPTER 25

Part Four: Chapters 25-29

1 These also are the proverbs of Solomon
that the men of Hezekiah, king of Judea, transcribed.
2 God is glorified by concealing a matter;
kings are glorified by searching out a matter.
3 As the heavens are for height, and the earth for depth,
so the hearts of kings are unsearchable.
4 Remove the dross from silver
and the smith has material for a vessel;

Part Four returns us to the Proverbs of Solomon, collected and **transcribed** (literally, "transferred") by Hezekiah's scribes, some 275 years after the death of Solomon (v. 1). We are deeply indebted to Hezekiah—one of the few good kings of Israel—for his insight into the value and need to publish them. Of course, the Spirit of God superintended all that was done.

Verses 2 through 5 deal with **kings**. Hezekiah tells us at the outset why these proverbs were copied: to **search out** not what God has *hidden* (cf. Deuteronomy 29:29), but what He has *revealed*. Counselors, and all Christians for that matter, should share Hezekiah's desire. **God is glorified** not only by what He reveals, but by what He **conceals**. It is important for counselors to know how to distinguish revealed from concealed truth. Counselees frequently demand to know things that God has not been pleased to tell us. They must be taught not to speculate, being informed that the Scriptures are sufficient for this life (cf. II Peter 1:3). The counselor must set a good example in this regard never speculating himself and always drawing the line where the Bible does.

Verse 3 speaks of the impossibility of determining the motives and reasons why a ruler acts as he does; indeed, it is as difficult as learning everything about **heaven and earth**. That fact should give us pause when reading columnists who claim to know all about the motives of government officials. It should also make us hesitant to judge.

Verses 4 and 5 make it very clear that **wicked** associations and evil counselors in government lead a ruler astray. When, as **dross is removed** and the pure **silver** alone is left, the **smith** *then* has **material** to make a **vessel**, so too the material for making a good ruler may emerge when his

5 remove the wicked from before the king
and his throne will be established by righteousness.
6 Don't honor yourself before a king,
and don't stand in the place of the great.
7 It is better for him to tell you, "Come up here,"
than for you to be moved down lower
before a noble that your eyes have seen.
8 Don't hastily go out to litigate a matter,
or what will you do in the end
when your neighbor has shamed you?
9 Debate your cause with your neighbor,
but don't disclose the secret of another.
10 Otherwise, he who hears will put you to shame
and you will never get over your bad reputation.

---

wicked advisers are removed. Thus his **throne will be established**. Evil associates will undermine it. The principle holds true in all areas of life, with leadership of every sort. But the importance of biblical counsel is strongly emphasized as well.

Verses 6 and 7 have to do with relationships to a king. But to see how much broader the principle lying within the proverb is, note how Jesus used it in a setting that did not involve kings (Luke 14:8-11). It is from this sort of New Testament usage of the Proverbs that the principles of interpretation and application I have used throughout have been gleaned (see the Introduction for more on this matter). The principle within the two proverbs involves the pride and pushiness of some whose self-esteem can be overbearing and must be taught their proper place. **Better** to have someone say **come up here** than to suffer the embarrassment of his **moving you down lower**. This is a vivid proverb that drives home the point that Solomon wished to make. Use it in cases where it is appropriate. Doubtless, our Lord thought it powerful too, since He did.

Verses 8 through 10 hold together, each having to do with **litigation**. Counselors should advise counselees who are anxious to go to court accordingly (cf. 18:13, 17). Ask, with Solomon, "How will you be able to handle it if you are **shamed** in the trial?" Discuss matters face to face in an informal way with others (see Matthew 18:15). And if that doesn't work, perhaps as a counselor you may be able to mediate between the parties (v. 9). In order to make a point, be careful not to disclose information that belongs to another who has not given you permission to do so. **Otherwise**, you will gain **a bad reputation** that you may never be able to

11 A word spoken at the appropriate time
is like apples of gold in settings of silver.
12 As a golden ring and an ornament of fine gold,
so is a wise reproof to a listening ear.
13 Like the coolness of snow at harvest time,
so is a faithful messenger to those who send him
since he restores the soul of his master.
14 He who boasts about a gift he didn't give
is like clouds and wind without rain.
15 Through patient holding back of anger
a ruler may be persuaded;
and a soft tongue breaks a bone.

---

shake (v. 10). It is unwise for counselors, under most situations, to advise a counselee to take legal action against another, and always wise to help a counselee who is bent on doing so to give careful and studied consideration before he charges ahead.

Verses 11 through 14 deal with speech, showing a variety of situations in which **words** do good or harm. In verse 11, the importance of timing is noted—something that overanxious counselees may not think about. It is not always *what* is said, but *when.* The beauty of well-timed, appropriate speech, when put in the proper **setting** or context, is like golden citrons (**apples**) set in **silver** in an oriental tapestry. Again, **a wise reproof** is like a **golden ring and an ornament of fine gold** when it is spoken to one with a **listening ear**. In other words, sensing the proper timing (when one is apt to **listen** sympathetically to the rebuke) is crucial. Counselors may learn much from these two verses. There is little profit that comes from plowing ahead, unconcerned about the state of receptivity in a counselee. Good counselors soon learn how to determine such things and wait for the right moment or conditions in which to give a **reproof wisely**. A **faithful messenger's** word is like **snow** brought down from the mountain to **cool** the drink of summer **harvesters**. It is welcome and refreshing (v. 13). But the proud liar who **boasts about a gift he didn't give** is like the desired clouds that one thought would bring rain, but which passed over without a drop falling upon the scorched earth. He is worse than worthless; he promises and fails to deliver. Boasters are often (always?) liars. It is cruel to arouse hopes that one never fulfills.

The next verse (v. 15) shows that one can restrain his **anger** if only he will do so. It also shows the benefit of restraint (cf. 15:1). Soft-tongued animals are carnivorous (they gnaw and break bones); rough tongued animals are herbivorous. Counselees will be well-advised about this matter.

16 Have you found honey? Eat only your fill.
Otherwise you will become satiated and vomit.
17 Let your foot seldom be in your neighbor's house
or he will be satiated with you and despise you.
18 A man who testifies as a false witness against his neighbor
is like a club, a sword and a sharp arrow.
19 Trust in a traitor in a time of trouble
is like a broken tooth or an unsteady foot.
20 He who sings to a person with a troubled heart
is like one who removes a garment on a cold day
and like vinegar on lye.

Verses 16 through 18 speak of unnecessary excesses. That is a new note in Proverbs. Moderation is important; it is a note you will find yourself striking in counseling all the time. As when eating too much **honey**, one is likely to get sick, so too must your visits to your neighbor's house be limited or he will soon **despise** you as a pest. When there is no need to testify against a neighbor, because he can only testify falsely, one who indulges himself in this highly unnecessary task is a fool who is viewed as a destructive instrument like a **club**, a **sword** or **a sharp arrow**. Many are far too anxious to put their two cents in when they don't even have that much to contribute! Some even make up data, just to get into the act. That is wrong and dangerous as well.

Verse 19 warns against gullibility. In the time when you need help it is better not to depend on an unfaithful person (**traitor**) than on no one at all. He will be like a **broken tooth** or a **foot** out of joint—neither can be depended on. It is not always good advice when someone recommends "any port in a storm." The question to ask is, "Which will be worse?" Some supposed "solutions" create greater and more serious problems.

Superficial, minimizing and the temporary relief offered by some counselors, are like a song to **a person with a troubled heart**: what it does is cheer him only for the moment. While dealing with symptoms only, it does nothing to solve his problem. This sort of counsel is like removing a warm jacket **on a cold day**. It does more harm than good. Indeed, it is doing exactly the opposite of what should be done. It is inappropriately calculated counsel. It is like **vinegar** poured on **lye** which causes an effervescence, in which both lose their essential qualities by being neutralized. Bubbles may seem to indicate that something's happening, but they are no more than feel good solutions; they are no solutions at all. In the end, while nothing is accomplished the matter only worsens.

21 If your enemy is hungry feed him bread;
if he is thirsty give him water to drink.
22 Thus you will heap coals of fire on his head,
and Yahweh will reward you.
23 The north wind brings rain,
and a secretly wagging tongue brings angry expressions.
24 It is better to dwell on the corner of a roof
than to share a house with a contentious woman.
25 As cold waters refresh a weary person
so is a good report from a distant country.
26 The righteous person giving way to the wicked
is like a polluted spring and a ruined fountain.
27 It isn't good to eat much honey,
but it is glory to search out glory.

Verses 21 and 22 are quoted in Romans 12:20. For a detailed exposition of these, and other verses in Romans 12, see my book *How to Overcome Evil.* To **heap coals of fire on an enemy's head** is to put him out of business *as an enemy.* The loving response of giving to meet needs turns enemies into friends.

Verse 23 states the inevitability of certain effects stemming from certain causes. The link is as sure as the **north wind** bringing **rain**. When a gossip (one with a **wagging tongue**) goes to work, this is sure to result in **angry expressions** from many who, otherwise, would have no need to think ill of or be angry with their friends or acquaintances.

Verse 24 has already been met in various forms (cf. 21:9).

Verse 25 probably throws some light on the kind of message mentioned in verse 13. It is good to keep in touch with family and friends who live at a distance (cf. 15:20; Genesis 45:27).

Verses 26 and 27 describe the way in which some counselees act in the face of opposition. You have the opportunity to encourage and help them to remain true to God. The sight of a believer caving in **by giving way** to **wicked** persons is like viewing the tragic fact that a once fine **spring** or **fountain** has become polluted. Fear is the problem. Teach counselees to be bold. In times of persecution, the search for glory—more and more of it (unlike the consumption of honey)—itself is glorious. Glory, here, is essentially that which brings God glory, and is opposed to **giving way to the wicked**.

28 A man who lacks self-control
is like a city without a wall.

A city without a wall is vulnerable to attack, exposing itself to ruin (v. 28). So too, a man without self-control lies under the same threat. He will ruin his opportunities to work, to have a happy home, etc. (cf. 29:11; the converse is found in 16:32). No matter what one's skills, abilities or knowledge, all of these can be undermined by failure to control one's temper, appetites, etc.

CHAPTER 26

1 As snow in summer and rain at harvest time,
so honor is not fitting for a stubborn fool.
2 Like a flitting sparrow or the swallow that flies about,
so the undeserved curse doesn't settle down.
3 A whip for the horse, a bridle for the ass,
and a rod for the back of stubborn fools.
4 Don't answer a stubborn fool according to his folly;
otherwise, you too will be like him.
5 Answer a stubborn fool according to his folly;
otherwise, he will be wise in his own eyes.

Verses 1 through 12 deal with the **stubborn fool** (*k^e sil*). He is viewed from various sides, including his attitudes, thinking and behavior. Here is the key passage having to do with this sort of person; it contains a better description than all the other passages put together. The word *k^e sil* is used over 50 times in the Book of Proverbs, indicating its importance in the thinking of the writers.

The first statement (v. 1) shows how inconsistent it is to give **honor** to a **stubborn fool**. It is like **snow in the summer or rain at harvest**. In Palestine those things simply don't happen. Verse 2 means that when he **utters** an undeserved **curse**, like a bird aimlessly flitting here and there, the curse never alights on the one it was aimed at. In other words, his invectives have no meaning to one who understands that they come from a fool. A counselee, worked up over such a curse is unwise; teach him to consider the source. This verse should supply you with the information that you need to do so.

What is fitting for the fool is not **honor** (v. 1) but a **rod** (v.3) laid across his **back**. He is like an animal that will respond only to a **whip** or **bridle**; there is no lesser way in which to correct and guide him. He will not listen to good counsel or reason. It is inappropriate, therefore, to continue to counsel one who proves to be a fool of this sort. The only thing that you can do, since you cannot use the **rod** on him, is to commend him to God Who, in His own way and time, will bring the equivalent of the rod into his life.

Verses 4 and 5 are not contradictory. Counselors should never resort to the **fool's** methods or manners in refuting him, or they too will act foolishly (v. 4). On the other hand, they must counter **his folly** or he will think

6 He who sends messages by the hand of a stubborn fool
cuts off his own feet and drinks injury.
7 As the legs of the cripple dangle uselessly,
so is a proverb in the mouth of stubborn fools.
8 Like one who attempts to bind a stone in a sling
is he who honors a stubborn fool.
9 As a thorn that pierces a drunkard's hand
so is a proverb in the mouth of stubborn fools.

---

that he has won the debate (v. 5). The second half of each verse spells out the objective of the first half. There is no contradiction. Counselors must become adept at following this clear advice both to avoid becoming foolish and to counter the fool's words. In this way, some times you *may* be able to awaken a fool to repentance.

To **send messages by a fool** is like **cutting off** one's **own feet** (so that the message cannot be delivered; v. 6). For all the good that it will do, you might as well not have legs at all. It is like drinking (guzzling down) **injury** (poison?) by the **gallons**!

The fool may be able to recite a **proverb** by rote, but it does him no good (v. 7). He cripples it by his folly. That is to say, the proverb is so weakened by him that it has no effect upon him. He neither understands it nor is able to apply it and benefit from it. The proverb **dangles** helplessly from his **mouth**. It is **useless**. So don't try to teach him truth until he has acknowledged his foolishness and is willing to change. Repentance will mean abandoning foolish ways and replacing them by their biblical alternatives.

To **honor** the fool (v. 1) is as silly as **binding a stone in a sling**. The purpose of a stone in a sling is not to fasten it to the **sling**; it is just the opposite. The idea is to freely loose the stone from the sling toward some object. It is sheer foolishness to bind the two together since that defeats the purpose of the operation. How incongruous then to **honor** a **fool** when the purpose of honor is to reward wisdom and righteousness—not foolishness!

When a **thorn pierces a drunkard's hand** he doesn't even feel it. So too, when a fool utters a **proverb** he may recite it correctly but it has no salutary effect upon him. He fails to understand or to take to heart the words that he speaks (cf. vv. 7, 9).

To **hire a fool** or a **drunkard** who happens to appear from somewhere or other is like putting into a careless **archer's** hands the **weapons** for **wounding indiscriminately** all and sundry (v. 10). What this proverb

10 Like an archer who wounds indiscriminately
is he who hires a stubborn fool or drunkard passing by.
11 As a dog returns to its vomit,
so does a stubborn fool repeat his folly.
12 Look at a man wise in his own eyes—
there is more hope for a stubborn fool than for him.
13 The sluggard says, "There is a lion in the road;
there's a lion in the midst of the streets!"
14 As the door turns on its hinge
so the sluggard does on his bed.
15 The sluggard dips his hand into the bowl;
he is too lazy to return it to his mouth.
16 The sluggard is wiser in his own eyes
than seven people who can answer reasonably.

---

implies is that there is no telling how much harm he will do to you or others. But harm he will do if you **hire** him; of that you can be certain.

Verse 11 is important to the counselor: to rescue a fool out of the consequences of his sin is unproductive. It does him little good. Unless the underlying pattern of foolish behavior and thought is replaced by a biblical pattern, the fool will repeat his folly. He never learns.(Cf. II Peter 2:22, where the disgusting figure of a **dog returning to** lap up his **vomit** is used for the equally disgusting fact that fools go back to lick up their old sins.)

Verse 12 holds out little hope for the fool so long as he continues his foolish ways. A proud person who **in his own eyes** is **wise** (when, of course, he is not) might not awaken to his misperceptions before a **stubborn fool** does.

The next set of verses (13-16) make fun of the **sluggard** for his lazy ways. To avoid going to work, as an excuse, he spins an absurd tale (cf. 22:13). He says, "I might be devoured by a lion in the streets." To this is added a vivid new picture: the lazy man is fixed to his bed as if by a creaking **hinge** on which he swings like a door from one side of the bed to the other. The picture is designed to prod him into action. The third image, again, is a repeat of 19:24 (q.v. for comment).

But in addition to his laziness, the sad part is that the sluggard will not listen to reason (v. 16). He knows better than everyone else (that is the meaning of **seven people**). Perhaps it is for this reason Solomon uses ridicule and sarcasm; he is trying to motivate the sluggard by shaming him.

17 A passerby who becomes emotionally involved in someone else's quarrel
is like one who grabs a dog by the ears.
18 Like a madman throwing fiery darts,
shooting arrows and dealing out death,
19 is the man who deceives his neighbor
and says, "I am only joking."
20 Where there is no wood the fire goes out;
and where there is no whisperer contention dies down.
21 As coal added to burning embers, and wood to the fire
so is a contentious man for kindling fights.
22 The words of a whisperer are like tasty morsels,
and they enter into the rooms of the heart.

You ought to learn from that methodology as it applies to such persons in counseling. Reasonable approaches simply fail.

In verses 17 through 19 you meet two kinds of troublemakers. The first is the one who loves quarreling so much that he will even become **involved** in disputes that have nothing to do with him. To do so is like **grabbing a dog by the ears** (presumably not Fido, but someone else's dog who is anything but friendly). He will get a reaction: often a hostile, possibly harmful one. He brings trouble on himself. You will encounter this counselee from time to time. The second is the person who does dangerous things (v. 18) like **deceiving** others (v. 19) and then says, "I didn't mean any harm; **I was only joking**." He too will show up in your counseling room. For the sake of testing your own knowledge and ability, why not write out the biblical alternatives to each of these lifestyles? Can you?

The way to curtail **contention** is to get rid of the **whisperer** (gossip). One woman on a telephone for just one week can destroy years of labor by a faithful pastor. Gossip has brought down families, churches, businesses, etc. Spreading gossip is like spreading a **fire**. Fires die out as a gossip repents and ceases his nefarious activities. If there is no repentance, the person must be put out of the church (v. 20). The **contentious man** is a pyromaniac; he **adds coal to burning embers** in order to set people ablaze. He loves a fight, as we say (v. 21). Gossip, the **wood and coal** of **contention**, is also likened to **tasty morsels**. People like to get the lowdown on others because they enjoy wallowing in dirt. Gossip is too easily accepted; your task, counselor, is to point out its poisonous effects on everyone involved (cf. 11:13, 18:8).

23 As silver dross is laid over an earthen vessel,
so are fervent lips and an evil heart.
24 He who hates pretends with his lips,
but inwardly he harbors deceit.
25 If his voice is gracious don't believe him;
seven detestable things are in his heart.
26 Though he covers his hatred by deception,
his evil will be exposed in the assembly.
27 He who digs a pit will fall into it,
and he who rolls a stone will have it roll back on him.
28 A lying tongue despises those it crushes,
and a flattering mouth works ruin.

The final cluster of verses (vv. 23-28) has to do with hypocritical speech. They warn about what to look for in insincere talk so that you may identify it. **Silver dross** looks like **silver**, but it is not; it is worthless. When spread over an **earthen vessel** it may deceive one into thinking that he is buying the real thing. Those who speak warmly may have, just beneath the surface, **hatred** stemming from **an evil heart** (v. 23). Indeed, one who **hates** another may **pretend** the opposite in order to draw him into his trap. **Inwardly**, he **harbors deceit** (v. 24). Be wary of those who, as we say, "lay it on thick;" what they are laying on may be dross! A **gracious voice** can be an alarm under certain circumstances. You should be aware of the dangers of soft talk and flattery in particular. It doesn't warrant consideration if there has been no prior repentance and reconciliation. A person's **heart** may be filled with **detestable** thoughts or plans to deceive and injure you (v. 25). One way or another, it will all come out before others if the individual is insincere (v. 26) because the one who plans evil for another will find it returning on himself (v. 27). In God's providence, He sees to it that this will happen. **Lying** covered **by flattery**, if not detected, is intended to **crush** people and bring them to **ruin** (v. 28). So be aware; enlighten counselees to these facts. Learn to read the signs of insincerity.

Chapter 27

1 Don't boast about tomorrow;
you don't know what a day may bring forth.
2 Let another praise you and not your own mouth;
let it be a stranger, and not your own lips.
3 A stone is heavy, and sand is a burden;
but the irritation a stupid fool causes is heavier than both.

James has appropriated and enlarged on verse 1 (James 4:13-16). See my commentary on James in this series for an exposition. But here, verse 2 accompanies it. Both verses have to do with pride. The first says, "I can be sure my plans will succeed." **Boasting** is asserting more than one is capable of pulling off; obviously, as Solomon observes, a person doesn't even know what the next day holds. To act as if one did is to attempt to take the place of God. The other way pride manifests itself is through **self praise**. **Self praise** is the *exercise* of pride. Some engage in this inwardly so that it is not always easy to detect, but others (as here) are quite vocal about it. Someone has said that the smallest package in the whole world is a person wrapped up in himself. Counselors will early recognize this latter manifestation when it is outward—they will, for instance, be regaled with a recital of the other's accomplishments. It is difficult to bring the proud person to a recognition of his problem, but, perhaps, one way to do so is to point out that he has lost friends right and left over the years—persons he has bored to tears with stories and claims about himself. If you don't know this for a fact, somewhere along the line ask, "Do you have trouble keeping friends?" The solution to the problem is found in verse 2: don't **praise** yourself. Let **another** do so. If there is any praise to be given, then others will give it. If they don't, either one's self-evaluation is askew or he may have to wait for God to say "Well done."

Perhaps the third verse follows hard upon the second because of the **irritation** a proud person, who proclaims his own worth, causes. It is, however, larger in scope. **Stupid fools** are hard to bear. If one is forced into keeping up regular contact with them he will soon find that to do so is a **burden** that grows heavy and wears him down. In many cases, it would be easier to carry a load of **sand** or **stone**. Tell **fools** this is how others see them.

Verse 4 deals with **jealousy**. Some jealousy is proper: God is jealous over His Name and over His people (cf. Exodus 20:5). He **ought** to be. He

4 Wrath is fierce and anger is overwhelming,
but who can stand before jealousy?
5 Better is open rebuke
than hidden love.
6 Faithful are the wounds of one who loves you,
while plentiful are the kisses of one who despises you.
7 A person who is full tramples a honeycomb,
but to a hungry person every bitter thing is sweet.

---

has a right and duty to defend both. He must maintain His place as the only true God. It is right for us to jealously guard God's reputation. **Jealousy** has to do with zeal (the two are connected etymologically). **Wrath** and **anger** are **overwhelming**, it is true, but they can't compare with jealousy which goes deeper than either. Here, Solomon focuses on human jealousy which, in counseling (as in Proverbs), often has to do with jealousy for one's wife (cf. 6:34, 35). Jealousy based on facts, testimony and evidence is one thing; that which is based on mere suspicion is quite another (on this, see I Corinthians 13:7). Jealousy of this suspicious sort does not grow out of love but out of lack of trust and expectation. Jealousy, then, can be either a demonstration of love or the lack of it. It is the counselor's task to help distinguish between these two.

Verses 5 and 6 are directions for counselors who truly **love** their counselees. One may protest that such love exists, but unless he is willing to manifest it by administering a **rebuke** when it is called for, his **hidden** "love" is doubtful (cf. Revelation 3:19). Such **wounds** as a counselor may inflict in love grow out of **faithfulness** to God and to his counselee. One must often wound in order to heal—as a doctor does. Those who, out of fear, refuse to rebuke when it is necessary, actually demonstrate to some extent a *lack* of love. Don't let them protest that they withhold the reproof because of love; that is but hiding behind love as a cloak, and an excuse for their own failure to love enough.

Verse 7 teaches something about self-restraint. Moderation, rather than overindulgence, actually increases enjoyment. One's capacity for enjoyment decreases with satiety. To teach self-restraint is to inculcate an important quality that is the fruit of the Spirit. For the part of the counselor and of the counselee in attaining it, see the section on the fruit of the Spirit entitled, "The Pursuit of Fruit" in my book *The Theology of Counseling*.

The person who can never settle down in a job, a church, a geographical location, because he is never content anywhere, is likened to the bird

8 Like a bird wandering from its nest
is a man wandering from his place.
9 Oil and perfume delight the heart,
and the sweetness of your friend
comes from his earnest counsel.
10 Don't forsake your friend or your father's friend,
and don't enter your brother's house in the day of your distress;
since a nearby neighbor is better than a far distant brother.
11 My son, be wise and delight my heart,
so that I may answer him who vilifies me.
12 A sensible person spots trouble and lies low;
naive persons continue on and suffer for it.
13 Take the garment of a person who is surety for a stranger,
and hold him to a pledge who is surety for an alien woman.

---

mentioned in verse 8. A wanderer rarely contributes much to others. He is always out to experience something new. Therefore, his focus is on himself, not on others. To minister well, one must usually have a base (here called **his place**—that is, the place where he *ought* to settle down). Even Jesus, Who had no place to lay His head, made Capernaum His headquarters.

Verses 9 and 10 deal with friendship (cf. v. 9 with vv. 5, 6). The blessing of having friends whose **counsel** is substantive (**earnest**), is described as **sweet oil** and **perfume**. A counselee without such a relationship lacks a valuable element. He must strive to build such a relationship by becoming such to others. How? Jesus described the essence of friendship as willingness to let others in on one's plans (John 15:15). And, says the writer, once a family friendship has been established, don't allow it to grow cold (v. 10). You'll find such a friend closer than a brother in time of need (cf. 18:24).

In verse 11, there is an admonition every counselor ought to take to heart. By the good effect that your counseling has on your counselees you will prove the value of biblical counseling to those who scoff at it. More than proving you are right, and they who **vilify** you are wrong, is the Name of God which you uphold thereby.

Verse 12 is sound advice for busybodies. Verse 13 also has been dealt with previously. But it adds to the concept of avoiding surety the idea that in adultery and prostitution the problem may also arise.

Verse 14 makes it clear that even the best intentions, carried out foolishly, negate themselves. Timing, for instance, can be crucial. Help counselees focus not only on **what** to do, but on how they are to do it.

14 He who rises early in the morning
and blesses his neighbor with a loud voice,
instead, his blessing will be considered a curse.
15 A constant dripping on a rainy day
and a contentious woman are alike.
16 To restrain her is like restraining the wind,
or to hold slippery oil by his right hand.
17 Iron sharpens iron,
and a man brightens his friend's face.
18 He who guards a fig tree eats its fruit;
likewise he who guards his master is honored.
19 As in water face reflects face,
so the heart of a man reflects that of another.

The commonly repeated problem with a **contentious woman** arises again in verses 15 and 16. To it is added the thought that to do anything about the problem is difficult. She is hard to **restrain**. Counselors, take note!

There is a play on the Hebrew verbs in verse 17 . The first means to **sharpen**, the second to **brighten**. The idea seems to be that one is made keener by contact and discussion, but the emphasis in the second line seems also to stress the joy such contact brings to both. Neither idea negates the other. The need for and the value of friendship is in view. A counselee without friends, with whom he may discuss matters briskly, is impoverished, and should be told so. He ought to be encouraged to cultivate such friendships. No Christian can be a loner and not suffer for it. God made us social beings; we need one another. The loner always turns out to be weird, miserable, etc.

In verse 18, the importance of caring for something valuable that God has given is the principle taught. A **fig tree** was a valuable asset. When needed, it will be there if one has **guarded** it from harm, and will meet the need of the hour. The application to the care of one's **master** in the second half of the couplet shows how the principle embedded in a proverb stretches out over larger territory than that of the immediate figure. As the fig provides food in the future because it is cared for in the present, so too the care for one's master will provide **honor** at a later time. The application of this verse to many circumstances in the lives of counselees is possible. Can you list at least five?

Verse 19 is of great importance to counselors. It teaches that one may learn about others by looking into his own **heart**. You cannot really know

20 Sheol and Abaddon are never satisfied;
so too the eyes of man are never satisfied.
21 The refining pot tests silver, and the furnace tests gold;
but a man is tested by what his mouth praises.
22 Though you mash a stupid fool in a mortar with a pestle
along with the grain,
his foolishness will not leave him.
23 Keep up on the state of your flock;
set your heart on your herds,
24 since riches are not forever,
nor the crown from generation to generation.
25 When the hay is removed and the green grass appears,
and the mountain plants are gathered,
26 the lambs will provide your clothing
and the goats the money for a field.
27 Then there will be enough goat's milk for your food—
for the food of your household
and the living of your maid servants.

---

another's heart except by self-reflection. It is by looking into your own heart, for instance, that you can fully understand Jeremiah 17:9. Greed and avarice are mentioned in verse 20. That is the way sin has constituted fallen man. Grace can overcome the problem (cf. Philippians 4:11-13). Note, also, that it is the **eye** that leads to **desire** (cf. I John 2:16). Counselees must be taught to train themselves not to let their eyes wander where they should not, nor to linger over those things that they cannot help but see (but do not need to continue to look at). Much difficulty could be avoided by this effort (cf. Job 31:1).

Verse 21 contains an insight particularly important to counselors: you can tell much about what a man is like by listening to him talk about his interests. What he praises is the **test** for what he is, what he loves, what he spends his time and money on, etc. Listen and learn.

What makes a **fool** a **fool** is the very fact that he will not listen or learn. The **grain** will yield to the **pestle**; he will not. Is then a **stupid fool** hopeless? Yes, so long as he remains impervious to the influences of God: **his foolishness will not leave him**. Keep that in mind and avoid wasting time with those who do not respond to the things of God.

Verses 23 through 27 draw a beautiful picture of the benefits of care and concern for one's responsibilities. Care today means provision tomorrow (see v. 18).

CHAPTER 28

1 The wicked flee when no one pursues them,
but the righteous are as confident as a lion.
2 Because of rebellion a land has many rulers,
but a discerning man of knowledge gives it stability.
3 A poor man who oppresses a weak person
is a driving rain that leaves no crops.

Verse 1 sets forth a very important observation from which counselors should learn much about **fear**. The one who fears (without any apparent cause) doesn't have some strange problem of "free floating anxiety" (a difficulty unknown in Scripture) or "paranoia" (of which the same may be said). Rather, when sleep loss and other physiological causes have been eliminated, he should remember this passage which speaks of the fearful behavior of those who because of *guilt* (real, but unknown to others) are looking over their shoulders. Evidence of this condition in a counselee is that **no one is pursuing** him. The righteous person behaves in the opposite manner (cf. Leviticus 26:17).

Rebellion by a people leads to an unstable government. Look for various changes of rulers (for example, note the history of some Central and South American countries). The passage applies, in principle, to leaders of churches, organizations, etc. as well. Those who are like the man described in the second half of the couplet, however, **give it stability**. **Stability**, therefore, is a function of the blessings of God's righteous government of the world. It is, of course, to be desired. Counselors may indicate to those who fear change that they may contribute to stability by becoming the kind of person that God blesses, and by doing what they can to insure that the right sort of leadership prevails in any body of which they are a part. **Discernment** among members of a country or a body lead to stability (v. 2).

Let a **poor**, penniless person assume power and he is likely to **oppress** others who remain in his former condition in the same ways in which he was **oppressed** (v. 3). He is like the **driving rain** that destroys **crops**. He will be destructive in all he does. An observation of this sort ought to be spread abroad in the church. It is not always wise to elect a person to a position which means too great a change for him; it may go to his head. He, rather, should progress up through the ranks. This proverb may be of help in electing elders and deacons, who should have already served faithfully in positions of less responsibility.

4 Those who forsake the law praise the wicked,
but those who keep the law strive with them.
5 Evil men don't understand justice,
but those who seek Yahweh understand everything.
6 Better is the poor person who walks in integrity
than a rich person who is a crooked, double-dealer.
7 He who keeps the law is a wise son,
but a friend of gluttons shames his father.

Verse 4 speaks of the way in which evil men (lawbreakers) sustain one another in their **wickedness**. They side with one another to justify their evil doings. But law-keepers will oppose them (cf. Romans 1:32). Watch out for this dynamic in those that you counsel. Just because you are told something that is backed by others, does not mean that it is true. Are they conspiratorial in their unity? That is always a question to keep in the back of your mind. False testimony is not an unknown concept.

The court system—and a large part of the American population as well—has departed from the idea of objective justice, exchanging it for some form of subjective "fairness," as they love to call it. Thus judges as well as others in places of authority, in the final analysis, appeal to no standard outside of themselves, leading to a condition that borders on anarchy. Rather than upholding the law, judges often "make" law by their decisions. But **those who seek Yahweh**, in contrast, **understand** that the Standard is His Word (v. 5). Knowing this, a Christian ought to deliberate his cause before believers in the church (I Corinthians 6; q.v.) as often as possible rather than going to law. Counselors ought to know about and understand that chapter in I Corinthians so thoroughly that they are ready and able to expound and recommend the procedures contained in it at all times.

The **poor person** with a lifestyle of integrity is better in God's sight (and leads a more satisfying, peaceful life) than a **rich person** whose ways are **wicked** and who speaks out of both sides of his mouth (v. 6). A **double-dealer** is one who is opportunistic, who lives according to no standard at all. His goal in life, in one way or another, is to advance himself. Many—far too many—counselees fall into this category. And there are counselees who will tell some people one thing and others another. The problem is not at all limited to counselees, many of whom may have more integrity than their counselors.

The sentiments of verse 7 have been expressed adequately elsewhere (see 23:19-21).

8 He who increases his wealth by interest and usury
gathers it for the person who pities the weak.
9 If one turns aside his ear from the hearing of the law
even his prayer is detestable.
10 One who leads the upright astray in an evil way
will fall into his own pit;
but a person of integrity will inherit good.
11 A rich man is wise in his own eyes,
but the poor man of discernment sees through him.

Verse 8 clearly indicates that the one who obtains money unlawfully (see 13:22) will soon lose it. God will see to it that his money is distributed to those who have no power. For additional information see Exodus 22:25, Leviticus 25:35-37, and Deuteronomy 23:19, 20.

If men will not listen to God, He will not listen to them (v. 9). There is a plain, unmistakable reference here to the importance of Scripture as the place in which God addresses men. In previous verses we have noted how the wicked ignore God's Word. Prayer, under conditions where man (not God) does all the talking, is **detestable** to Him. Make that clear to counselees who wonder why God doesn't answer their prayers (cf. also I Peter 3:7). The fact is, in many cases, God has already answered the questions that counselees ask, but since they don't read the Bible, they don't know the answers. In such cases where you know that the answer is plainly stated in Scripture, you might say something like the following: "Ah, but God *has* answered your prayer. If you would only stop asking Him questions and, instead, read what He has said about it, you would know. The trouble is that you want to do all the talking; God has something to say too!"

Counselees sometimes would like to bring others down with themselves (v. 10). Here you read God's estimate of such people and what He intends to do about their behavior. He says that if they continue leading others **astray**, He will see that they are captured in **their own pits**. On the other hand, those who refuse to be led astray, but maintain their integrity in the face of temptation, will **inherit good** things. The choice is clear, and counselees who are deciding which way to go should be faced with the consequences of both decisions.

It doesn't take much intellectual power for a **wise poor person** to **see through** the rich man who may have money, but little else (v. 11). He is shallow and hollow. Wisdom and **discernment** have little to do with whether a person is **rich or poor**. A poor man can be **wise** in God's sight as, indeed, many are. A rich person may be foolish—as many are. But in the long run, each receives the sort of "riches" he deserves.

12 When the righteous have cause to rejoice there is a great celebration,
but when the wicked prevail, a man has to be sought.
13 He who hides his sins will not succeed,
but the one who confesses and forsakes them will receive mercy.
14 The man who constantly dreads sinning is happy,
but the one who hardens his heart falls into trouble.
15 A wicked ruler of a weak people
is a roaring lion and a raging bear.
16 A ruler without discernment even adds oppression;
but one who despises unjust gain prolongs his days.

Verse 12 does not teach a new thought. Persons abundantly show up and **celebrate when the righteous** prevail, but let the **wicked** take charge and you'll have a hard time finding anyone.

Verse 13 is crucial for counselors. All counselees who must begin to change must first **confess** their **sins** to God and make plans about how to **forsake** them (by replacing them with their biblical alternatives, and by radically amputating those temptations that induce them to sin). Don't forget this important factor in bringing about change. No pagan counseling system can succeed because it omits both (indeed, all too often, Christian counselors also neglect this important matter). God will be **merciful** to them in Christ when they do. Counselors will find themselves frequently quoting the first half of the couplet as well as the second. There is no way to **succeed** if a counselee **hides his sins**. How foolish! He cannot hide them from *God*! (See also 17:9; Psalm 32:5.)

Verse 14 doesn't mean some slavish fear should drive the righteous man. Strong words (**constantly dreads**) are used to denote a forceful determination pursued throughout each day. The **hardhearted** person (one whose heart has been hardened against God and His Word) will **fall into trouble** precisely because he doesn't care about whether he follows God's Word or not. Thus, he shows that he cares little about God. Regularly, throughout Proverbs, the wicked person is *contrasted* with one who is pleasing to God. This is in order to give the counselee a sharper understanding of God's will.

The **raging bear and the roaring lion** are dangerous; they are out to kill, and there is no restraint on them (v. 15). A **wicked ruler of a people** who have no power to resist is like those two beasts. The ruler who **has no discernment adds repression** to his other vices. But he will not last long; only the just ruler can look forward to **prolonged days**.

17 A man depressed over shedding another's blood
will flee to the pit;
let no one help him.
18 He who walks in integrity will be saved,
but a crooked, double-dealer will suddenly fall.
19 He who tills his ground will have plenty of bread,
but he who is involved in worthless pursuits will have plenty of poverty.
20 A faithful man will be full of blessings,
but a person rushing after riches won't be acquitted.
21 It isn't good to show partiality;
when even for a piece of bread a man will do wrong.
22 A stingy man is in a hurry to acquire wealth,
but he doesn't know that poverty will overtake him.
23 One who rebukes a man, afterwards finds favor
more than he who flatters with his tongue.

Depression stems from sin. Here (v. 17) in the example given, it is the sin of murder that is in view. The torture of the memory of one's foul deed drives him toward death (**the pit**). He deserves no **help** (but in our society is given abundant help by do-gooder groups). Note well what is said to cause **depression**. Whenever someone talks about suicide, in a depressed state, check out what sin (or sins) may be behind it.

For verse 18 see verse 6.

Verses 19 through 22 are of a piece. They speak of **wealth** and **poverty**. Laziness or industry have a lot to do with it (v. 19). The person who is **faithful** to God and to others can expect God to bless **him richly** (though not always monetarily; there are riches and "riches"), but the one whose goal is making money will be dealt with accordingly (cf. v. 20: I Timothy 6). If someone will do wrong for so little, think of what he will try to get away with when **shown** partiality! One's rush for wealth actually turns out to be a rush toward poverty which, to be sure, will soon catch up with him no matter how hard he runs (v. 22).

Most faithful counselors have experienced the truth of verse 23 (cf. 27:5, 6).

24 He who robs his father or mother
and says, "It isn't wrong,"
is a partner of a destroyer.
25 A greedy person stirs up strife,
but one who trusts Yahweh will prosper.
26 He who trusts his own heart is a stubborn fool,
but he who walks in wisdom will avoid danger.
27 One who gives to the poor lacks nothing,
but he who hides his eyes will be cursed profusely.
28 When the wicked prevail a man hides himself,
but when they perish the righteous come out in force.

The person who destroys a home, a relationship, etc. is the one who **robs** his parents and then justifies it (v. 24). He thinks he is building for his own future; God says he is tearing it down! Warn children about this all-too-frequent problem.

Greed always leads to contention. The way to **prosper** is through ignoring things and money while concentrating on **Yahweh** (v. 25; Cf. Matthew 6). True riches come only from Him.

According to verse 26, **wisdom** from God, found in His Word, is what men need; not their own ideas (cf. Isaiah 55:6-11). There could hardly be a more anti-Rogerian statement than that found in this verse. Divine **wisdom** alone (not one's own **heart**) can point out the safe road in life or in death. Counselees' opinions are worth nothing unless they accord with God's.

God provides for the needs of those who help the poor (cf. 14:21); and the converse is also true (v. 27). This sentiment is common in the Book of Proverbs.

See the final verse of this chapter with verse 12. They teach the same thing.

CHAPTER 29

1 A man who after many rebukes stiffens his neck
will be destroyed suddenly and without healing.
2 When the righteous increase the people rejoice,
but when the wicked rule people sigh.
3 A man who loves wisdom gladdens his father,
but a friend of prostitutes wastes wealth.
4 A king stabilizes a land by justice,
but a man who accepts bribes tears it apart.
5 A man who flatters his neighbor
is spreading a net for his steps.

The first verse of this chapter begins with a strong warning. It is one faithful counselors from time to time will find themselves repeating to counselees. To be **destroyed**—that is powerful; **suddenly—**that is fearful; **without healing**—that is devastating! It is a word from God that should make **stiff-necked** counselees think twice before turning their backs on biblical **rebuke**.

Compare verse 2 with 28:28. Surely, every society that has problems of the sort mentioned will experience the weariness and frustration to which the latter half of the couplet refers. Counselees may carry that malaise over into various aspects of life. Think of the ups and downs of our own country in recent years with the various reports of wickedness and chicanery that seem to prevail.

There are many parallels to verse 3 found in Part One of the Book of Proverbs.

If government officials can be **bribed** they will be. And, as a result, there will be a diminution of **justice** which, in turn, will rip a society to pieces (v. 4). Counselees must be made aware of the fact that, since Adam, there has been a lack of justice in the world; they should expect that some day (not necessarily in this life) God will right all wrongs. But in the meanwhile, correct theology on this point will help carry them through without grandiose expectations.

To try to win over a neighbor by **flattery** is only to **spread a net** for one's self (v. 5). In other words, flattery is superficial, thin; it soon falls apart and one has to eat his own words. That is the teaching of this verse. Then, more generally, verse 6 says virtually the same thing: when an **evil man** sins (by flattery, or whatever) in one way or another that sin becomes a trap in which, at length, he will find himself enmeshed.

6 In the transgression of an evil man there is a trap,
but the righteous sing and rejoice.
7 A righteous person knows the plea of the weak,
but the wicked don't discern such knowledge.
8 Scornful men inflame a city,
but the wise avert anger.
9 A wise man litigates with a foolish man,
but the latter shakes and sneers and there is no settlement.
10 Bloodthirsty men despise a person of integrity,
and the upright seek to save him.

Wicked people care nothing about those who are powerless (v. 7). The **righteous person**, on the other hand, pays attention when **weak people plead** for help (or mercy). This is a very helpful verse for use in counseling. When a counselee obstinately refuses to show mercy to another, why not read the verse and then ask, "On the basis of your response, how would you characterize yourself—as **righteous** or **wicked**?" That should bring him to his senses if anything will.

In verse 8, the power of **scorn** in stirring up trouble is highlighted. The danger of media gone wild is of importance here; demagoguery can be vocal or in print. **Wise** people, however, know how to combat this, and thus **avert** the **danger** that scorners might otherwise cause. Wise counselors, with reason and truth, must counter the mockery and slander that sets things ablaze. A counselor should be a steadying influence. If wise persons do not speak up to do so (whether they be counselors or not) they too will be responsible for the omission, and in part responsible for the consequences. What is true of a city can be every bit as true of homes, churches, businesses, etc.

There is no way to get any sense out of a **foolish man** in a trial. He is agitated, irrational and says anything that comes to mind—no matter how absurd (v. 9). He, therefore, can be dangerous, and you will probably reach no satisfactory outcome. The answer? Put him in God's providentially working hands. Men can do little with him.

Verse 10 once more speaks of how the **upright** must help when they see wicked persons running roughshod over those with **integrity**. Here is as direct a call to service as one could wish (cf. v. 8; 24:11, 12). The counselor must always be on the right side here and endeavor to enlist counselees in the same cause.

11 A stubborn fool fully ventilates his anger,
but the wise, holding his back, quiets it.
12 If a ruler listens to lies
all his ministers will be wicked.
13 The poor and the oppressor have this in common:
Yahweh gives light to the eyes of both.
14 The throne of a king who judges the weak according to truth
will be established perpetually.
15 The rod and reproof impart wisdom,
but a youth allowed to be on his own disgraces his mother.
16 When the wicked increase transgression increases,
but the righteous will see them fall.
17 Correct your son and you will have rest;
and he will give you many delights.

According to verse 11, Freudian **ventilation** is the sin of a **fool**. Counselors who advise it are propagating sin and foolishness. The solution to anger is self-control (cf. Galatians 5:23). It is not ventilation. This fruit of the Spirit is sufficient to enable one to **hold back** anger, no matter what form it may take. If one restrains anger, it **will quiet** down. Isn't that good to know in order to encourage counselees to do the right thing? You don't have to guess about what to advise; you don't have to go wrong in advising!

Verse 12 is a straightforward statement of the same problem mentioned in 25:4 and 5. On the other hand, verse 14 shows how a ruler *should* act. The thrust of the verses has to do with maintaining one's rule by the practice of justice for the powerless. (Cf. also v. 7.)

This important verse on child discipline (v. 15) stresses not only the **rod** but also **reproof** (verbal counsel). It is parallel to Ephesians 6:4 where both again are coupled. **Reproof** alone is insufficient, as is the **rod** alone. Both must be used if discipline is to succeed. **Wisdom** comes from the balanced use of the two in tandem. When you read of studies in which it is said that corporal punishment fails, ask whether the studies had anything to do with the joint activities always advised in the Word of God. You can be sure that they do not.

Verse 16 shows that bad times will come and why. But it brings encouragement as well: they won't continue indefinitely. If **the righteous will see the wicked fall**, one may expect things to change for better during the course of a normal life span.

On verse 17, see verse 15.

18 Where there is no prophetic vision people are unrestrained,
but one who keeps the law is blessed.
19 A servant can't be corrected by words;
though he understands, he won't respond.
20 Look at the glib man—
there is more hope for a stubborn fool than for him.
21 If one pampers his servant from youth
afterwards he will become his son.
22 One prone to anger stirs up contention,
and a man of great fury abounds in transgressions.
23 A man's pride brings him low,
but the person lowly of spirit receives honor.
24 He who shares loot with a thief despises himself;
he hears the oath, but won't testify.

The Scriptures provide the answer to any society gone amuck (v. 18). Without the **prophetic** message, there is no way to restrain evil. The law-abiding society is blessed by God. Each counselee either contributes to the upbuilding of a society or to its demise.

It takes more than words to get the message across to many a **servant** (v. 19). In those days, a beating might be in view; today, threats of firing, etc. Many have trouble following through this way with workmen. But, as this verse says, it is essential to do so when those in the business place fail to **respond**. Threats of punishment are the only things that motivate some.

You can't cut it with a **glib** approach to life; there must be substance to what one says and does (v. 20). The **stubborn fool** has little to offer; the superficial person who depends on a gift of gab instead of study and work, has less. It is a tragedy to see someone try to get by this way. Read this verse to him and ask him what he has to say. His reply to that question might not be so glib!

Verse 21 states a fact. Depending on the situation, it could be either a promise or a threat!

Many other verses accord with verse 22. No angry person can avoid causing much sin and **contention**. His life is characterized by these two things. Until he learns self-control (cf. v. 11) neither will cease.

Pride leads to the opposite of humility (v. 23). The former brings one down (often that is why he comes for counseling); the latter lifts him up (that is what he needs to learn in counseling).

The **oath** mentioned in verse 24 is the oath a witness must take. He hears it administered, but because he is involved in the crime (one way or

25 The fear of man lays a trap,
but one who trusts Yahweh is safely set on high.
26 Many seek a ruler's favor,
but justice for each man comes from Yahweh.
27 An unjust man is detestable to a righteous person,
and the upright in his ways is detestable to the wicked.

---

another) he refuses to give an honest testimony. This is dangerous to him; he really **despises himself** by doing so, since he places himself in a precarious position should his association with the **thief** be found out. Urge counselees to come clean.

Many are caught in the **fear trap** when they come for counseling (v. 25). Love and faith in **Yahweh** alone can release them. The fear of God is the one fear that removes all other fears. It is by relinquishing one's fear of God that he muddies the spring (25:26).

Lobbying isn't the way to do it; seeking God's favor instead is the way to find and obtain justice (v. 26),

Verse 27 emphasizes the fact that there can be no common cause between Christ and Belial. The concept of becoming "co-belligerents" with Romanists, Mormons, etc. is not acceptable.

CHAPTER 30

Part Five: Chapter 30

1 The words of Agur, Jakeh's son,
The oracle that the man spoke to Ithiel,
to Ithiel and to Ueal.
2 I am too stupid to be a man;
I don't have a man's understanding
3 and haven't learned wisdom.
But I do know the holy One.
4 Who has ascended to the heavens and returned?
Who has gathered the wind in His fists?
Who has wrapped the waters in His garment?
Who has established all the ends of the earth?
What is His Name—and His Son's Name?
Tell me if you know.
5 Every Word from God has stood the test;
He is a Shield to those who take refuge in Him.
6 Don't add to His Words;
otherwise, He will rebuke you and you will be proven a liar.

The words of **Agur** are from a person identified only by his father's name and the ones to whom he delivered God's Word (oracle). The only problem with this is, today we know nothing of any of the five names mentioned in verse 1.

Agur begins with a humble acknowledgment of his own **stupidity**; he looks on himself more like an animal than a man (v. 2). So, what he has to say, he says, comes not from him, but from the Holy One (God; vv. 2, 3). Yet he also asserts that the God Whose Word he has received as a prophet is far beyond his own comprehension (v. 4). The intriguing question about **His Son's Name** is just that—no more. I cannot fully fathom it. Surely, you and I know that His Name is Jesus.

Agur has a high view of the Scriptures; they are true and unfailing (they have **stood the test**). Indeed, he sees no difference between any parts of God's Word (as some liberals do): **every Word of God** is reliable (v. 5). He also sees the believer finding his **refuge** behind God who is a **Shield** to protect him from the vicissitudes of life. How wonderful if all who call themselves "Christian counselors" had similar views!

7 I have asked two things from You;
don't deny them to me before I die:
8 remove far from me vanity and lies;
give me neither poverty nor riches;
apportion to me only my share of bread.
9 Otherwise, I may be full and deny You
and say, "Who is Yahweh?"
Or I may become poor and steal,
violating the Name of my God.
10 Don't slander a servant to his master
or he may curse you, and you will be found guilty.
11 One age curses its father
and doesn't bless its mother;
12 an age pure in its own eyes,
yet not washed from its filth;
13 an age—how lofty is its eyes—
and how its eyelids are lifted up!
14 It is an age whose teeth are swords
and its jaws knives
to devour the poor from the earth
and the needy from among men.

Because he believes these things, Agur strongly warns against **adding** to God's words, as many careless counselors do today with their frivolous ways of handling the Bible. How sad to hear people attributing temperament theories, self-esteem dogma, twelve-step programs, etc. to God by misconstruing His Word; indeed, by adding to it. Some day they will be **rebuked** and **proven to be liars**. This concern is what makes me hesitate over the interpretation of verse 4, for instance, where many more confidently plunge ahead with what I believe could be little more than speculation.

Verses 7 through 9 provide a very fine viewpoint on wealth: there are dangers in both too little and too much. Either circumstance may lead to strong **temptations** (v. 9). That does not mean God will not provide vast riches to some (cf. David and Solomon) and withhold much from others. He is able to sustain us in either extreme (cf. Philippians 4:11-13). But most of us find it easier (as does Agur) to fall somewhere in between the extremes. Many counselees, who don't recognize the temptations in the extremes, need to be brought to the place where they genuinely are able to pray this prayer.

Verse 10 raises a question: *who* is it that may **curse you**—the servant or his master? Presumably, the servant does the cursing; the master does the investigating and, as a result, may find you guilty.

15 The leech has two daughters who cry,
"Give! Give!"
Three things are not satisfied;
and four never say, "Enough:"
16 Sheol and the barren womb,
earth not satisfied with water,
and fire have never said, "Enough!"
17 The eye that mocks his father,
and scoffs at obeying its mother,
the ravens from the valley will pick it out.
18 Three things are too wonderful for me,
and four I don't understand:
19 the path of an eagle in the sky,
the way of a snake on a rock,
the road of a ship in the midst of the sea,
and the way of a man with a virgin.
20 This is the way of an adulterous woman:
she eats and wipes her mouth,
and she says, "I didn't do anything wrong."

We turn next to verses 11 through 14 in which four types of people are listed, all of which are equally **detestable** to God. The word **generations** may mean "classes" of individuals. They are ungrateful children who show disrespect for parents, self-conceited persons who have high self-esteem, proud and scornful people, and those who are cruel and oppressive toward the **needy**.

"There is not **enough**," say the bloodsucking **leech**, the **barren womb**, the parched **earth** and the **fire** that is running low on fuel (vv. 15, 16). Presumably, the verses speak of human greed. Greed is like these things. Show the greedy person that this is how he comes across to others.

Verse 17, in a forceful figure, warns that God will judge the children who **mock** and **scoff** at their parents. An important word of warning for rebellious children to hear, if there ever was one! If the exact fulfillment does not occur (there being few **ravens** about to do the job), one may be sure that God can provide a suitable punishment of equal severity!

Verses 18 through 20 describe four things that are difficult to understand. None of these leaves a trace of its presence. Again, this is an observation—to be used for whatever profit it may have in various situations. It points out the uncertainty of certain claims. The **adulteress** is the one to whom the analogies are applied. She does what she does, cleans up and goes on to her next victim. It is to her all in a day's work!

21 Under three things the earth quakes,
and under four it cannot bear up:
22 under a servant when he rules,
under a shameless fool when he is filled,
23 under a despised woman when she is married,
under a maidservant when she succeeds her mistress.
24 Four things are small on the earth,
but they are the wisest of the wise.
25 The ants are not a powerful people,
yet they lay up their food in the summer.
26 The rock badgers are a people without strength,
yet they make their homes in the rock.
27 The locusts have no king,
yet they all go out in formation.
28 The lizard you can catch with your hands,
but it is in king's palaces.
29 There are three things that are impressive in their stride;
indeed, four move well when walking:
30 a lion is mighty among the beasts
and doesn't retreat before any other;
31 the strutting cock, and a he-goat;
and a king at the head of his army.
32 If you have been foolish in exalting yourself
or if you have planned evil,

Verses 21 through 23 list four things equally unacceptable; there can issue nothing but trouble from any such happenings. The **servant** is unfit for the task of ruling, as is the **maidservant**. The **shameless fool** can't handle success and the **despised** woman is unbearable when she captures a man.

Verses 24 through 28 speak of four **small, weak** creatures that, nevertheless, because of other qualities they possess, do quite well in spite of their insignificance. Counselees need to hear that emphasizing their strengths (as these creatures do) they too may succeed. Don't let them concentrate on their weaknesses.

In verses 29 through 31 four creatures that look good as they **move** are listed. They **impress** those who see them. An observation to which is attached no clear lesson, unless it be that which follows in verses 32 and 33.

Verse 32 warns that one must cease **exalting himself** just as he must back off from **planning** other **evil**. The **covering** of the **mouth** here refers

cover your mouth with your hand,
33 because from the squeezing of milk out come curds,
from the squeezing of the nose out comes blood;
so too from the squeezing of anger out comes strife.

---

to silencing this kind of self-praise. If one doesn't (v. 33) he will suffer the consequences as surely as the **curds, blood and strife** attend the actions that produce them. There are inevitable consequences to sinful practices.

Chapter 31

Part Six: Chapter 31:1-9

1 The words of King Lemuel;
the prophecy that his mother taught him:
2 O my son! O son of my womb! O son of my vows!
3 Don't give your strength to women
or your ways to those who wipe out kings.
4 O Lemuel, it is not for kings to drink wine
or for rulers to desire strong drink.
5 If they drink, they forget what is decreed
and pervert the right of all the oppressed.
6 Give strong drink to a person who is dying
and wine to one in painful anguish.
7 Let him drink and forget his poverty
and not remember his misery anymore.
8 Open your mouth for the speechless;
for the cause of all who are left orphaned.

Neither king Lemuel nor his mother is known from any other writing. His mother either received the following prophecy from which she taught him or, having obtained it elsewhere, taught it to him (v. 1).

Verse 2 (literally, "What" where the English has **O**) sets forth her deep concern for her son the king in this emotional outburst. She knew the great temptations that people in power must face.

Verses 3 through 7 warn against **wine** and **women**, two interests that have destroyed many kings—and persons in lesser stations of life. How many have become weak and dissipated as the result of indulgence in them.

Verses 4 through 7 focus on drink alone. Drunkenness leads to forgetting the **decrees** of God and to **perverting** the biblical **rights** of those who are weak and defenseless. Drink, indeed, may be used to help someone in a medical way if dying, or one in excruciating **pain**. Such a person may need to **forget** (in the sense of not feeling) his poverty (of health and strength). This verse has something to say about the use of pain killers in *extreme* situations.

The prophecy goes on to urge king Lemuel to stand up for the weak and oppressed, the orphan and the one who has no proper representative at court (the **speechless**). He, himself, is to take up their **cause**. Today, coun-

9 Open your mouth;
judge righteously,
and defend the poor and needy.

Part Seven: Chapter 31:10-31

10 Who can find a fully-capable woman?
Her value is far above precious jewels.
11 Her husband's heart trusts in her
so that he shall have no lack of gain.
12 She does him good and not evil
all the days of her life.
13 She seeks wool and flax
and works in willing delight with her hands.

---

selors are often in a position to take up the **cause** of those without power or influence.

The alphabetic acrostic that begins at verse 10 and with which the Book of Proverbs ends, is unique. Nothing elsewhere in all of literature approximates it. It is a poem of unparalleled magnificence, yet preeminently practical.

The poem begins by asking where one can find a **fully-capable woman**. Evidently, she is rare. She is a many-sided person who, as the writer describes her, is well-balanced in all ways. The **value** of such a person to her husband and her family goes far beyond the worth of **precious jewels** (v. 10).

According to verse 11, she is trustworthy; **her husband's heart trusts in her** (something that can be seen in the following verses where, it is obvious, he has given her great latitude in decision-making). To gain this freedom, a wife must prove she can handle it. The ideal wife, pictured here, does so. Indeed, she is able to see to it that, rather than draining his resources—as some wives do—she is able to increase them. Continuing to speak of her relationship to her husband, we are told, she is an asset, **doing him good and not evil**, so long as she lives (v. 12). The woman who concentrates on doing good to her husband continually will be praised. In verses 10 through 12, one sees that she is husband and family oriented. The three or four jobs that she will be said to have all *help* the home. She is not career oriented. Verse 12 is the answer to many counseling problems.

14 She is like trading vessels:
she brings in food from a distance.
15 She also rises while it is still night
and gives game to her family
and assignments to her maids.
16 She examines a field and buys it;
from the fruit of her hands she plants a vineyard.
17 She girds her loins with strength
and strengthens her arms.
18 She perceives that her trading is good;
her lamp doesn't go out at night.
19 She puts her hands to the distaff,
and her hands hold the spindle.
20 She opens her hands to the poor;
yes, she reaches out her hands to the needy.
21 She doesn't fear the snow for her family
since all her family are clothed in scarlet.

In those days there were no supermarkets. Consequently, she often had to go here and there to obtain everything needed to supply her household with food (v. 14).

And in order to cook meat (game) and assign duties for the day to her **maids** she rises early—while it is still dark. "Oh," you say, "she has maids. If I did, I could be like her!" Wait a minute, counselee, you have maids like she'd love to have had—refrigerators, stoves, freezers, microwaves, dishwashers, etc. And while they may need repair from time to time, they don't go after your husband!

This woman is into real estate transactions: she **buys** a field. In it she **plants a vineyard**. All of this from other earnings she has received (**the fruit of her hands**). She works hard physically and does heavy work (vv. 16, 17).

Because as she barters and **trades** she does well, she works long into the night, and what she does is productive (v. 18).

The next two verses (19, 20) are lovely. The same hands that work at the **distaff** and that hold the **spindle** to earn more money, as a result, are able **to reach out to the poor and needy**. She makes enough to help others. She is not ingrown.

And she doesn't **fear** cold weather (even **snow**) for her household. Why? She clothes them all in red flannels (literally, in **scarlet**). Beautiful, warm clothing is what she provides the family. She prepares ahead of time (v. 21).

22 She makes bedspreads for herself;
her clothing is fine linen and purple.
23 Her husband is known in the gates
where he sits with the elders of the land.
24 She makes linen garments and sells them,
and delivers belts to the merchant.
25 Strength and dignity are her clothing,
and she laughs at the future.
26 She opens her mouth in wisdom,
and the law of kindness is on her tongue.
27 She looks after the ways of her family
and doesn't eat the bread of idleness.
28 Her children rise up and call her blessed;
her husband also praises her.
29 "Many daughters have done well,
but you're the greatest!"
30 Charm is deceitful and beauty is empty,
but a woman who fears Yahweh will be praised.

She also makes her own **bedspreads** and expensive **clothing** (**fine linen and purple**). She wants her home and her family to look attractive (v. 22).

In verse 23, you must understand that her **husband** is not loafing as she works. Because he has a wife like her, he has risen to a place of prominence in the town, so that he sits as one of the elders (town fathers) **in the gates** (the city hall). The verse is speaking about her in terms of what she has done for her husband.

She also makes clothing to sell: **linen garments and belts**. How many tasks of this sort does she undertake? Four? Five? It is hard to tell, but many.

She is a woman of **strength**, but also **dignity** (she is not a mere drudge, v. 25). And because she has such foresight, and prepares so well for it, she is able to **laugh at the future**.

Indeed, she is well versed in biblical teaching and can speak wisely to others, including her children. She is not gruff, sarcastic, short-tempered or careless in speech. Her words are kind (v. 26).

She cares for her family (making sure they are cared for spiritually as well as materially). She is not an idle gossip or busybody (v. 27).

For all this her **children and her husband praise her**. He says, "Honey, you're the greatest" (vv. 28, 29).

31 Give her credit for the fruit of her hands,
and let her works praise her in the gates.

Beauty, or physical attractiveness, can become a curse to those who depend on it. Here is a woman with inner beauty (v. 30; cf. I Peter 3:1-6). She must be given **credit** for all she does (she is action and task driven) and **her works** (exhibited by the clothing her husband wears) **will praise her in the city hall**.

For a complete list of all Jay Adams'
titles published by the Institute for
Nouthetic Studies, scan this QR code.
It will take you to our online bookstore.

www.ingramcontent.com/pod-product-compliance
Lightning Source LLC
LaVergne TN
LVHW010056110826
845155LV00028B/361

* 9 7 8 1 9 4 9 7 3 7 2 1 9 *